The Governments of
GERMANY

The Governments of

GERMANY

Arnold J. Heidenheimer

UNIVERSITY OF FLORIDA

CROWELL COMPARATIVE GOVERNMENT SERIES

Thomas Y. Crowell Company

NEW YORK   ESTABLISHED 1834

EDITOR'S FOREWORD

In our time the study of comparative government constitutes one of many fields or specialities in political science. But it is worth recalling that the most distinguished political scientists of the ancient world would have had difficulty recognizing the present-day distinction between the study of comparative government and study in other subject areas of the discipline. Think of Plato, for example, whose works abound in references to the political systems of his own and earlier days. Or consider Aristotle, whose *Politics* and related writings were based on an examination of more than one hundred constitutions. Twenty centuries after Aristotle the comparative emphasis continued strong in the work of Montesquieu and Rousseau, among others. In the nineteenth century the comparative tradition entered upon a period of decline, but there are signs that the merits of comparative political analysis are once more gaining recognition. At many colleges and universities, the introductory course in political science is no longer focused exclusively on American government. The comparative approach—in politics, in law, in administration—is becoming increasingly important in the political science curriculum.

This booklet, one of a series, is designed to reflect that approach, without, however, marking a sharp departure from the substance and method of most comparative government courses. With one exception (Arnold J. Heidenheimer, *The Government of Germany: West and East*), each booklet deals with one national government, but the booklets are distinctively comparative in at least two senses. Most of them include material descriptive of other political systems, especially that of the United States. In addition, the booklets follow a common outline, so far as possible, and are designed to promote comparative treatment. Of course, there is nothing to keep the instructor or student from treating a particular governmental system in isolation, if he chooses to do so. On the other hand, his approach to political institutions and functions can be as comparative as he wishes.

A further advantage of this series is that each booklet has been written by a distinguished scholar and authority in the field; each author is personally and professionally familiar with the political system he treats. Finally, the separate booklets make it possible for the instructor to design his course in accordance with his own interest or the interests of his students. One booklet may be substituted for another or any booklet put aside for one semester without affecting the others. The booklets, in short, unlike most one-volume textbooks, give the instructor maximum freedom in organizing his course. This freedom will be virtually unlimited as the forthcoming titles in this series complete a survey of representative governments of the world.

But to return to Aristotle once again, it remains true that the best judges of the feast are not the cooks but the guests. I have tried to indicate why, in my view, the recipe for the series is a good one. Let all those who teach comparative government, and all those who take courses in that field, proceed to judge the booklets for themselves.

ARNOLD A. ROGOW

INTRODUCTION

So recently led by a fanatical Fuehrer who promised to expand their "Lebensraum" far beyond the borders of Europe, the German people are now contained in two areas the size of Oregon and Pennsylvania. One of these, the German Federal Republic, has re-established democratic parliamentary institutions and has entered into close partnership with the West. The other, which has given itself the name of the German Democratic Republic, has taken over the institutions and ways of life of totalitarian communism and has become closely integrated with the Soviet bloc. Thus within one lifetime present-day Germans have experienced on their own soil almost all the forms of political rule which have been exercised from the chancellories of the Western world in modern times. The authoritarian rule of Emperor and army; a model but ill-fated parliamentary democracy; government based on the president's emergency decree power; the unchecked exercise of power by a revolutionary totalitarian movement of the right; government by foreign military occupation; a modified parliamentary democracy; and a Communist-dominated "people's democracy"—all these forms of government and political rule have left their imprint on Germany in the past half century.

This book is intended to serve as an introduction to contemporary German politics for the student of comparative government and the interested general reader. One thing which it seeks to do, by counterpointing elements of continuity against those of innovation, is to show how this complex political heritage has shaped German attitudes and political conduct. But if politics cannot be considered in a historical vacuum, neither can it be considered apart from the way of life and the dominant patterns of economic and social structure. With this in mind considerable attention is focused on the socioeconomic profiles of the two states whose political systems are here under discussion. The text then proceeds to an examination of the political forces which serve

as the main instruments in shaping decisions within the political
process—the political parties and their leaders, the economic
interest groups, the religious communities, the civil service, and
the communication media. The policies about which these groups
have contended, as well as the style and rules of the discussion,
are analyzed within the framework provided by the operation of
the governmental institutions. This basic framework of analysis
is especially useful in the case of the Federal Republic where
such governmental institutions as the Chancellorship and the
Constitutional Court can be shown to reflect basic characteristics
of the political system as a whole. In the case of the "Democratic
Republic" quite different relationships exist, and hence the focus
is much more on the power-structure of the Communist party
(SED) rather than on governmental institutions, though these
are also discussed.

The fact that this volume deals with two political systems
which are so disparate and yet so closely interrelated has presented
certain problems of organization. In essence the pattern chosen
introduces the reader first—through a thumb-nail sketch—to the
common historical heritage and then to the contrasting social
and economic systems of the two states as they have evolved since
1945. From this initial overview he will perhaps be better prepared to consider the two sections which then examine each
political system separately. In the last two chapters the problems
of German politics and of the two systems are again discussed
within an "all-German" setting, against the larger European and
international background.

As the footnotes and bibliography of this little volume will
make evident, the author has drawn heavily on the work of many
scholars and writers. It is good to be able to present to students a
synthesis based on the efforts of as capable a group of men as
have devoted themselves to the study of German politics in the
postwar period, particularly in the United States. But one able
mind and vigorous personality must be singled out for special
mention. Professor Otto Kirchheimer, of Columbia University,
has generously provided inspiration and criticism which have
contributed greatly to improving the finished product. A number
of others have read portions of the manuscript and made excellent
suggestions which I appreciated. These include Professors Kurt
Steiner, of Stanford University; Gerhard Loewenberg, of Mt.
Holyoke College; Fred Hartmann, of the University of Florida;
Karl Roskamp and Maurice Ramsey, of Wayne State University;
and Herr Andreas von Lovenberg, of Muenster, Germany.

Appreciation must also be expressed to a number of German officials and authorities who generously supplied information. These include Dr. Walter Strauss, State Secretary in the Ministry of Justice; Dr. Hans Kutscher, Judge of the Constitutional Court; Ministerialrat Dr. Seifert, of the Ministry of Interior; Dr. Karl Lohmann, of the Bundestag; Dr. Hans Schuster, of the *Sueddeutsche Zeitung;* Dr. Richard Moennig, of Internationes; and Dr. Murawski, of the Ministry of All-German Affairs. I would also like to thank Mr. Keith Panter-Brick, of the London School of Economics and Political Science, for allowing me to use some material which I had originally worked up for him, and Wayne State University, whose support facilitated my work during the early stages.

Finally my thanks to my assistant, Mr. Daniel Fine, and to the autocrats of the typing table—Mrs. Mary Aprile, of Detroit, and Mrs. Clare Lewis, of Gainesville—and of the editorial bench, Mrs. Susan La Farge.

At the end of each chapter, except the last, is a short bibliography. The better known American political science periodicals have been abbreviated as follows:

APSR	*American Political Science Review*
FA	*Foreign Affairs*
JP	*Journal of Politics*
PSQ	*Political Science Quarterly*
WP	*World Politics*
WPQ	*Western Political Quarterly*

A. J. H.

Gainesville, Florida
June, 1961

CONTENTS

The Governments of
GERMANY

PART I

GERMANY: ITS HISTORY, PEOPLE, AND SOCIETIES

1 - The Molding of Modern Germany

The Long Road to Unification

An understanding of the tumultuous character of much twentieth century German political experience requires some appreciation of the complex political history of the country and its people. The existence of a German state, characterized by a central government and a uniform splotch of color within definite boundaries on a map, has been, historically speaking, a very short-term phenomenon. When Hitler came to power in 1933 with dreams of subjecting all Europe to German rule, Germany itself had existed in this form for only two generations. For centuries before that, from the Middle Ages right into the nineteenth century, Germany consisted merely of those areas of central Europe whose inhabitants spoke one or another of the German dialects. They had no common flag, no common rulers, and not much in the way of shared history. This situation was in marked contrast to that of most other countries of northern and western Europe, particularly England and France, where a feeling of national identity had been fostered by many centuries of rule by powerful kings who had imposed uniform systems of law and administration.

The common political traditions that Germans could look back upon were remote in time, such as the heritage presumed to have been left by the old Germanic tribes which Tacitus had described. In these early German communities there was little in the way of organized government, the settlement of breaches of the law being left to the person injured and his near relatives. There was an emphasis on liberty, but in the peculiar autarchic sense that any man had a right to freedom if he was strong

1

enough to defend his rights by himself. This old Germanic tradition was established in pre-Christian times and continued to be
powerful into the Middle Ages when it was superceded by legal
and other institutions based on Roman influences.

A second German political tradition looked back to the
unity Germans had enjoyed within the latter-day Roman Empire,
particularly under Charlemagne. This tradition emphasized the
bonds that—through institutions like Christianity, the inheritance of Roman law and a common European culture—tied
Germany to the Western and the Latin world. Indeed, German
princes inherited the nominal leadership of the remnants of the
old Roman Empire (First Reich), within which the German
areas remained very loosely held together until the time of Napoleon. The emperorship rotated among various German princes
and electors until the fifteenth century, when it was finally
bequeathed as an empty relic to the Hapsburgs, rulers of Austria.

The decay of the Imperial power led to the decentralization
of political power and to the complex sets of loyalty typical of
the feudal structure, with prelates, free cities, princes, and even
minor nobility carving out their own realms. By the thirteenth
century there were ninety-three ecclesiastical and fourteen lay
princes. A century later there were forty-four lay princes, and
their number continued to multiply as partitions took place between heirs. Many parts of the country were converted into tiny
fragments of territory incapable of fulfilling the tasks of a state.
During this time the free German cities, ruled by a wealthy
merchant class, reached the pinnacle of their political and economic power. But changing trade routes, misdirected invest-
ments, and war led to their decline in the sixteenth century, thus
preventing the further development of a strong German middle
class. The weakness of the kings and lay political power allowed
the church not only to claim for its clergy exemption from the
criminal jurisdiction of the state, but the right to try laymen in
its ecclesiastical courts. In England such courts were gradually
integrated into the king's courts, where application of the Common Law discouraged localism. In Germany royal courts did not
endure, and lay justice was administered by territorial judges
applying laws of a strictly local character. When, later in the
Middle Ages, lawyers trained in the Roman law entered on the
scene, they did so as allies of the princes, rather than as servants
of the Emperor.

Administration, too, evolved strictly on the local, or at most
regional, level. In the smaller territories the prince often ex-

ercised a personal kind of rule, and the evolution of a professional officialdom was slow. Representative institutions contributed little in the way of a centralizing force. Originally the Imperial Reichstag consisted only of those great princes who elected the Emperor. In the fifteenth century the admission of lesser princes and free towns gave this institution a somewhat greater representative character. But the great lords, the lesser princes, and the representatives of the towns met in separate colleges, with the effect that the Reichstag was both less representative and more divided than the English parliament. In this way did German particularism manifest itself in a multiplicity of political institutions which for centuries defied effective integration. At the same time the narrow outlook and lack of awareness of a common bond were not only obstacles to unification, but actually contributed to the formation of deep historical prejudices among the peoples of the different German states and regions.

The great social and economic changes which marked the gradual transition from a predominantly agricultural and feudal to a predominantly capitalist and urban society might yet have generated enough centralizing forces to bring some measure of unity to the German lands. But two factors prevented such a culmination: Germany became the storm center of a European ideological struggle of unprecedented dimensions; and her geographical position, which had allowed her cities to achieve such great prosperity, became more than ever before a great political handicap as her territories became a battleground for rival foreign armies. The Reformation constituted a revolution rending the Christian web which had maintained a European cultural unity, despite feudal particularism. It superimposed on regional and dynastic divisions schisms based on divergent faiths. The paradox that Luther united Germans as no other before him had —both religiously, in the wake of his movement, and culturally, by establishing a uniform style of written German—while also leaving a heritage of denominational strife which virtually split Germans in two, is characteristic of the contradictory German historical development.

For the cause of German unity and the development of German liberalism, the Reformation, however, had disastrous consequences. Its effect on the rulers was less significant than on the ruled. Much to Luther's annoyance, his followers did not content themselves with breaking theological ties to Rome, but in many regions sought to convert the movement into a large-scale social revolution. A peasant rising of unprecedented proportions was initially successful in large sections of southwest Germany, and many princes were forced to accept reforms such as the abolition of serfdom, the lowering of taxes, and the right of the people to elect their own parsons. But, although vastly superior in numbers to the princes, who lacked standing armies, the peasants suffered from a severe lack of discipline. Their cause was already on the decline when they were bitterly attacked by Luther himself, who called them "murderers and robbers who must be stabbed, smashed or strangled, and should be killed as mad dogs." Increasingly, the emphasis of Lutheranism on the freedom of the spirit gave way to new dogmas and rites and a new, bigoted priesthood. Moreover, Luther's interpretation of the Sermon on the Mount, to the effect that every ruling power, whether tyrannical or not, was ordained by God and hence to be obeyed, placed a heavy political mortgage on German Protestantism. It led to the development of separate state churches, each recognizing the suzerainty of the local prince, and becoming so identified with the prevailing social and political order that they opposed manifestations of liberalism with misplaced fervour and remained insulated from the misery which plagued the lower classes as a result of war and economic change.

The struggles carried on between princes and Emperor in the aftermath of the Reformation brought Germany to a new low ebb of impoverishment and humiliation, and her once proud cities declined. In the early seventeenth century the Hapsburgs made themselves temporary masters over most of an exhausted Germany. But the wars continued as the more powerful rulers of Sweden and France intervened, and for decades foreign armies ravaged the German lands. When the Thirty Years' War came to a close in 1648 Germany was as divided as ever, with power distributed between weak princes and an impotent Emperor.

However, while foreigners lorded over Germans, at least one German ruling house, the electors of the eastern province of Brandenburg, were expanding their realm at the expense of their Slavic neighbors, whom they ruled with unrestrained absolutism. Building in part on the crusading tradition of the Teutonic orders, these rulers gradually shaped the kingdom of Prussia, in which military priorities reigned supreme. In this impoverished and culturally backward area, a succession of brilliant rulers developed politics of a style new to Germany, with an efficient state machinery and an excellent army ruled by kings who knew how to harness their nobles to the task. Frederick the Great turned the Junkers (the East Prussian landed aristocracy) into administrators, spent the bulk of his resources on the army, and while demanding great sacrifices from his subjects engaged in a series of limited wars which moved Prussia into the ranks of the great powers, a rival to the Hapsburg Emperors for the political leadership of Germany. For a century and a half it was difficult to predict who would become the instrument of unification—the Hapsburgs, who were Catholic, cosmopolitan members of the traditional European "establishment," or the Prussians, who were upstart, disciplined, rough, and, together with their Junker adjutants, oriented much more towards the East than the West.

After the Napoleonic period developments were greatly influenced by the rise of liberalism and nationalism, the two great political movements of nineteenth century Germany. The Napoleonic storm swept away most of the decrepit little dynasties, united them into new states and, most importantly, gave Germans the first taste of those political rights which the middle classes in the western countries had established. Feudal privileges of church and nobility were abolished; civil liberties and other Enlightenment ideas found entry into Germany and were warmly welcomed by the hitherto politically apathetic middle classes. But what had been won through revolution in France was imposed on Germany by a foreign administration. Later, when Prussia and Austria joined the grand alliance which sealed Napoleon's doom, most of the middle classes were ready to hail the Battle of Leipzig as signalling the birth of a new Germany.

However, when the Congress of Vienna returned most of the old rulers to their thrones, they still refused to ally themselves with a national movement which they identified with bourgeois radicalism. Some of them granted constitutions, but in Prussia and Austria reaction remained dominant. The German Federation (under Austrian chairmanship) which succeeded the Empire was a sham, and the various Customs Unions had little impact. Nationalist agitation was left to the urban middle class, particularly to the professional class, who still formed a very small segment of a country whose total town population was not much greater than that of contemporary Paris. Their chance came, again as a consequence of outside initiative, when the Paris Revolution of 1848 touched off popular disturbances in Vienna, Berlin, and elsewhere, which the weak and vacillating regimes could not master. The rulers in most of the states were all but overthrown, and agreed to subordinate themselves to the authority of a national government.

The hour of German liberalism had struck, and several hundred delegates of the educated upper-middle classes met in Frankfurt to draw up a national constitution. But their opportunity slipped away as the delegates lost themselves in rhetoric, argued whether to offer the position of constitutional monarch to Austria or Prussia, waxed indignant when Czechs, Poles, and Danes sought to claim national rights for themselves as well, and lost contact with the German masses. This allowed the princes to re-establish themselves, so that when the Frankfurt Parliament finally offered the German Emperorship to King Frederick William of Prussia, he turned it down as a "jester's cap lined in red." The few radical members of Parliament who continued to claim power in Frankfurt were chased out by Prussian and Austrian troops. Reactionaries breathed a sigh of relief. In Frankfurt, the great German philosopher, Schopenhauer, enthusiastically sent his opera-glasses to the officer directing the mop-up from a near-by roof and deeded money to the families of Prussian troops who had participated in restoring order.

Twenty years later a Prussian king did deign to accept the Imperial crown. Speaking in 1871 at the field headquarters for his successful campaign against France, King William agreed to respond to "the unanimous call of the princes and free cities to create the German Reich . . . and to reestablish the Imperial crown." Significantly, he accepted the commission from the princes and not from his subjects. The political happenings of the two previous decades were crucial for this culmination. These included the expansion of Prussian political power in North Germany, the gradual rapprochement between the nationally-oriented middle classes and the ruling forces of militarist-aristocratic Prussia, the deathblow to Austrian ambitions delivered in the brief Austro-Prussian War of 1866, and the subsequent creation of a North German Confederation. The Franco-German War merely served to arouse the patriotic sentiment which swept the reluctant South German states (except Austria) into the Imperial fold. In doing so they acted true to the blueprint of Otto von Bismarck, who had risen from a provincial East Prussian background to become chief minister of Prussia and, through immensely skillful use of the forces of diplomacy, military power, and political blackmail, the real creator of the Second German Reich.

Bismarck's influence continued to be dominant for another two decades, during which he firmly established the constitutional traditions of the Empire and indirectly influenced those of subsequent regimes. His genius synthesized the contradictory elements in the German political tradition. How did it prove possible to reconcile German regional diversity and the continued existence of most of the smaller kingdoms and principalities with Prussia's desire to give strong unified leadership? Bismarck devised a federal structure within which the various states had equal standing but assured Prussian dominance by providing that Prussia's chief minister would automatically become Imperial Chancellor. How to reconcile the middle and lower classes' demands for political equality with the upper classes' insistence on the retention of their special privileges? Bismarck responded with a clever dual policy under which elections to the national legislature, the Reichstag, were held on the basis of universal suffrage, while the Prussian state legislature, which shaped the lion's share of domestic legislation affecting most Germans, retained an archaic electoral system which allowed the reactionaries to remain in control. In like manner, the Chancellor met the problem of reconciling demands for constitutionalism with the autocratic traditions of Prussia by allowing the Constitution to give the illusion of popular influence on the government, while in fact the real decision-making powers remained lodged in the hands of those tried servants of hierarchical authority, the civil service and the army.

The Reich Constitution of 1871 combined elements of political institutions of the "old" Empire with those of the Constitution of the North German Federation of 1866, parts of which were taken over intact. The Emperor's powers had a dual basis: as Emperor he controlled foreign and military affairs and appointed the Imperial Chancellor; as King of Prussia he ruled over the domestic affairs of his state, as did the other German princes. The integrating function within the federal system was played by the *Bundesrat,* which was composed of delegates from the various states. This body, under dominant Prussian influence, met in secret and had extensive powers both in the legislative and executive areas. (In effect, it combined most of the functions that in the United States are divided among the Cabinet, the Senate, and the Governors' Conference.) Its president, the Imperial Chancellor, who held his job by virtue of Imperial confidence, while being at the same time the only minister responsible to the popularly elected Reichstag, was the pivot about which the German constitutional system revolved.

This extremely complex structure functioned with reason-able efficiency as long as the pivotal position was occupied by its architect. But in its relations with Parliament the Imperial government was involved in strenuous constitutional conflict from the very start. For in pursuit of his policy of killing parlia-mentarism through Parliament, the Iron Chancellor sought both to limit the Reichstag's powers to nonessentials, and to harass and discomfit the legislative parties so that they would fear-fully respond to his wishes. He largely succeeded in depriving the Reichstag of ministers whom it could hold responsible for policy, and he almost succeeded in depriving it of its most basic power, that of approving the budget. Even so, he frequently bullied the legislature into voting military appropriations for as long as seven years at a time. In this way the legislature was placed in a position where it could neither affect the tenure of the Chancellor and his ministers, nor effectively hamper passage of the most important pieces of legislation. Furthermore, the Constitution prohibited simultaneous membership in the govern-ment and the legislature, thus setting a legal barrier to the introduction of parliamentary government. In contrast to the British system, where ministers sit amongst their parliamentary colleagues on the front bench of the government party, the members of the government in Germany sat on a raised rostrum, looking down on the semicircle of deputies.

Because of his clever and unscrupulous manipulations, Bis-marck was never matched against the whole of the Reichstag in his greatest political struggles, but always managed to isolate the parties in an attempt to crush them one at a time. He was ready to cooperate with almost any party in order to achieve his ends, but he usually destroyed them when they gained enough confidence to make strong demands. In turn, he collided with the Zentrum, representing the Catholics of West Germany, the Conservatives, representing the Prussian old guard, the National Liberals, representing the democratic middle class, and the Social Democrats, representing the Marxist-influenced working class. His successive campaigns against the Catholics and the Socialists involved an all-out use of police power, the suppression of meet-ings and newspapers, and the imprisonment of priests and party leaders. These attempts at suppression backfired. The two parties whom the Chancellor accused of "opposing national development by international methods and fighting against the nation state" were able to resist, not because of aid from the Vatican or the

Socialist International, but because of the stubborn cohesion
of their adherents, who greatly increased their party voting turnout in the face of official repression. But on the whole Bismarck
did succeed in intimidating the parties. By limiting them to
ineffective debate, he prevented them from forming effective
competition to the administrative elite. By blocking their leaders'
roads to public office, he prevented them from recruiting the
best political talents of their time.

To understand German politics under the Empire it is
necessary also to understand the prevailing political goals, and
their degree of acceptance. It might have been expected that
nationalist fervor would ebb after the achievement of unification.
But Germany's rulers would not have it so. They could not resist
the temptation of averting criticism of their policies by keeping
the attention of both the educated elite and ordinary folk fixed
on the promises implicit in a policy of national expansion. Talk
of German colonies, German preparedness, and the superiority
of German culture were the order of the day. New generations
were inculcated with memories of the Franco-German War, and
under Emperor William II a vigorous start was made on the
creation of a navy which would eventually rival Britain's. The
virtue of war was the subject of sustained glorification. Whereas
earlier philosophers like Kant had written of the hope of achieving a state of perpetual peace, now generals like Moltke attested
that, "Perpetual peace is a dream and an unlovely one at that,
while war is a link in the divine order of the world. In it are
developed man's purest virtues, courage, faithfulness to duty and
the willingness to make sacrifices. Without war the world would
sink in the swamp of materialism." Such sentiments were expressed outside of Germany as well, but nowhere else were they
so well received as in a country permeated with militaristic influences, through institutions like the reserve officer corps and the
martial figure of the Emperor himself.

Consensus on national goals was, however, far from complete.
Sentiment in South and West Germany remained skeptical of
the military ambitions of the Prussian rulers. Catholics found it
difficult to identify with a dynasty which had allowed their
persecution. Radicals poked fun at the self-conscious posturing
of members of the official establishment. Historians like Momm-
sen bemoaned a "miscarriage of national feeling." Marxists
resisted demands for the strengthening of national power by
calling for international solidarity of the workers. Each of these
groups, as well as the various factions supporting the govern-

ment, developed complex philosophical systems to buttress their
political positions. These ideologies or *Weltanschauungen* did
much to shape political movements and at the same time to lend
intellectual reinforcement to the divisions that continued to
exist among the German people despite the cloak of unity their
rulers imposed. The ideologies of the more extreme left and right
promoted militancy, but at the center the middle-class liberals
reacted in the main by retreating from active participation in
politics. Writing at the turn of the century, Friedrich Naumann
noted that forty years earlier a bond had still tied the educated
classes to liberalism. "But this tradition was lost as Bismarck's
greatness crushed liberalism. The majority of the educated . . .
believed in the greatness and power of the single great man.
. . . The disdain with which Bismarck treated the parliamentarians was taken over as though it was a permanently valid
value judgment. And as Bismarck was forced aside and then
died . . . a great vacuum remained in the intellectual consciousness of the educated German. He fell back into the apolitical attitudes of the eighteenth century."

Thus, by the time that socioeconomic developments came
increasingly to favor the German middle classes in terms of
wealth and numbers, their political ideas were adulterated and
they had lost their self-confidence. In England, where the difficult
stages of industrial "takeoff" had been completed in the early
nineteenth century, the self-confident middle classes could press
gradually toward a political victory over the aristocracy. In
Germany, on the other hand, the middle classes looked back on
a string of political defeats and became increasingly worried
about a working class which was only then being exposed to the
hardships and strains through which the British workers had
passed earlier. By playing the middle classes off against the
Marxist-led workers, Bismarck's regime managed to retain absolute political control.

Though it arrived belatedly, German industrialization assumed tremendous momentum in the decades after unification.
Backed by a dynamic banking system, built on the fruit of
intense scientific and technical research, and developed within
tight cartel structures, German industry grew phenomenally on
all fronts. In the four decades after 1870 German iron production
increased ten-fold, surpassing Britain's output along the way. In
the course of this period Germany was transformed from a land
where two out of three people lived in villages and hamlets to
one where three out of five lived in urban, predominantly indus-

trialized centers. The Ruhr developed into a mighty arsenal of cartelized heavy industry, ready to forge the Emperor's weapons. The new industries demanded and got high tariff protection, while the small tradesmen were pushed increasingly to the side. These changes did place the hierarchical order under great strain, but buttressed by a phalanx of bureaucratic, academic, and military supporters, it held fast without having to make too many concessions, except to the new captains of industry, who were granted places within the ruling class. Kaiser Wilhelm II, who assumed personal control after Bismarck was eased out of office in 1890, was still basically ruling a great industrial nation much as his forefathers had imposed discipline on the ignorant peasants of a frontier province.

Outwardly, German society presented a picture of sobriety and orderliness. Its members knew their place according to their titles and ranks, whether as reserve officers, commercial counsellors, or assistant deputy street cleaners. But in the twilight zones new forces were generating strength. The Socialist-led working class, embittered by its exclusion from decision-making, sought to beat the state at its own game by developing a supremely disciplined political organization, drawing on those same qualities of sacrifice and courage which the militarists had idealized. Growing stronger with every election, until they received almost one-third of the vote in 1912, the Socialists represented a vast unintegrated political element, which was divided between its commitment to revolution and its eagerness to display its political responsibility, if only given the chance. Among the artisans and shopkeepers a movement based on political anti-Semitism found considerable response. Despite the Emperor's friendship with leading Jewish capitalists, many of his subjects and even his court chaplain participated in the movement, though it was not nearly as strong as in Austria and some other countries. Elsewhere, too, dissatisfaction was rife. In East Prussia the great landowners were alarmed at their worsening economic position, and sought to compensate by retaining political power on the basis of the reactionary Prussian election law. There was strong pressure to extend the vast welfare program, including health insurance and social security which Bismarck had introduced. But efforts to introduce reforms from above, even through an incorruptible civil service, lost much of their value, because the masses were not allowed to feel that they had won victories for themselves.

The acid test of the political system which Emperor William

II developed on Bismarck's foundations came in World War I, unleashed in good part by hazardous German diplomacy. At first the system and the German population lived up to the Emperor's highest expectations. Regional jealousies disappeared as the nation dedicated itself to the national cause. The Reichstag voted huge military credits with barely a murmur. Even most of the Socialists gave wholehearted support to the war effort, rationalizing their disavowal of previous commitments to international workers' solidarity with the assertion that they were aiding the cause of progress by helping a conservative regime to defeat an even more reactionary one, that of the Russian Czar. But as the German victory failed to eventuate, the tensions which the Bismarckian system had sought to submerge came to the surface. Liberal and Catholic politicians asked themselves why they were supporting an autocratic regime against countries whose governments had granted their citizens the privileges of parliamentary government and ministerial responsibility. The workers, tired of providing cannon fodder and bearing the brunt of economic sacrifices, were encouraged by their leaders to ask why they were dying for an Emperor who did not deem them worthy of an equal vote in the Prussian legislature. Awkwardly the Emperor made promises of reform, but they came too late. Under the impact of unceasing Allied pressure, morale on the home-front sagged noticeably. Then, in November, 1918, inevitable defeat was hastened by the political unrest in German cities which quickly developed into demonstrations demanding bread, an end to hostilities, and the overthrow of the regime. As the revolutionary spirit spread to units of the army and navy, German leaders saw the ground slip beneath their feet. The army high command, which had indirectly ruled Germany since the outbreak of war, advised the Emperor that further resistance was useless and suggested that he seek refuge in neutral Holland. Thus did the German Empire crumble.

The Weimar Republic, 1918–33

After the downfall of the Emperor's regime, Germans were suddenly presented with the opportunity to follow the dominant political tradition of the West by establishing democratic political institutions. Surprisingly, the opportunity caught most German political parties unprepared. Even the progressive groups had prepared only piecemeal reform plans looking at most toward a constitutional monarchy. There were virtually no republicans.

Earlier liberal democratic sentiment had atrophied or been stunted. Of all the German parties only one carried the word "democratic" in its name, and this by its program was pledged to achieve a socialist revolution. To most Germans domestic democrats seemed like political animals out of the dim pre-Bismarckian past. They thought of great-grandfathers who in the early nineteenth century had cursed into their beer at the arrogance of the local prince, or had climbed grandiloquently onto makeshift barricades in the picture-book revolutions of 1848.

In the interval, the vast bulk of educated German opinion had drawn broad philosophical conclusions from limited historical experience, so that they saw in the decay of liberal movements proof that democratic forms were not suited to German politics. The experiences of the Western countries were dismissed as inapplicable. The German upper-middle class tended to share the snobbish ethos of the old ruling classes, who looked askance at Britain as a country of traders where even the nobility had accepted mercantile values. Parliamentary institutions were conceived as suitable for the compromise of sordid economic interests, but not adequate for a nation of poets and philosophers. As Thomas Mann wrote in 1918: "Away with the foreign and repulsive slogan 'democratic.' The mechanical democratic political institutions of the West will never take root here."

The dominant influence of the tradition of philosophical idealism deriving from Hegel, which depreciated the significance of objective phenomena, had an important influence in causing Germans to reject Western political values. Western concepts of liberty, which stressed the absence of inhibitions on such external acts as freedom of speech and assembly, were dismissed as vulgar and superficial. *German* freedom was conceived as the freedom of the inner man to engage in poetic flights of the imagination and daring metaphysical speculation. Its exercise depended little on the will of the official legislator, except that the passions aroused under a popular form of government were likely to disturb the tranquility required by the creative mind. Moreover, the sharp class cleavages in German society had led to the perpetuation of exaggerated notions of the intellectual and moral weakness of the average voter, whose voice would be decisive under a democratic system. Although Germany had achieved a higher degree of literacy than any country, much educated opinion—the crucial elite who controlled German administration, culture, and education—expected that "the masses" would give

free rein to their low instincts and install a political system
which would smash the proud achievements of German culture.
Conservative German constitutional lawyers argued that if a
people sought to exercise sovereign rights through a legislature,
power would inevitably fall into the hands of parties and factions
which would corrupt the national will by tearing it into little
pieces.

It was a tradition molded by such concepts which had to be
overcome by the politicians entrusted with the task of drafting
Germany's first republican constitution. Their meeting place,
Weimar, the city of Goethe and Schiller, was symbolic of the
democrats' attempt to link up with an earlier, pre-Bismarckian
tradition which, if not democratic, was at least humanistic.
Significantly, they did not meet in Hamburg, Berlin, or one of
the other large cities where revolutionary skirmishes had actually
taken place and where radical sections of the working class movement were strongly in favor of emulating the Bolshevik precedent
set in Russia. Actually the Socialist government which took over
responsibility for maintaining order did set up workers' soviets,
but, though Marxist in programmatic commitment, the majority
of the Socialist leaders had come to accept gradualist aims. They
opposed the radicals' suggestion that they establish a proletarian
dictatorship and initiate a sweeping revision of the social and
economic systems, which could only have been achieved through
the use of force. When the radicals sought to enact their
plans anyhow, they were suppressed by their fellow Socialists with the aid of regular troops and reactionary volunteers.
This led to a division within the German working-class movement, and the beginning of that tradition of hostility between
German Socialists and Communists which was to contribute to
the downfall of the Weimar Republic.

Having split with their own left wing, the majority of the
Socialists cooperated in drafting the constitution with the two
other parties which by 1919 had accepted the republic, namely,
the progressive German Democratic party (DDP) and the Catholic Center party (Zentrum). That the constitution was to bear a
primarily liberal democratic, rather than Socialist, character was
borne out by the fact that the drafting work was entrusted to a
Democratic party constitutional law professor. There was wide
agreement that the constitution should establish a parliamentary
system, but little in the way of German traditions to build on.
Looking abroad, the drafters found appeal in the relative stability of British governments, but mistakenly attributed this to a

constitutional balance of power between the King and Parliament. Thus they concentrated on creating a constitutional figure, the president, who would take the place of the British monarch as the authoritative balancing force which could help shape order out of the diversity of opinions represented in the powerful and popularly elected legislature.

The changes between the Weimar Constitution and its predecessor are well brought out by the different sequence of sections in the two documents. In the 1871 document the section dealing with the princes' organ, the *Bundesrat,* was followed by those dealing with the executive and the popularly elected Reichstag. In the Weimar Constitution, the section dealing with the popularly elected legislature took first place. The Reichstag was given the predominant share of legislative power and, in contrast to earlier practice, the power of approving and dismissing the Chancellor and his ministers. Second place, but potentially equal power, was given to the president as head of state, elected directly by the people so that his mandate would be as strong as that of the Reichstag. He was also given the power to nominate the Chancellor, dissolve the Reichstag, and rule through emergency decree. Closely linked to the sections dealing with the presidency came those dealing with the political executive, the Chancellor and the cabinet. The cabinet was viewed as a link between president and Parliament, and thus made dependent on both institutions. Finally, in last place, were the sections dealing with the considerably weakened federal element within the Constitution. As befitted a constitution with a strong centralist bias, the second chamber, the *Reichsrat,* which included representatives of the *Land* (state) governments, was endowed with extremely limited powers, mainly of an administrative nature.

Structurally, the experiment with the creation of a dual authority, Reichstag and president, neither of which carried executive responsibility, was a dubious one. The two Weimar presidents were distrusted by large segments of the population; Friedrich Ebert (1919–1925), because he was a Socialist ex-saddler, Otto von Hindenburg (1925–1934), because he was a conservative ex-general. Most precarious of all was the constitutional position of that organ which was most important in shaping the political prestige of the regime. For the cabinet was given little power to maintain itself against a demanding legislature, and successive ministries found themselves at the mercy of either the president's pleasure, or shifting legislative majorities, or both. The weakness of the cabinet, moreover, was directly related to the functioning of the party system, which the Constitution's drafters did not adequately take into account. In order to stay in power, cabinets had to retain the confidence of a legislative majority, which meant the confidence of parties. Parties were thus the supremely important institutions, but the Constitution neither recognized nor regulated their position. The stability of the larger democratic parties was threatened by the ease with which splinter groups could sap their strength because of the prevailing system of proportional representation, which allowed even minute parties to gain parliamentary representation. Finally, the ease with which anticonstitutional parties could contribute to the overthrow of successive governments made the position of the parties supporting the regime increasingly difficult.

In many respects the Weimar Constitution was a very progressive document. But its drafters lacked sufficient understanding of practical political relationships, and in too many ways they tried to face in two directions at once. A good example lies in their treatment of civil rights. Compared to the Constitution of the Second Reich, which had left civil rights entirely to the Land constitutions, the Weimar charter pledged the national government to protect the citizen against the many threats to his liberties. Then, having enumerated civil rights admirably, they added another article (Article 48), which gave the president power to cancel the same guarantees if the public security were threatened. The same sweeping article also provided the president with power to suspend large parts of the Constitution, by allowing him during crises to direct the Chancellor to enact legislation even without the support of the Reichstag.

The Weimar Constitution might nevertheless have served as the basis for a stable democratic state if subsequent political conditions had been more favorable. As it was, the antidemocratic groups were given an initial advantage by the fact that the democratic parties, who acted as midwives to the Constitution, also had to take responsibility for accepting what practically all Germans regarded as a humiliating and ruthless peace treaty. "Versailles" became a club for the extreme nationalist groups which soon organized amidst the chaos caused by civil strife and economic hardship, followed by ruinous inflation. By arguing that "traitors" on the home-front had caused defeat by stabbing the army in the back, the extremists won the cooperation of many reactionary officers, who had lost economic position and social status as a result of the virtual disbanding of the German army. (The peace treaty provided for a Reichswehr of only

100,000.) The nationalist fanatics showed their determination by assassinating some of the most prominent of the new republic's statesmen, including the ministers Erzberger and Rathenau, who belonged respectively to the Center and Democratic parties. Further difficulties for the regime were caused by the French occupation of the Rhineland and the need to pay large reparations to the victor nations, in addition to having to renounce claim to all German colonies.

By the mid-twenties, however, the regime was beginning to gain stability amid world-wide prosperity. The working class reaffirmed its support of the moderate constitutional policies of the Social Democrats, who remained the most solid backbone of the regime. The SPD (Sozialdemokratische Partei Deutschlands) discarded much of its semirevolutionary ideology and, together with the dominant trade union movement to which it was affiliated, supplied the bulk of the mass electorate, local officials, and grass roots support which sustained the regime among the people. From its ranks also came most of the volunteers who joined the prorepublican organizations which kept the Nazi and Communist street gangs in check. The other of the two original "Weimar" or prorepublican parties proved less stable. Most of the German Democratic party's middle-class voters deserted it in the course of the twenties, mainly in favor of two more conservative parties, the moderate right-wing German Peoples' party (DVP) and the nationalist-Protestant German National Peoples' party (DNVP), whose attitude toward the republic was much more critical. Gradually these two parties shared in assuming governmental responsibility, and the DVP even produced the single outstanding parliamentary figure of the Weimar Republic, Gustav Stresemann, who as Foreign Minister went furthest in seeking to strengthen German ties to the Western world, particularly to France. Cabinets including representatives of these parties alternated throughout the twenties. Even the victory in the 1925 elections for the presidency of the right-wing parties' candidate, Hindenburg, caused no grave concern, for the venerable ex-general pledged himself to support the republican Constitution.

But the regime proved unable to radiate the political magnetism necessary to convert either its grudging supporters or its open enemies, or to solve through political means the social and economic problems which served to keep Germans deeply divided among themselves. Some of its most serious weaknesses lay within the governmental structure. Large proportions of the civil servants and judges carried over from the preceding regime served the republic with questionable loyalty. Relying on the sacrosanct German tradition of civil service tenure and on the lack of qualified candidates for high office from outside the old ruling classes, these officials felt free to flaunt their reactionary commitments. Right-wing agitators, libellers of republican politicians, and virulent anti-Semites could pursue their aims with relative impunity, for the republic's courts were rarely severe with their kind. Even those clearly guilty of assisting Adolf Hitler in his attempt to initiate an overthrow of the government in Munich in 1923 were sentenced to only a few years' imprisonment. In the Reichswehr, which became an increasingly important political factor during the last years of the republic, officers with democratic sentiments were a distinct rarity. Outside these official circles, a considerable portion of the intellectuals allied themselves with a movement which called for a "conservative revolution" to end the party quarreling of Weimar and which sought to replace the parliamentary system with some form of authoritarianism based on national solidarity.

But while considerable portions of the educated elite served as the republic's grave-diggers, the most direct threats were to come from political movements which attracted large segments of the masses. Leading the groups which sought to destroy democracy through the use of democratic elections were the National Socialists and the Communists. Both recruited strong cores of members dedicated to the establishment, respectively, of Fascist or proletarian dictatorships. But, though well organized and able to agitate with relative impunity, these movements proved no serious threat during the period of prosperity. In 1928 the total anticonstitutional vote of these and similar movements was less than 15 per cent. (The Nazis polled only 2.6 per cent.) But the repercussions of the world depression aggravated the underlying economic and social tensions. The failure of the market mechanism seemed to lend support to those prophets of doom who had long predicted that both liberal democracy and capitalism were on their last legs. Large social groups became disaffected because of very severe grievances. Small businessmen felt themselves driven to ruin by the bankers and the cartels. Farmers rallied to use force to prevent foreclosures. Skilled artisans rebelled against the pressure to join the industrial proletariat or even the long line of the unemployed. Workers of all kinds lent a ready ear to radical exhortation, as the cutbacks in production cost them their jobs and the government's attempt to maintain balanced budgets cut into their meagre unemployment benefits. University-trained intellectuals and technicians, unable to find responsible jobs, joined the antidemocratic forces in droves, and the universities became hotbeds of radicalism, mainly of the rightist kind. Finally, the disgruntled among the insecure lower-middle classes rallied in large numbers to the siren songs of the splinter groups and the totalitarian movements.

Under the resulting pressures, the party alliances which had supported the regime began to crumble. Interest groups within the larger parties made irreconcilable demands and frequently split off into special interest parties. On election day the voter was wooed by as many as twenty parties. The air was full of party strife as policies based on economic interest calculations were superimposed on older programs based on ideological traditions. If there was little agreement on substantive questions there was even less on procedural ones. Extremist groups espoused a variety of radical solutions. Among the larger parties, the DNVP and the DVP began to edge away from their earlier, partial commitment to the Constitution and called for the creation of a presidential regime and other strong-man solutions. The workers shifted their strength from the Socialists to the Communists. But the biggest gains were made by the Nazis.

The real political crisis of the republic began with the 1930 elections, brought about by the inability of the democratic parties to agree on basic economic policies. They showed a sharp increase of public support for both the right-wing and Nazi parties (the latter jumped from 12 to 107 seats) which began to coalesce into a powerful anticonstitutional force. Viewed with suspicion by the moderate left and denied the cooperation of the right, the Center party Chancellor, Heinrich Bruening, sustained his government even without the support of a parliamentary majority, as a result of President Hindenburg's delegation of powers to rule by emergency decree. From that point on, government on the basis of democratic legitimation ceased, and administration based on a negative impasse began. The decrees issued by the Bruening government remained in force, not because they were accepted by the legislature, but because the Social Democrats dared not vote to annul them for fear that the Chancellor's resignation would lead to new elections in which the antidemocratic parties would make still greater gains. But the Nazis were gaining strength steadily—in membership, in the size of their paramilitary formations, and in local and Land elections. In July, 1932, after they had succeeded in forcing new Reichstag elections which resulted in their capture of 230 Reichstag seats, they became by far the largest party. At this point the pro-democratic parties ceased to be influential forces altogether. Widespread rioting, unceasing economic crisis, and virulent agitation by nationalist, Nazi and Communist forces made the state's continued existence dependent on the limited power of the Reichswehr and the fading will power of the aging president. From then on, the only alternatives open to Hindenburg were to entrust the government to military-conservative groups who would seek to ignore the deeply divided Parliament and public opinion, or to appoint as Chancellor the leader of a party openly dedicated to using its control of government to suppress all political opposition. Hindenburg was loath to turn power over to the "Austrian corporal," but he was equally tired of bearing lonely responsibility for controlling a political system whose forces he did not understand. In the final negotiations, Hitler proved extremely adept at playing up to the image which both the right-wing parties and the president wanted to form of him, that of a leader who would forget his more excessive commitments once entrusted with the mantle of authority. The DNVP supported his claim to the Chancellorship and so did many of the president's military and civilian advisers. On January 30, 1933, Hitler was duly invested as the last Chancellor of the Weimar regime which he had sworn to replace with a one-party dictatorship.

With the wisdom of hindsight, we can easily deduce that the German democratic system of the interwar period was not adequately prepared to sustain itself against the threat of totalitarian movements seeking to capture it from within. But can we pinpoint the faults? Was the constitutional system badly designed, or was distortion caused by the political forces which operated it? Were the electoral machinery and party leaders at fault, or were the Germans so hopelessly divided that neither leadership nor constitutional devices could save them? Was the republic doomed because of the German's want of experience with self-government and lack of commitment to democratic values, or because powerful minority groups unscrupulously encouraged a demagogic leader's mad ambitions? Experts are still very much divided on these questions, but a number of statements can be made about the lessons of Weimar, especially as perceived by those Germans who sought to reinstate democracy after the Nazi regime had collapsed:

(1) The Germans' first national experiment with self-govern-

ment occurred both under extraordinarily unfavorable circumstances and at a time when too many Germans were still too divided on too many basic political ends, as well as on how to achieve them. A basic prerequisite of parliamentary democracy is a wide consensus on national goals, or at least on acceptable alternatives. This did not exist in Germany for most of the period of the republic.

(2) German political and interest group organizations, and especially the leaders who guided them, were not well adapted to functioning within a democratic system. Too much influenced by outdated ideological systems and/or narrow concern for special interests, they were unable to grow beyond their earlier subordinate positions and to produce leaders who could define, shape, and confront the larger issues. Even parties which were intellectually committed to democracy proved unable to redirect their energies from the effective criticism of an authoritarian state to the effective strengthening of a democratic state.

(3) The Weimar Constitution was not well adapted to regulate the political system and in part contained the seeds of its own destruction. The ease with which methods contrary to the spirit of the Constitution were legally invoked through use of emergency powers weakened appreciation of the importance of rules and procedures. The creation of a strong presidency encouraged the legislature to act irresponsibly, while the cabinet's lack of political power led to executive instability and administrative irresponsibility. The legislature failed to evolve basic rules which would lead to meaningful decision-making within the parliamentary system. The liberal spirit of the Constitution also led its defenders to display misguided tolerance toward the regime's open enemies.

(4) While the Nazi movement built its large popular support on the basis of the chauvinism, gullibility, and short-sightedness of the German middle classes especially, it also found fertile ground among the frustrated and embittered German masses at large. It could not have developed momentum without the tolerance of large sections of the intellectual elite and the active support of influential power-holders, particularly among the industrial leaders. Unable to distinguish their distaste for democracy from the fear of communism, many who held the highest positions in Germany's economic and social life gave the Nazis both the financial means and the cover of respectability which they needed to make possible their swift rise from the gutter to the Chancellery.

Nazi Totalitarianism

With Hitler's assumption of the Chancellorship Germany was rapidly coordinated into a totalitarian state and society, and eventually into an armed camp for the subordination of other peoples. To emphasize the theme of national revival, the regime was called the Third Reich. In guiding its course, Hitler, as Fuehrer and dictator, aroused intensities of blind loyalty and immeasurable hatred matched by no other modern politician. He amazed the world and delighted most Germans by rapidly turning an economically listless, politically divided, and dispirited country into a prosperous, self-confident, and aggressive world power. Vast construction projects were undertaken, welfare programs were greatly strengthened, and the wholesale annihilation of millions of human beings was commenced. In little over a decade his regime produced so staggering an exhibit of deliberate violations of basic human, individual rights that it cast the dismal records of other totalitarian regimes into the shade. Indeed, his ability to appeal to the hidden, irrational motivations of an educated nation has had a lasting, dampening effect on the optimistic political assumptions of Western liberal democrats.

Nazi Germany produced many variants of the characteristics usually associated with totalitarian dictatorships. Ideologically, the Nazi movement created initial appeal by exciting popular resentments and jealousies. It promised to protect a "downtrodden" Germany from the evil machinations of "international" Jewry, the "decadent" rapaciousness of Western democracies, and "subhuman" Marxists. The center of its crude philosophical basis was a melodramatically developed concept of race, according to which the Aryans (i.e., Germans) were the master race and all other peoples were destined to either subservience or extermination. An attempt was made to explain all aspects of man's existence in terms of the Nazi racial theories, much as extreme Marxists seek to explain all phenomena in terms of materialistic causation. Finally, the Nazi ideology also promised the future paradise typical of totalitarian appeals. Under the "new order," carefully bred blond Aryans were to create a new culture on the ruins of a decadent Western civilization. These were the aims of the Nazi party which, as in other totalitarian one-party states, was organized on a hierarchical principle and completely intertwined with the state machinery. It recognized neither constitution nor law, only the will of the leader. Leader and party in turn felt free to employ a system of police terror to achieve those ends which enticement and threats could not attain. Under the Fuehrer, the Nazi party and its allied organizations finally assumed complete control not only over the machinery of the state, but also over communications and most social organizations, and indirect control over the armed forces and all branches of the economy.

Adolf Hitler was born into a minor Austrian official's family, had a difficult childhood, some scrappy art training, and while still in his youth began to imbibe the virulent racialism that sprouted in the occult intellectual underworld of prewar Vienna. After volunteer service in the wartime German army, he was demobilized in Munich as a corporal and found temporary employment as an observer of radical political groups for an army intelligence unit. Finding one of these groups to his liking, he took out membership (he had card No. 7) and began to display extraordinary speaking abilities in public meetings. Attacking the West and the Jews, he soon drew beerhall crowds in thousands and achieved a prominence which brought him into contact with other extreme nationalists, including reactionary generals. He played a leading role in drawing together the diverse elements which feared or hated Communists, democrats, and labor unions, synthesizing them into a new movement. Officially, the German National Socialist party was born in 1920 in Salzburg as a result of the merger of various small groups which had support on both sides of the border. (Most Germans at this time wanted to bring Austria into the Reich.) Its party symbols brought out the hotchpotch of influences which it sought to reflect: the swastika was taken over from the reactionary Free Corps who were fighting the Marxists, the red color from revolutionary socialism, the "Heil" from older German usage, the raised-hand salute from the Italian Fascists. The following year Hitler became the movement's official head, and began to receive support from "respectable" people in society and big business who hoped that he would cut the ground from under the leftist movements. The Nazis promised the masses radical action in the name of "national" rather than "Marxist" socialism. In November, 1923, working hand-in-glove with reactionary confederates in the army and government, Hitler gambled all to lead a coup d'état which sought to overthrow the Bavarian government in Munich as a prelude to a march on Berlin. The attempt was squashed, but because of friends in high places (the Bavarian Justice Minister entered Hitler's cabinet a decade later), Hitler was given a prison sentence just long enough to permit him to write *Mein Kampf,* which was to become the movement's bible. During the middle twenties the movement was reorganized and established roots all over Germany, building up an organization of several hundred thousand devoted members and activists in its tough fighting formations, the brown-shirted SA and the black-shirted SS, the latter sworn to personal loyalty to the Fuehrer.

The defeat of the Munich putsch persuaded the Nazi leaders to abandon attempts at violent overthrow of the state and to concentrate instead on winning strength in electoral contests. As early as 1928 Joseph Goebbels, whose name later became a byword for propaganda lies, openly stated the party's intent: "We are going into the Reichstag in order to seize our supply of weapons in the very arsenal of democracy. We are becoming deputies only in order to use its own institutions to undermine the values of the system. If the democrats are so stupid as to reward us for this . . . with legislators' pay and free railroad tickets, that is their affair."

CONSOLIDATION. When he assumed the Chancellorship many conservative Germans believed that under pressure from Hindenburg and the other parties Hitler would forget his extreme statements and settle down to rule together with the Nazi and conservative ministers who made up his cabinet. They failed to understand how fanatically he was committed to his program and underestimated his ruthless acumen. Confident that he could force the divided opposition to yield him complete power legally if he played his cards right, Hitler exploited Nazi control of the pressure and communications channels of the Reich and Prussian governments in an attempt to win an outright majority in the elections scheduled for March, 1933. Events played into his hands. In late February, a heroically demented Dutch anarchist, whom the Nazis used as an unwitting tool, set fire to the Reichstag building. The Nazis blamed this sensational act on the Communists, and demanded and received an emergency decree from the dazed President Hindenburg which allowed the Chancellor to suspend civil liberties and to take over police control in *Laender* (states) where "threats to public security were not being adequately met." This allowed the Nazis to imprison political opponents with the appearance of legality, seize police power where it was held by non-Nazi Land ministers, and use it for purposes of getting out an immense Nazi vote. For the record, the election results demonstrated the stubbornness of non-Nazis, for despite terrorism and propaganda, the Nazis did not quite succeed in winning the desired majority. But the seventeen million votes cast for their ticket constituted 44 per cent of the total vote; together with his German National allies, Hitler had a majority.

After outlawing the Communist party and arresting most of its deputies, Hitler resorted to the idea of getting the Reichstag to pass an Enabling Act under which the legislature would yield its powers to the Chancellor, in effect liquidating itself without formal constitutional amendment. By means of threats, promises, and pledges of good behavior, the Nazis succeeded in inducing the Center party and the remaining Liberal and Conservative deputies to vote for the ignominious act which marked the formal end of the Weimar system. Only the remaining Socialists stood firm to vote against Hitler. A few months later all non-Nazi parties were declared illegal and dissolved.

In the following year the Nazis laid the basis of their dictatorship, even though the senile Hindenburg remained president. Large numbers of Socialists, intellectuals, and other potential opponents were arrested, and the concentration camps were organized. Jews began to be weeded out of the civil service and the professions. Editors unfriendly to the regime were forced to resign and were replaced by Nazis. Free trade unions were taken over and converted into a state-controlled Labor Front. Nazi-oriented clergy were encouraged to take over the Protestant churches, and Catholic opposition was cleverly diminished by Hitler's promise to respect church rights in a Concordat with the Vatican. Leaders of all mass organizations were put under pressure to give evidence of their loyalty to the new regime, and the ranks of the party expanded greatly as they and many others sought to climb onto the bandwagon. The use of terror became widespread as the dread secret political police (Gestapo) expanded its network. Although the scales fell from the eyes of many Germans who had previously evaded the dark side of nazism, there was little active resistance. Just as the democratic mass organizations, such as the trade unions, had surrendered without struggle, so most of the moderate officials, officers, and professors lacked the civil courage to make a show of protest. Some even took heart from the fact that in April, 1934, Hitler purged that part of the Nazi leadership which had advocated radical anticapitalist action. But the blood-bath which annihilated some of his oldest party comrades also claimed many conservative opponents and should have served notice of things to come. Opposition, however, occurred only underground, mainly among Socialist and Communist groups in contact with their exiled colleagues abroad. In August, 1934, the death of Hindenburg finally allowed Hitler to do away with the last shred of constitutionalism. He declared himself both head of state and Chancellor, and as Fuehrer demanded and received a personal oath of loyalty from all servants of the state.

Like the masters of all totalitarian systems, the Nazis were not content with seizing control of the state and merely expanding its functions, but aimed at controlling all phases of economic, social, and even personal life. Gradually, satellite organizations were developed to carry the Nazi ideology and the Fuehrer principle into the most remote sectors of the social structure. But complete control could not be brought about at once by the party alone, even in highly organized Germany and with a rapidly swelling party apparatus. Instead, the party infiltrated and took over the most crucial organizations, taking some into partnership, and making concessions to others (such as the Catholic church) to buy a benevolent neutrality until the regime was stronger.

For the first five years, something of a division of authority was arrived at between the Nazi hierarchy on the one side and its allies in the army and business on the other. The latter groups were generally left alone as long as they followed over-all government policy. They were allowed to continue as a kind of second force, not politically, but in the sense of commanding executive positions parallel to those of the government and party. Thus the expanding army organization, based on its corps of professional officers, as well as the business-controlled sector of the economy, were allowed for a time to resist open nazification. This also held in part for the state bureaucracy, another institution with a tightly organized group life which the Nazis did not want to disturb since they depended on it to carry out their orders.

But all other economic, professional, and labor organizations were taken over directly by the placement of tried Nazis at their helm. The Labor Front became an important subsidiary organization of the state, as the Nazis tried to lure the workers over to their cause. Welfare benefits were expanded, the unemployed were guided to new jobs created by the armaments industry and the vastly expanded public works program, and recreation and vacation programs were set up in which amusement and propaganda were cleverly mixed. Less complex were the problems of enlisting the support of peasant and artisan groups. These had been strongly pro-Nazi even before the take-over, their loyalty won by the way the party glorified romantic pre-industrial ideals. Their antidemocratic sentiments were now redirected so as to bring about identification with the party's political and economic programs. Some trouble occurred when the artisans found that the Nazis were not going to carry out their earlier promises of carving up or taking over their hated big business rivals. But the Nazis succeeded in persuading these lower-middle class groups to see their enemy only in Jewish-controlled big business, and to regard the German capitalists as fellow workers in the Fuehrer's vineyard.

"National solidarity" was the slogan successfully employed to bring the uncommitted into line, especially as the Fuehrer's policies led to such successes as the return of the Saar by a referendum of its population, Western acceptance of the illegal German militarization of the Rhineland, prestigious German intervention in the Spanish Civil War, and the "bringing home" of Austria in 1938. But as the Nazis' domestic strength grew and plans for military aggression were developed, it was found advisable to extend party control over sectors previously left a certain independence. Thus the army was "nazified," at least at the top, by the retirement of its traditional leaders and their replacement by generals loyal to the regime. Civil servants were no longer allowed to remain aloof but were expected to join the party. Business also was drawn more completely under state influence, though it remained in private ownership until the end.

The Nazi state was based squarely on the cult of one individual. Submission to the will of the leader who somehow embodied the national will was the beginning and the end of Nazi political theory. The party saw itself only as an instrument for rendering the state completely submissive to the Fuehrer's will. Hitler was fond of telling young party fanatics that the only basic rules were "blind discipline and the absolute recognition of authority." Even a top-ranking leader like Hermann Goering proclaimed, "I have no personal conscience; Adolf Hitler is my only conscience." This dependence on the personal whim of one person was difficult to reconcile with the efficient running of even an autocratic administration, which would normally be based on some coherent set of rules. But Hitler wanted to be bound by nothing. Neither the Weimar Constitution nor most pre-Nazi laws were ever really replaced because Hitler refused to be bound by any kind of legal norms. He placed supreme confidence in his ability to make correct decisions based on intuition.

But since Hitler could not make every decision necessary for the running of a state, it was inevitable that a division of powers should develop within the Nazi state, lack of legal basis notwithstanding. Basically, the authority of the various Nazi organizations and ministries depended on the degree of confidence that Hitler had in their leaders at any one time. In the resulting competition among the Nazi paladins, Heinrich Himmler, the head of the SS, gained a dominant position soon after the take-over, which he solidified by gaining effective control over the entire German police system. Vital areas of administration were taken away from regular government agencies and placed under his indirect control. The SS quickly eclipsed in authority the party bureaucracy itself, which was preoccupied with integrating its vast membership and exercising indirect control on the local level. The party organization in fact was relegated to the status of a control organ over the masses, making sure that non-Nazi groups and individuals were deprived of any opportunity to make effective decisions.

Throughout the Hitler period power ebbed and flowed among the Nazi leaders in the party organization, the SS, the army, the bureaucracy, and their subdivisions. After 1941, when Martin Bormann was named party secretary, the party organization began to reclaim much power from the SS apparatus. But in the meantime, the SS had built up a virtual state within a state. It had suborganizations that competed in foreign policy with the Foreign Ministry, agencies that developed occupation policies which conflicted with those of commanding generals, and it also ran its own system of prison and extermination camps. It even developed its own army, the Waffen-SS, which, recruited all over Europe, grew to almost a million and was beyond the jurisdiction of the army high command. After the war it expected to carve out its own model state, which was to be made up of sections of France and Belgium with the capital at either Ghent or Dijon. The official language was to be German, but at the beginning the people were to be allowed to continue to speak French.

While the Nazi leaders fought each other for power and control over the vast conquered areas of Europe, the rest of the German administrative and military elite worked with customary efficiency to keep the vastly swollen state machinery functioning relatively smoothly. It was this elite that worked out the difficulties arising from the erratic policies and battle commands which emerged from the Fuehrer's headquarters in an endless stream, and prevented the contradictory pressures from the various Nazi cliques from causing fatal internal conflicts. Though largely excluded from the inner councils, members of the elite maintained an extraordinarily high discipline which allowed Hitler to make even greater demands. Though many secretly rejected the Nazi regime or even belonged to the "inner immigration," they followed the dictates of obedience and duty to the Fatherland which generations of forebears had shaped. The idea of measuring orders and official policies by the moral yardstick of personal values was alien to the German bureaucratic outlook. It took even the bravest among them years of soul-searching before they could bring themselves to attempt what reason and basic concern for the national destiny commended as the only possible solution, to end the Nazi regime by overthrowing Hitler. The attempt on Hitler's life in his East Prussian command headquarters on July 20, 1944, was the culmination of years of planning in a number of highly secret resistance groups which consisted mainly of the most courageous members of conservative German social groups. But the handful of aristocrats, generals, high civil servants and labor leaders failed in their endeavor to end the regime which was leading Germany to the abyss. Their attempt did achieve symbolic value for postwar Germans seeking to restore some measure of national self-respect.

The horrors inflicted on European populations during World War II finally convinced the world of Hitler's earnest determination to carry out the program first outlined in *Mein Kampf,* and subsequently elaborated in his tirades before the Nazi party meetings and in the private conversations since published in his *Secret Conversations.* Developments bore out his declaration of November, 1933, that he had not become Chancellor in order to do otherwise than he had preached for the past fourteen years. His phenomenal success in carrying out seemingly fantastic plans, first of internal, then of world revolution, can be attributed in large part to his extraordinary readiness to gamble all previous achievements for yet higher stakes. Because of his unchallengeable position he was able first to use the party as an instrument to capture Germany, and then Germany as an instrument to capture control of Europe. When by 1942 German armies had overrun almost the entire continent of Europe and also penetrated into North Africa, his promise of turning the Germans into a master race seemed well on the way toward realization. Hitler took personal command of operations on the warfront, and the success of operations based on his intuition impressed not only the generals, but his people and the world.

However Hitler was not content with fulfilling the positive promises of greater "Lebensraum." Confident of eventual victory almost to the end, he ordered an energetic start to the "reforms" which formed part and parcel of the establishment of the new order. High priority was given to the elimination of "the Jewish problem." First in Germany and then in the occupied countries Jews were deprived of all civil rights, herded together into ghettos, and eventually transported to areas in Poland and Czechoslovakia. Ostensibly they were to be resettled in isolated "pales," but in reality this was the road to the awful "final solution" that led to the mass murder of millions of human beings in the gas chambers and ovens of the extermination camps. Carried through with terrifying efficiency by special SS and other units under the direction of genocide engineers like Adolf Eichmann, this operation was duplicated on a smaller scale by many other programs designed to eliminate groups considered undesirable under Nazi racial theories. Thus gypsies and the mentally retarded were methodically dispatched, as were hundreds of thousands of political opponents, resistance fighters, and civilian hostages. Seldom had absolute power corrupted so absolutely what had initially been accepted by many as an idealistic program for national regeneration.

The extermination programs were kept relatively secret, and after the war most Germans declared that they had known nothing of these and other abominations. Indeed, only a small minority of selected party fanatics had been shaped so completely by the totalitarian mold that they were able to suppress their consciences altogether. But large numbers of "average" Germans who held positions in the party and its affiliated organizations had come to adapt themselves to the regime's excesses, rationalizing acceptance with the argument that they were inevitable or that they were more than balanced off by the regime's positive achievements. Even the very large number who conformed only outwardly could not help but be carried along by an unceasing propaganda campaign. The exposure to years of uninterrupted nationalist frenzy, exhortations to discipline, acceptance of party orders, and self-submersion in racialist mystique made such a deep impression on Germans of all backgrounds that those few thinking of recreating a democratic order after the inevitable defeat frequently had to ask themselves whether Hitler's handiwork might not require several generations to undo.

THE AFTERMATH. With the collapse of the Nazi regime and Hitler's suicide in Berlin in April, 1945, as the Soviet and Western armies swept their way deep into German territory, German political development had turned full cycle. What had begun a century earlier as an attempt to unify diverse states culminated, after sporadic attempts at domestic integration and external expansion, in the complete disintegration of the German Reich and the assumption of German sovereignty by the victorious occupying powers. As a result of inter-Allied agreements reached at Yalta and Potsdam, the central European map was completely recast. Territories which Germany had annexed from Poland and Czechoslovakia in 1939 were returned, and Austria was recreated. In addition, very large sections of Germany east of the Oder and Neisse rivers, which were German even before 1933, were turned over to Poland and the Soviet Union "for administration." Although their final status was to be determined in the peace treaty, they were in fact annexed, and their indigenous German population of about ten million was driven out. Finally, the rump of German territory was divided into zones of occupation, administered respectively by American, British, Soviet, and French military governments, while Berlin was divided into sectors occupied by the same powers.

The Allied agreements had left open the question of what final political status Germany was to be granted. East-West tensions soon began to hamper the operation of the Inter-Allied Control Council, which never succeeded in coming to grips with the problem of reconciling contradictory policies among the occupying powers, and ceased to function in 1947. For a time Germany was divided into what were in effect four zonal states. The three Western powers gradually moved first toward the economic and then toward the political, merger of their zones. This process culminated in 1949 in the creation of the Federal Republic (West Germany), to which the Soviets responded by quickly establishing a rival German Democratic Republic (East Germany) in their zone.

Bibliography

Germany to 1918

Alexander, Edgar, "Church and Society in Germany," in J. Moody, ed., *Church and Society* (New York, 1953).

Clapham, J. H., *Economic Development of France and Germany, 1815–1914* (Cambridge, 1936).

Craig, Gordon A., *From Bismarck to Adenauer: Aspects of German Statecraft* (Baltimore, 1958).

——, *The Politics of the Prussian Army, 1640–1945* (Oxford, 1955).

Eyck, Erich, *Bismarck and the German Empire* (London, 1950).

Hallowell, John H., *The Decline of Liberalism as an Ideology with Particular Reference to German Political-Legal Thought* (Los Angeles, 1943).

Hamerow, Theodore S., *Restoration, Revolution, Reaction: Economics and Politics in Germany, 1815–1871* (Princeton, 1958).

Hertz, Friedrich, *The German Public Mind* (London, 1957).

Holborn, Hajo, *History of Modern Germany* (New York, 1959).

Kohn, Hans, ed., *German History: Some New German Views* (Boston, 1954).

Krieger, Leonard, *The German Idea of Freedom* (Boston, 1957).

Meinecke, Friedrich, *Weltbuergertum und Nationalstaat*, 4th ed. (Munich, 1917).

Naumann, Friedrich, *Die Politische Parteien* (Berlin, 1913).

Pross, Harry, *Die Zerstoerung der Deutschen Politik: Dokumente 1871–1933* (Frankfurt, 1959).

Sell, Friedrich, *Die Tragödie des deutschen Liberalismus* (Stuttgart, 1953).

Taylor, A. J. P., *The Course of German History* (London, 1948).

Valentin, Veit, *The German People* (New York, 1953).

Verweil, Edmund, *Germany in the 20th Century* (New York, 1956).

The Weimar Republic

Blachley, F. F., and Oatman, M. R., *The Government and Administration of Germany* (Baltimore, 1928).

Bracher, K. D., *Die Aufloesung der Weimarer Republik*, 2d ed. (Stuttgart, 1957).

Brecht, Arnold, *Prelude to Silence* (New York, 1944).

Eschenburg, Theodor, *Die Improvisierte Demokratie der Weimarer Republik* (Laupheim, 1954).

Eyck, Erich, *Geschichte der Weimarer Republik*, 2 vols. (Munich, 1956–57).

Flechtheim, Ossip K., *Die Kommunistische Partei Deutschlands in der Weimarer Republik* (Offenbach, 1948).

Halpern, S. William, *Germany Tried Political Democracy* (New York, 1946).

Heberle, Rudolf, *From Democracy to Nazism* (Baton Rouge, 1945).

Klemperer, Klemens von, *Germany's New Conservatism* (Princeton, 1957).

Rosenberg, Arthur, *A History of the German Republic* (London, 1936).

Sontheimer, Kurt, "Antidemokratisches Denken in der Weimarer Republik," *Vierteljahreshefte fuer Zeitgeschichte*, V (1957), 42–62.

Watkins, Frederick M., *The Failure of Constitutional Emergency Powers Under the German Republic* (Cambridge, Mass., 1939).

Wheeler-Bennett, John W., *The Nemesis of Power* (New York, 1954).

The Nazi Period

Baumont, Maurice, *et. al.*, eds., *The Third Reich* (Praeger, 1955).

Bracher, Karl Dietrich, Sauer, Wolfgang, and Schulz, Gerhardt, *Die Nationalsozialistische Machtergreifung* (Cologne, 1960).

Bullock, Alan L. C., *Hitler: A Study in Tyranny* (New York, 1952).

Friedrich, Carl, and Brzezinski, Zbigniew, *Totalitarian Dictatorship and Autocracy* (Cambridge, Mass., 1956).

Grebing, Helga, *Der Nationalsozialismus: Ursprung und Wesen* (Munich, 1959).

Hassell, Ulrich von, *The von Hassell Diaries, 1938–44* (Garden City, 1947).

Heiden, Konrad, *Der Fuehrer* (Boston, 1944).
Hitler, Adolf, *Mein Kampf* (Boston, 1943).
Jarman, T. J., *The Rise and Fall of Nazi Germany* (New York, 1956).
Kogon, Eugene, *The Theory and Practice of Hell* (New York, 1950).
Meinecke, Friedrich, *The German Catastrophe* (Cambridge, Mass., 1950).
Nazi Conspiracy and Aggression (The Nuremberg War Crimes Trials), 10 vols. (Washington, 1946–48).
Neumann, Franz, *Behemoth* (New York, 1942).
Neumann, Sigmund, *Permanent Revolution* (New York, 1942).
Reitlinger, Gerald, *The Final Solution: The Attempt to Exterminate the Jews of Europe, 1938–1945* (New York, 1953).
Schweitzer, Arthur. "Organisierter Kapitalismus und Parteidiktatur, 1933 bis 1936," *Schmoller's Jahrbuch*, LXXIX (1959), 37–79.
Seabury, Paul, *The Wilhelmstrasse: A Study of German Diplomats under the Nazi Regime* (Berkeley, 1954).
Shirer, William L., *The Third Reich* (New York, 1960).
Taylor, Telford, *Sword and Swastika* (New York, 1952).
Trevor-Roper, H. R., ed., *Hitler's Secret Conversations, 1941–44* (New York, 1953).

2 - West and East Germany: Contrasts between Societies and Economic Systems

Population Structure

It is important to remember that the Germans constitute the largest national group in all of Europe west of the Soviet Union. It was this fact which led the French to build the Maginot Line and which today makes unification so much more difficult. There are many on both sides of the Iron Curtain who do not relish the idea of a powerful state made up of some seventy-five million Germans. As things stand, war and its aftermath brought considerable dislocation of large population groups, particularly expulsion of the bulk of the German population from East Prussia, Silesia, and the other "Oder-Neisse" territories, as well as from the Sudetenland in Czechoslovakia and German populated areas in the Balkans. The following figures suggest the magnitude of these changes:

44361

German population changes, 1939–58 (in millions)

	1939	1958	Gain or loss
West Germany (Fed'l Republic)	40.2	52.5	+12.3
East Germany (Dem. Republic)	15.1	16.3	+ 1.2
West Berlin	2.7	2.2	− 0.5
East Berlin	1.6	1.1	− 0.5
"Oder-Neisse" territories	9.6	1.1	− 8.5
TOTAL	69.2	73.2	+ 4

It is noticeable that the over-all effect of the redistribution has been to increase greatly the population of West Germany. This is because the bulk of the expellees did not care to remain in the Soviet zone but headed for the western parts of the country. In addition, the "Democratic Republic" has suffered an exodus of some two to three million, mostly younger, productive inhabitants who crossed into West Berlin and the Federal Republic between 1949 and 1960. In recent years its population has remained almost static, since the number of those leaving has about balanced with the natural population increase. By contrast, the population of the Federal Republic has increased by some eight million between 1947 and 1958. The over-all increase in the German population is explained by the fact that the influx of ethnic Germans who had previously lived outside the Reich (i.e., in Poland, Yugoslavia, Rumania) plus the natural population increase has more than made up for the six to seven million military and civilian casualties of World War II.

The German population in both East and West is predominantly urban. In West Germany (including West Berlin) about a fifth of the population lives in eleven large cities with more than 500,000 inhabitants each, about 45 per cent in small and medium-sized towns and cities with populations of over 5,000, while slightly over one-third lives in smaller, rural communities. In the Democratic Republic there is a somewhat greater population concentration in rural communities and medium-sized towns, but there too population tends to be concentrated in heavily industrialized areas. Thus the heavily industrialized Land Northrhine-Westphalia and the Dresden-Leipzig-Karl-Marx-Stadt district each contain a third of the population of the two states.

In the East the administrative districts have relatively equal populations, but in the West the Laender, embodying in part traditional boundaries, vary greatly in population, almost as much as American states. Some Laender embody strong regional traditions, especially those like the Hanseatic city-states of Hamburg and Bremen or heavily agricultural Bavaria. The dialects of simple people from these areas vary quite as much as do the accents of a New Yorker and a South Carolinian. Another distinct group are the Rhinelanders, proud that after a century of rule from Berlin the West German capital was established in one of their towns by one of their own political leaders. But Land boundaries do not necessarily correspond to traditional loyalties. The occupying powers caused the Rhinelanders to be divided between two Laender, while the citizens of Wuerttemberg and Baden subsequently found themselves united into one Land. Natives did not always welcome the influx of expellees, who were at first heavily concentrated in the poorer agricultural areas of Schleswig-Holstein, Lower Saxony, and Bavaria. However, as cities and factories were rebuilt, they spread out more evenly.

Considerable political significance attaches to the religious structure of the population, and not only to the proportions between Protestants and Catholics, but also to their regional distribution. Since the formation of the Second Reich, Catholics, though predominant in certain sections, have been outnumbered about two to one in the country as a whole. They were always influential in predominantly Catholic areas like Bavaria, the Rhineland, and Silesia, but they lacked power nationally. The division of Germany has changed this situation radically. Within the Federal Republic they now claim almost half (45 per cent) of the population, a fact which has been of much greater advantage to the West German Christian Democrats than to the Social Democrats. The religious affiliation of East Germans is by contrast predominantly Protestant; only 11 per cent are Catholics. Traditionally, the Catholic church has been both better organized and more successful in maintaining touch with its following than have the Protestant churches. This is due to the fact that the Protestant churches were organized predominantly on a Land and regional level, and only loosely unified within several national church organizations. In addition, the Protestant churches almost completely lost contact with the working-class population, while the Catholics were much more successful in sponsoring a whole network of working-class organizations which helped maintain this important link. Up to 1960 the churches continued as one of the few organizations able to transcend the boundaries of the two states, although they have frequently been in conflict with the authorities of the Democratic Republic.

The West German Economic System

The differences in economic policy between West and East Germany were not as stark initially as they were to become later. This was because under the crisis conditions of the immediate postwar years it was found necessary in both West and East to continue the system of rationing and tight economic control introduced under the Nazis. The critical parting of the ways occurred in June, 1948, when the futility of attempts to achieve unified Allied policy had become evident and the United States and Britain introduced a new currency in their zones and allowed the German economic administration to initiate a policy of radical decontrol of the economy. This policy was carried through under the direction of the future Federal German Minister of Economics, Ludwig Erhard, who, with the support of the non-Socialist parties, gambled that the incentives of a free market economy would serve to liberate long dormant productive capacities. His policy proved phenomenally successful as Germans

West Germany's postwar economic recovery

	1948	1950	1953	1957	1960
Crude steel production (million tons)	5.6	12.1	15.4	24.5	34.1
Employment (millions)	13.5	14.3	16.0	19.0	20.4
Unemployment (millions)	.8	1.3	.9	.4	.1
Standard of living (private per capita consumption compared to prewar standard; 1936 = 100)	——	92	114	151	171

SOURCE: UN Statistical Yearbooks; Wolfgang Stolper, *Germany between East and West* (Washington, 1960); unofficial estimates for 1960.

eagerly sought to earn more of the new hard currency in order to buy goods which shopkeepers had previously withheld, while manufacturers rapidly expanded production facilities in order to keep up with the swelling demand for goods which were now made available on a nonrationed basis for the first time in almost a decade.[1]

The subsequent increases in production were impressive. In many industries production doubled within six months. Total industrial production, which had stood at barely half the prewar (1936) figure in mid-1948, surpassed this mark by the end of 1949. With characteristic vigor Germans of all classes—managers, workers, and foremen—worked longer hours than anybody else in Europe in order to expand productive capacities, modernize communication facilities, and rebuild housing. Differences between labor and management were subordinated to the common task. Trade union leaders showed great restraint in making wage demands in order not to impede the German drive to recapture overseas markets, thus setting the stage for a low wage, high profit growth. German technical ingenuity met the challenge of the time to improve production methods and product design in order to catch up with competitors in the United States and elsewhere. Primarily, however, industry sought to fill the demands of the domestic market, shaped by the great acquisitive fervor that gripped the German population once it saw the opportunities for satisfying material wants.

Production continued to increase without any significant recession or real levelling off. Steel production climbed from five million tons in 1945, and by the time it reached thirty million tons in 1960 West Germany had far surpassed Britain to become the world's third largest producer (after the United States and Soviet Union). Total industrial production doubled once again between 1950 and 1957 as the West Germans marked up annual growth rates averaging 10 per cent, roughly four times the American figure. The Federal Republic's gross national product had already surpassed the 1936 level in 1950, and this figure was doubled by 1957. Records like these were made possible through extremely high investment figures, which continued at a rate of from 20 to 25 per cent of the national income. Though especially encouraged by tax legislation, this indicated that Germans were working not merely to satisfy current demand, but because they possessed real confidence in the future potential of their economy.

Immediately after 1945, considerable amounts of industrial equipment concentrated in the Ruhr area had been dismantled and shipped to countries which German armies had despoiled.

[1] Henry C. Wallich, *Mainsprings of German Revival* (New Haven, 1955), Chap. 4.

The French particularly called for the internationalization of this region, the most powerful industrial complex in Europe. This extreme solution was avoided through a series of events which eventually led to the inclusion of German heavy industry in the European Steel and Coal Community. With the gradual lifting of Allied production limitations, German industry undertook an energetic drive to regain prewar markets and to capture new ones. Conditions were favorable, for in the period following the Korean crisis German industry could supply at low prices goods which had become scarce as a result of the shift to military production in other countries. Success in this endeavor led to a strong interlacing among the economies of West Germany and other Western countries.[2] The great increase in trade between Germany and the Western countries not only made up for lost markets in traditional areas like the Balkans, but also provided a substitute for the intra-German trade which used to be carried on with East Germany and which declined to one-tenth of its prewar significance. Thus whereas in 1936 West Germany had spent 8.6 per cent of its gross national product on imports from East Germany, in 1958 it spent less than 1 per cent, while imports from other countries (mainly in the West) increased from 5.6 per cent to about 13 per cent of gross national product during the same period.[3]

American Marshall Plan aid played a considerable part in supplying the crucial initial capital required for expansion, but further investment was made possible by the very considerable profits which manufacturers and businessmen were able to plough back into their firms. The attempt to restore private business as a dynamic economic factor in the reconstruction of Germany was supported by extremely generous tax policies which favored the creation of new wealth and brought economically powerful groups to identify their fortunes with those of the state whose economic basis they were helping to shape. The question of ownership and control of industry was settled in their favor. Originally there had been much sentiment, especially among Socialists and the trade unions, for nationalizing heavy industry, but this impulse was unable to prevail over the newly found enthusiasm for private enterprise. Instead, the Co-determination Law of 1951 gave the trade unions the opportunity to help in-

[2] Ludwig Erhard, *Germany's Comeback in the World Market* (New York, 1954), Chap. 1.

[3] Wolfgang Stolper, *Germany between East and West* (Washington, 1960), pp. 10–11.

fluence company policies by sending representatives to the board of directors of the large steel and coal companies.[4]

The power of the owners and managers of the very large industrial and commercial firms, who are organized in tightly knit industrial and trade associations, was demonstrated in their ability to undo many of the deconcentration measures introduced under the Occupation. Firms like Krupp, which had been ordered to divest themselves of parts of their industrial empires, were able to avoid the implementation of these orders and even to acquire other large firms which increased their dominance. A similar development occurred in banking. The Allies had broken up the "Big Three" banks which had dominated German banking into thirty independent units. By 1952 these had been reconcentrated into nine banks and by 1957 the "Big Three" were reestablished.

Thus postwar West German economic development has been marked not only by large production increases but also by a return to earlier patterns under which control over large sectors of the economy rests in the hands of a relatively small number of managers and bankers. In view of continued prosperity and full employment this fact has not caused any serious conflicts affecting large parts of the population, but it worries many critics of German big business as well as adherents of the free market economy. Obviously, if concentration of ownership and interlocking directorates continue unabated, the doctrine of free competition will become less and less meaningful. Official policy has sought to deal with these problems, but it has been handicapped by the fact that the government's political backers in industry have opposed the necessary stringent regulations. However, while not making much progress in the area of concentration of ownership, in 1957 the government did pass Germany's first anticartel law,[5] and such formerly typical German business practices as price-fixing and market-sharing have been somewhat curtailed. But the organizations representing industry and big business remain the most powerful of economic groups. Where they have led, other economic groups have followed. Labor, farmers, white collar workers, artisans, and civil servants are all highly organized and seek to achieve their ends through the political process as well as through economic bargaining. As in other advanced industrial

---

[4] Wallich, *op. cit.*, pp. 307 ff.

[5] E. Guenther, "Das Gesetz gegen Wettbewerbsbeschraenkungen im Rahmen der deutschen Wirtschaftspolitik," *Wirtschaft und Wettbewerb*, X (November, 1960), 747 ff.

countries, the government has become the embattled regulatory mechanism of a complex economic system.

From Rags to Riches

A politically significant aspect of the German recovery program is that it allowed the West German economy to integrate the millions of exiles from former German areas in Eastern Europe, who had for years been forced to remain in makeshift refugee camps or had been quartered with resentful local families. As new production and service facilities were created, more jobs opened up. This was not immediately the case, for the currency reform caused shortages of credit and capital which led to considerable unemployment. At one time it surpassed the two million mark, and there was some unrest as it continued to hover over the million mark well into the 1950's.[6] But by 1954 the demand for labor began to increase much more rapidly than did the supply, even though the work force continued to be augmented not only by youths reaching working age, but by refugees from East Germany and those returning late from Russian prison camps. Employment increased most markedly in industry and commerce, but significantly also in the restaurant and tavern trades, where it doubled between 1950 and 1956, a phenomenon by no means accounted for by foreign tourists alone. By 1959, unemployment was almost nil (1.3 per cent). Employment had increased by more than 50 per cent in the course of a decade, prosperous housewives were leaving the labor market, and German businessmen were forced to import workers from Italy and even Spain. In 1960, 276,000 foreign workers were employed in West Germany, and personnel chiefs were sending agents all over Europe to recruit factory hands willing to work for the German mark.

While the economic miracle doubled the number of West German millionaires in four years (1936: 1,957; 1953: 1,566; 1957: 3,502), benefits deriving from economic expansion were fairly widespread. Industrial wages rose gradually. In 1950 the average industrial worker was paid the equivalent of about thirty cents an hour, much to the annoyance of British and other competitors whose labor was more expensive and who felt that German union leaders were not militant enough. By 1958, however, German unions had succeeded in raising the average hourly rate to

[6] Wallich, *op. cit.*, pp. 79 ff.

more than fifty cents an hour[7] without delaying economic expansion by more than a minimum of work stoppages. Throughout the 1950's the average German worked close to fifty hours a week, but by the end of the decade the unions were pressing for a reduction, with posters showing a little girl saying, "I want my daddy at home on weekends." Tax returns also showed the general increase in prosperity. In 1950, 54 per cent of all wage and salary earners made less than 900 dollars; in 1957 only 16 per cent were in this category while 53 per cent were earning from 900 to 1,800 dollars a year.[8] During the same interval the number of workers and employees earning more than 2,400 dollars increased from 800,000 to 5.3 million, while the currency maintained its purchasing power better than almost any other, price increases being held to an annual average of less than 2 per cent. Real personal per capita consumption increased by about 6 per cent annually in the first eight years of the existence of the Federal Republic. And between 1954 and 1960 the number of privately owned cars increased four-fold (to four million), those owned by workers twenty-fold (to one million). Inevitably, there were some who failed to win their share. In 1956 the bottom third of the population received only 11 per cent of all personal income.[9] And in 1960 there were still people living in the abandoned barracks of the former Nazi concentration camp at Dachau. But the vast majority of Germans had benefitted immensely from the economic recovery program.

What have been the social consequences of this economic revival? For some years observers of German society detected a so-called "restorationist" trend which led Germans to seek to regain social position by competing for material and status symbols. This appears to have been an essentially short-term effect associated with the unexpected rapid ascent from rags to riches of many social groups. A more fundamental trend may

[7] Figures in Deutschmark (DM) are here given at the official exchange rate prevailing since 1960 ($1 = DM 4), after the 5 per cent upward revaluation carried out that year. However, it should be noted, particularly in regard to personal income figures, that specific amounts of money have a much higher purchasing value in Germany than in the United States, perhaps almost double. Thus a German worker earning the German equivalent of fifty cents an hour could probably purchase as much with that amount as an American worker could with one dollar.

[8] Gerhard Zeitel, "Einkommenstatistik," *Handwoerterbuch der Sozialwissenschaften,* Section 28, p. 65.

[9] Martin Lohmann, "Die Westdeutschen Investitionen 1948–1957 und ihre Soziale Problematik," *Hamburger Jahrbuch fuer Wirtschafts und Gesellschaftspolitik,* III (1958), 56.

be a development toward the kind of society based on personal achievement typical of the United States. Traditional external signs of status are becoming outdated. Rank in the governmental hierarchy has lost significance as the civil service bureaucracy has become only one among many. Cosmopolitan experience no longer suffices, as millions of workers stream across the Alps to vacation by the shores of the Adriatic. Domestic servants are becoming museum pieces as country girls find that they can earn twice as much in the factory as in the nursery. Family background has declined in importance as vast numbers now leave their native towns in search of new homes or job possibilities. There are many signs to indicate that Germany's social stratification is becoming strikingly similar to that of other industrial countries where feudal traditions were eclipsed earlier or were nonexistent. If the over-all picture still shows somewhat less social mobility than, for instance, the United States, this is partly because of the greater numerical significance of stable groups like professionals (2.9 per cent versus 1.4 per cent in the United States), small entrepreneurs (10.7 per cent versus 6 per cent), and farmers (10.6 per cent versus 5.9 per cent), who tend to pass on positions and status to their children, and the lesser significance of mobile groups like technical and other employees (18.8 per cent versus 30.8 per cent).[10] But basic socio-economic trends tend to bring West Germany closer to the American pattern.

One institution which does not contribute as much to increasing social mobility as it might, or as its equivalents do in countries as different as the United States and the Democratic Republic, is the educational system. The quality of the general German educational system is rightfully held in world-wide esteem both for its successes in bringing literacy to the masses and for its traditional ability to produce outstanding scholars and scientists. But as in most continental countries there tends to be a strong class bias as to who gets advanced education, which is for many the only route to higher social status. Four-fifths of the pupils leave school at the age of fourteen, and those who do go on proceed to the *Gymnasien*, the academic high schools which prepare for university entrance. *Gymnasien* students, however, have always been drawn disproportionately from middle-class families which supply both the incentive and the financial means. In Britain a concerted effort has been made to remove

[10] Morris Janowitz, "Social Stratification and Mobility in West Germany," *American Journal of Sociology*, LXIV (1958), 8.

at least the financial barriers for working-class children by providing aid to families which keep their children in secondary school; there is also a generous public scholarship program for university students. West Germany has not seen fit to follow this example, and one result is that only 5 to 10 per cent of university students come from working-class families, even though all universities in Germany are public, their tuition rates are quite low, and the state does provide other marginal subsidies and a limited scholarship program.

However, most socially-conscious Germans have come to feel fairly satisfied with the social system. As one wrote in 1960:

Tonight, as I dine on oysters flown in by Air France . . . I don't have a bad social conscience. The taxi driver out there could, if he wanted to, occasionally afford oysters and wine. . . . The expellees have been resettled and the manner in which they are looked after is an extraordinary accomplishment of our society. The drug store down the street glitters in chrome, its neon signs promise to bring back lost slenderness. The goodlooking druggist gracefully dims the golden ray of lights as if she were a stage goddess, and gets ready to meet her boy-friend outside an entrance designed by a student of Picasso. They drive off in a white sports car. . . . while the radio plays a soft American tune all about the beauty of Virginia. The girls don't look the way they used to in the days of the Hitler youth movement. They are dressed like their equivalents in New York or Paris, and they wear their hair and cosmetics just as they do in London or Rome. . . . I live in the Federal Republic. Do I live in paradise? [11]

Others emphasize how much changes in German values have eclipsed the traditional stereotypes which foreigners held of the German mentality:

These new Germans don't just live to work, rather they know quite well how to combine self-improvement with all possible comforts. . . . Where once ideals motivated, indifference now reigns. The somber impulses of the "Faustian man" have given way to the clearest sort of calculation. Once-popular concepts of "destiny" are received with knowledgeable smiles and expressions of a "sense of mission" are dismissed with shrugs of the shoulder. Is it possible that a people who before could never do without a rich assortment of *Weltanschauungen* and *ideologies* now yawns at the mention of the thinkers who shaped its traditions? [12]

If this intellectual's evaluation sounds ambiguous, a student writes on a more positive note. He sees West German values

[11] Wolfgang Koeppen, *Die Welt,* June 11, 1960.
[12] Herman Proebst, *Magnum,* April, 1960, p. 14.

shaped by the satisfaction of personal wants generally and by a
fascination with the American style of life in particular, but
thinks this is not a bad thing.

This outlook is based on enthusiasm for a better standard of living. . . .
The fellow who can figure out how soon he too can own a motor bike
or a Volkswagen won't dream any longer of the day when there will
be a *Gauleiter's* job opening up in Central Asia. . . . One result of
this outlook is that politics is no longer regarded as a matter of pas-
sion, but rather as a matter of choosing between a variety of possible
solutions.[13]

Another intellectual refuses to accept this optimistic line.

How happily one would entertain the hope that the Western "part-
Germans" with all their American civilization have foresworn nationalism. But one can in fact only ascertain that up till now they are a
blank page. I refuse to regard the plebiscites for refrigerators which
are held every four years as real political decisions. It all depends on
who gets the chance to write what on this blank page in times to come.[14]

East German Development

About the same time that the West moved to decentralize
economic control through adoption of the "social market policy,"
the East began to move energetically in the other direction. In
1945 only the larger industrial and business enterprises had been
socialized, and even these remained under the control of communal and Land authorities. The change-over to centralized
control and planning began in 1948 and found expression in the
Two-Year Plan adopted for 1949 and 1950. Subsequently a state
planning commission was created on the Soviet model, and it
was this agency which developed two additional Five-Year Plans
which initially sought to concentrate all energies on the creation
of a previously almost nonexistent heavy industrial base. Despite
lack of adequate coal and iron resources, steel production was
increased tenfold in the period from 1948 to 1958, though at
this point West Germany was still outproducing the East by a
ratio of twenty-six to three million tons annually.

More recently, within the framework of a new Seven-Year
Plan (1958 to 1965) which parallels that of the Soviet Union,
the East German economy has been closely integrated with the
economies of the entire East European bloc. Thus, East Germany

[13] "Schlacken," *Deutsche Studentenzeitung*, January, 1954, p. 3.
[14] Erich Kuby, *Magnum*, April, 1960, p. 544.

Indices of the comparative development of the West and East German economies

	1936	1950	1957
Aggregate Gross National Product			
West Germany	100	116	200
East Germany	100	77	122
Per capita Gross National Product			
West Germany	100	92	151
East Germany	100	69	112
Industrial, mining, & electricity output			
West Germany	100	117	233
East Germany	100	75	144
Per capita consumption			
West Germany	100	92	151
East Germany	100	37	95

SOURCE: Wolfgang Stolper, *Germany between East and West* (Washington, 1960), p. 14.

has come to concentrate on expanding its chemical, heavy mechanical, and electro-technical industries so as to serve as a specialized supplier to the other "peoples' democracies" as well as to the Soviet Union, for whom it has become the most important foreign source of investment goods. In little more than a decade East Germany has set up not only a planned economy in sharp contrast to the West German system, but has gradually extended the framework within which the planning takes place from the local, to the national, to the supranational level.

The experimentation with planning formulas caused considerable waste and privation, but this did not deter the East German regime from gradually eliminating the remaining private sectors of the economy in line with its ideological goals. Small private factory owners found it increasingly difficult to secure the materials necessary for achieving assigned production targets. Frequently the authorities would find minor infringements of planning or tax regulations and, while the owners were thus under pressure, offer to provide public capital to help modernize the plant.[15] In this way the state became the dominant partner even of enterprises which it did not directly run, and the private sector, which had still made up almost a quarter of East German industry in 1950, was gradually reduced to the vanishing point (1959: 5 per cent). A similar development occurred in areas like

[15] John Herz, "East Germany: Progress and Prospects," *Social Research* (1960), 147.

the construction industry and wholesale trade, where the "social-ist" sector became predominant in the course of the 1950's. Private farmers, artisans, and retail store owners continued to be tolerated as long as they were useful to the state, which was anxious not to overload its economic agencies to the point of organizational breakdown. Ingenious types of "socialist" organization, such as producers' collectives and state-controlled trading cooperatives, were set up with the aim of encouraging the smaller owners to place themselves voluntarily in dependent positions, thus allowing the state to carry out complete socialization at a later date with a minimum of struggle or interruption of economic activity.

The process which by 1960 led to the virtual elimination of private property in agriculture serves to illustrate the manner in which East German collectivization was carried through and its similarity to the earlier Soviet model. The first stage actually created an increased number of private farmers, since the 1945 land reform program distributed the best part of some 7,000 large estates among approximately 300,000 expellees, land-poor farm-ers, and farm laborers, most of whom received less than ten acres. After a period of consolidation comparable to the "New Eco-nomic Policy" period in the Soviet Union, pressure began to be brought against middle-sized farmers who owned between twenty and one hundred acres. By means of political propaganda and economic pressure much of their land was incorporated into agricultural collectives. But by 1952 still only about one-quarter of the total land area was in the "socialist" sector, half of this in collectives and half under direct state operation.[16]

When pressure caused the large-scale flight of peasants to the West, the regime substituted a propaganda campaign urging small-scale farmers to deed their land voluntarily to collectives in order to benefit from the preferred position in terms of better machine tractor service and lower production quotas. The pres-sure was maintained with varying degrees of intensity; it was relaxed during crisis periods like those following the June 17, 1953, uprising and the Polish and Hungarian revolts of 1956, and intensified when conditions stabilized. Between 1953 and 1958 the proportion of land in collective ownership increased from 13.8 per cent to 29.4 per cent, climbing to 45 per cent by 1959. Then in the spring of 1960, the regime decided to stage an intensive drive to complete collectivization. Thousands of

[16] Frieda Wunderlich, *Farmer and Farm Labor in the Soviet Zone of Ger-many* (New York, 1958).

Communist activists descended on the villages to undertake a personalized pressure campaign on the peasants still holding out, who were made to see that jail or flight were the only real alternatives to "voluntary entry" into at least a "class-one" collective, in which the peasants gave up their land but kept title to their animals and implements. As newspapers reported district after district achieving 100 per cent collectivization the peasants realized their hopeless position and surrendered title to their land.

The elimination of entire social groups, such as the independent peasants and industrial and commercial entrepreneurs, has been part of the huge social revolution engineered in East Germany. Social mobility has been tremendous as elements of the old middle and lower-middle classes have been forced down the social scale while large masses of workers have been carried upwards. Although the denazification and expropriation processes were most important in eliminating the middle classes' position of influence, other techniques were employed for groups like professionals. Independent practice has been made all but impossible for lawyers and doctors. Like managers, they have been forced to accept positions as employees of the state or one of its subsidiary organizations. Members of the intelligentsia, especially teachers and professors, have had to conform to the twisting party line in their instruction and writings. Many of those who remember better times, or hear of conditions in the West in broadcasts from West Berlin, tend to escape to West Germany.

In an attempt to replace these groups, the East German regime has from the beginning sponsored a far-reaching program of training workers and peasants for entry into positions in the intelligentsia, the bureaucracy, and managerial positions. Typical perhaps is the engineer, Rosemarie Gutermuth. Originally a humble construction worker, she distinguished herself by winning commendation as an "activist," was promoted to forewoman of her brigade and was then sent to study engineering on a government scholarship. She ended up as a responsible bureaucrat working in the Ministry of Reconstruction and was widely quoted as saying: "What I am and the way I live I owe entirely to our Workers' and Peasants' state." [17] The relatively high salaried elite groups of engineers, managers, and intellectuals who have been funnelled into the new positions created within the ap-

[17] Otto Stammer, "Sozialstruktur und System der Werthaltungen der Sowjetischen Besatzungszone Deutschlands," *Schmoller's Jahrbuch*, LXXVI (1956), 103.

paratus of the planned society after proper ideological indoctrination, form one of the key social bases for the regime.

But workers in the public enterprises can also gain significant
rewards if they are willing to pursue the manifold opportunities
offered and to assume political responsibilities by membership in
a party or political youth group. Active campaigns in the shops
encourage them to read serious literature and to discuss it in
discussion groups. They may be delegated to pursue part-time
home study of advanced technical subjects, or to spend their
evening hours attending night classes in philosophy or economics
at the local university. Many are encouraged to write contributions for newspapers and magazines, in the expectation that their
coworkers will lend greater credence to their articles than to
those of professional propagandists. Between these activities an
active and ambitious East German worker can earn quite a good
living, but his educational and political activities take up virtually all his spare time. In addition, he is required to train with
his unit of the workers' militia, preparing for the day when he
might have to capture a group of "Western imperialist infiltra-
tors." All in all, the East German regime has certainly discovered
ingenious ways to combat the monotony characteristic of the
modern industrial worker's mode of living. But woe to the
worker if his performance in one of his manifold tasks should
fall below expectations, or if he should say the wrong things in
the party political discussion, since a decision by his superiors
can relegate him overnight to a menial job paying less than half
of what he had become used to earning.[18]

The economic achievements of the German Democratic
Republic were for many years far less impressive than those of
the Federal Republic. It took the East Germans far longer to
reach prewar levels of production and even longer to supply the
average citizen with something like his prewar standard of living.
This was due not only to successive changes in policy relating
to the basic restructuring of the economy and to the losses
incurred in the process of the socialization of industry, trade,
and agriculture, but also to the fact that East Germany lacked a
heavy industry base. Another initial handicap was the fact that
the Russians carried through the dismantling program much
more thoroughly than the Western Allies, with the result that the
East was deprived of a far larger share of its productive capacity.
Though possessing only a third of total German resources, the
Soviet zone was forced to supply over three quarters of all

[18] Erika von Hornstein, *Die Deutsche Not* (Cologne, 1960).

German reparations, to the value of perhaps ten billion dollars. These factors, together with the problem of a continued labor shortage due in good part to the flight to the West of skilled workers and technicians, handicapped East German reconstruction. It was only in 1954 that the regime achieved the equivalent of prewar production levels.

Well into the 1950's, however, the emphasis on increasing production goods led to continuing shortages of consumer goods, which caused the regime to maintain rationing until 1958. Until this time currency in East Germany really had two values. Rationed goods were sold at quite low prices, while many goods purchased in the state-run "HO" stores required no ration coupons but were priced much higher. In this way the regime was able to ensure minimum standards of living and at the same time to limit excessive consumer expenditure. Dissatisfaction with the standard of living was one of the causes of the 1953 uprising, since it had been little improved for the past several years and was then some 50 per cent below West German standards. In the following years greater emphasis was placed on consumer goods in East Germany, just as in Soviet Russia, and by 1957 the gap between the average East and West German workers' standard of living was reduced to about 30 to 40 per cent.[19] East Germans were gradually able to afford luxury items like radios and vacuum cleaners, while the quality of clothing and similar products improved considerably. By 1960 a correspondent for the London *Economist* could report that "The East Germans are once again enjoying most of the creature comforts. . . . They are wearing markedly better clothes. There are more private cars and motor bikes on the road. There are generally more goods in the shops, not merely in the shop windows. The average German's conception of a square meal—plenty of fresh meat or sausage, and beer or wine—is procurable anywhere at a reasonable price."[20] But these gains did not obscure the fact that East Germany did not even come close to achieving its propaganda goal of overtaking West Germany by 1961 in consumption of the most important consumer goods and foodstuffs, and had to admit this publicly.

Nevertheless, despite initial handicaps and continuing problems due to planning difficulties and population flight, East Germany in the course of the fifties almost caught up with the

[19] Heinz Markmann, "Lohn und Kaufkraft in der Sowjetzone," *Wirtschaft-wissenschaftliche Mitteilungen*, 1959, No. 3, p. 13.

[20] *Economist*, June 25, 1960, p. 1350.

Federal Republic in the crucial matter of ability to expand its economy. Average annual growth rates in both West and East ranged between 8 and 10 per cent, with a slight Western advantage due mainly to its population increase. Although both West and East devote an unusually high share of the national product to investment, the East increased its ratio spectacularly from 18 per cent to 28 per cent, thus slightly overtaking the Federal Republic (1958: 24 per cent).[21] The greater part of investment went into industry, thus enabling East Germany to almost double industrial production between 1950 and 1957. On balance, the economic achievements of the Democratic Republic should not be underrated. As Professor Wolfgang Stolper observed in 1960: "Of course the continuing depressed level of East German living standards should be noted; on the other hand it is likely that this disparity will lessen and there is a distinct possibility that East Germany may for a while actually register a higher future per capita rate [of growth] than the Federal Republic." [22]

Bibliography

Economic Structure

Arnold, Felix, *Die Sozialistische Planwirtschaft und der Demokratische Zentralismus in der Volkswirtschaft der DDR* (Berlin, 1959).

Erhard, Ludwig, *Germany's Comeback in the World Market* (New York, 1954).

Hartmann, Heinz, *Authority and Organization in German Management* (Princeton, 1959).

Lohmann, Martin, "Die Westdeutschen Investitionen 1948–1957 und ihre Soziale Problematik," *Hamburger Jahrbuch fuer Wirtschafts und Gesellschaftspolitik*, III (1958), 32–56.

Markmann, Heinz, "Lohn und Kaufkraft in der Sowjetzone," *Wirtschaftswissenschaftliche Mitteilungen* (1959), Nos. 2 & 3.

Ortlieb, H. D., "Unsere Konsumgesellschaft," *Hamburger Jahrbuch fuer Wirtschafts und Gesellschaftspolitik*, IV (1959), 225–45.

Stolper, Wolfgang, *Germany between East and West* (Washington, 1960).

——, and Roskamp, Karl, *The Structure of the East German Economy* (Cambridge, Mass., 1960).

Wallich, Henry C., *Mainsprings of German Revival* (New Haven, 1955).

Wunderlich, Frieda, *Farmer and Farm Labor in the Soviet Zone of Germany* (New York, 1958).

Social Systems

Herz, John, "East Germany: Progress and Prospects," *Social Research* (1960), XXVII, 139–56.

Hornstein, Erika von, *Die Deutsche Not* (Cologne, 1960).

[21] Stolper, *op. cit.*, pp. 33, 44.
[22] *Ibid.*, p. 12.

Janowitz, Morris, "Social Stratification and Mobility in West Germany," *American Jl. of Sociology*, LXIV (1958), 6–24.

Lowie, Robert H., *Toward Understanding Germany* (Chicago, 1954).

Pross, Helge, "Die Soziale Schichtung in der Bundesrepublik," *Deutsche Rundschau*, LXXXIV (October, 1958), 916–26.

Reigrotsky, Erich, *Soziale Verflechtungen in der Bundesrepublik* (Tuebingen, 1956).

Stammer, Otto, "Sozialstruktur und System der Werthaltungen der Sowjetischen Besatzungszone Deutschlands," *Schmoller's Jahrbuch*, LXXVI (1956), 55–105.

Stern, Carola, *et al.*, "Ulbricht's Germany: Studies in Intellectual Gleichschaltung," *Soviet Survey* (1960), No. 34, 30–73.

Wagner, Helmut R., "The Cultural Sovietization of East Germany," *Social Research*, XXIV (1957), 395–426.

PART II

THE FEDERAL REPUBLIC

3 - Political Structure and Behavior

Origins, Conditioning, and Constitution

OCCUPATION THERAPY. Now that the West and the Federal Republic are allies, there is a tendency to look back to the postwar period and see the occupying powers as benevolent Dutch uncles pooling their collective political experience in order to come up with the right solution for the new democratic Germany. Initially, however, the Germans were regarded as defeated enemies, rule over whom was placed predominantly in the hands of military officers with a minimal understanding of long-range political aims. When political policies were gradually given a certain amount of priority, these were applied during the first years on a largely uncoordinated basis by zonal commanders reflecting the interests and predilections of their own national governments. Thus the French sought to bring about the dismemberment of Germany, while the British and Americans espoused, respectively, a centralized political system based on the nationalization of industry, and a federal system based on the maintenance of maximal private property rights. When, during the latter part of the Occupation, the Western Allies finally bridged their own differences in the face of mutual rejection of Soviet aims, they were already sharing the bulk of political power with German politicians, and it became increasingly difficult to distinguish between Allied and German policy. Nevertheless, there is no doubt that the occupation did have considerable effect both in recasting many elements of the framework of postwar German politics and in conditioning German political behavior.

The most immediate impact on the largest number of Germans occurred as the result of Allied policies to uproot nazism, and to punish those who had assisted the Hitler regime.

The highest ranking survivors of the Nazi hierarchy and its military and civilian appendices were of course held to account in the Nuremberg War Trials (in which the Soviet Union also participated). But, in addition, millions of Germans were subjected to denazification proceedings in which the attempt was made to investigate the degree of assistance they had given the Nazi regime and to punish them accordingly. Sentences ranged from prolonged imprisonment, through dismissal from office (418,000 in the United States zone) and the payment of heavy fines, to the obligation to spend stipulated periods of time working as ordinary laborers helping to clear up the rubble or repair desecrated Jewish gravestones. But the difficulty was that obvious criteria, such as membership in the Nazi party and its numerous affiliates, were a dubious key to the identity of the worst offenders. In the British and French zones there was relatively little emphasis on punishing the small-time party member, and it was possible to channel considerable energy into a program designed to punish the more active agents of the regime. The Americans, however, decided to have denazification boards review the cases of no less than 3.6 million out of 16 million adults in the United States zone, thus creating a staggering task for the relatively few Americans and proven anti-Nazis who had to carry it out. The result was that denazification proceedings deteriorated; the boards became less thorough and more lenient just at the time when they began to deal with the more serious cases.[1] The Germans, among whom the collective guilt doctrine had created a kind of negative solidarity, were quick to develop theories of self-justification which minimized their role in Nazi excesses and maximized the weaknesses of the denazification process. Gradually the program was replaced by purely German proceedings against individuals guilty of criminal acts under German law.

Denazification proceedings did, however, serve a vital purpose in removing individuals with Nazi records from positions of public responsibility, at least for the time being. Thus, many were forced out of the judiciary, the civil service, the teaching profession, and the communication media. In private business check-ups were less rigorous, although about a quarter of the managerial personnel were removed at least temporarily, and many large corporations were at first taken over directly by trustees of Allied military government.[2]

[1] John D. Montgomery, *Forced to Be Free: The Artificial Revolution in Germany and Japan* (Chicago, 1957), pp. 10 ff.
[2] *Ibid.*, pp. 94–125.

The Allies were sufficiently wise to recognize that they could not uproot one elite without replacing it with another, and so their policy manuals prescribed that denazification steps were to be matched by democratization actions, not only through the appointment of demonstrated anti-Nazis to public positions, but also through the creation of new institutions which would help Germans with impressive democratic credentials assume positions of influence. In this manner, the leaders of the pre-Hitler trade unions were reinstalled in office long before similar invitations were extended to business and professional groups whose over-all record was far more ambiguous. Similarly, the Occupation authorities began to divest themselves of their initial monopoly in the communications field by issuing licenses allowing certain anti-Nazis to publish newspapers and by replacing the personnel of the state-run radio works. But the most important political instruments of democratization were the political parties, which were licensed only after their programs and membership lists had been screened. Although procedures differed in the various zones, four parties usually received Allied encouragement. These included the Communists, whose credentials as active anti-Nazis were at first rated high everywhere; the Socialists, who with an equally clear political record, re-established their party organization; and finally the Christian Democrats and the Liberals, who, though their organizations had played very little role in the anti-Nazi resistance, were nevertheless recognized as the spokesmen for democratically inclined population groups which, before Hitler, had supported such relatively loyal "Weimar parties" as the Center and the German Democratic party.[3]

LAENDER AND ZONES. In addition to uprooting Nazis and nurturing new, or reinstating pre-Nazi, political leaders, the Allies set up the governmental structure from which the Federal Republic was to evolve. The basic units resuscitated were the Laender, the traditional German states which had been abolished by the Nazis. In setting up the Laender two kinds of problem were encountered. In south and southwest Germany, loyalty to the Laender was still very much alive, but Occupation geometry had caused zonal boundaries to cut across traditional Land boundaries. In northwest Germany, on the other hand, a century-long Prussian hegemony had largely destroyed regional loyalties, so that after the abolition of Prussia the British had to

[3] Richard D. Scammon, "Political Parties," in E. H. Litchfield, ed., *Governing Postwar Germany* (Ithaca, 1953), pp. 471–500.

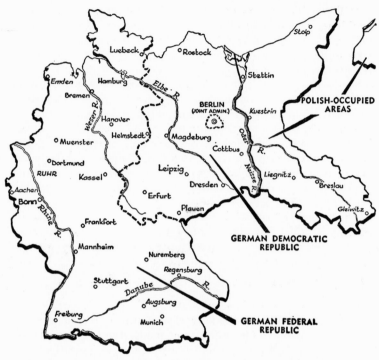

Germany (*From* The New York Times, *June 12, 1955*)

set up Laender without much regard to local traditions. Apart
from the two city states of Hamburg and Bremen, the only
revived Land possessing both live historical traditions and prewar
boundaries was Bavaria, a fact which has helped the Bavarians
maintain a long-term gain of influence in national politics.
With the hope of preventing the re-creation of a strong central
government, the French, and to some extent also the Americans,
encouraged the small Laender in their zones to set up elaborate
governmental machinery and encouraged a largely artificial Land
patriotism. The British on the other hand exercised centralized
control through zonal authorities, and though they too set up
such new Laender as Lower Saxony, Rhineland-Westphalia, and
Schleswig-Holstein, they did not attempt to revive archaic boundaries or to encourage Land governments to exaggerate their
political significance.[4]

Thus during the period 1946 to 1947 each of the zones was

[4] Roger H. Wells, "State Government," in Litchfield, *op. cit.*, pp. 84–117.

developing its own peculiar flavor and institutions. The North Germans looked down on the officials in the French and American zones as provincial and even "separatists," while the South German officials regarded their compatriots from the Ruhr northwards as undemocratic "centralist lackeys," who lacked understanding of grass-roots democracy. Since the different occupation powers naturally encouraged the teaching of their language in the local schools, it was soon suggested that if the trend toward zoning were to continue Germans would start speaking with French, British, and American accents. A change in the situation was brought about, however, by a combination of economic necessity and Soviet intransigence. The Americans and the British were the first to plan the merger of the economic administrations of their economically complementary zones. When the Russians and French refused invitations to join, they began the gradual build-up of interzonal agencies which culminated in the creation of the bizonal Economic Council. The French, recognizing the futility of attempts to hold out for a loose confederation of German states, gradually fell into line, thus turning the bizone into the trizone. This expansion of German government allowed the German party politicians to look beyond the horizons of their Laender and to think concretely of vying for national power. The two strongest parties, the Social Democrats (SPD) and the Christian Democrats (CDU), staked out their positions in the Economic Council, where the CDU together with the smaller parties upheld Erhard's free market policy. The Socialists, still loyal to the idea of a planned economy, were confident that Erhard would fail and that the support of the impoverished masses would then make them the dominant party.

Meanwhile, the widening rift between the Western powers and Soviet Russia in effect reduced the number of potential alternatives. West Germans could either continue to hope that despite the failure of successive foreign ministers' conferences the Allies would come to an agreement paving the way to an all-German government; or else they could support the much more immediate efforts to create a German rump state based only on the territory of the three Western zones.

By the summer of 1948 the mass of West German political opinion was moving toward acceptance of the "Western" solution. All the major party groups were now organizationally cut off from their counterparts in the Soviet zone, while Soviet rejection of the Marshall Plan, followed soon thereafter by the launching of the Berlin Blockade, tended to undercut the argu-

ments of the minority that Germans should support no constitutional arrangements unless based on the unification of all
four zones. With varying shades of reluctance, the West German
politicians thus accepted the Western Allies' proposal that a
constituent assembly be called to draw up a constitution for a
West German state, to which the Occupation powers would be
prepared to yield the bulk of German political authority. They
gave legalistic expression to their reservations by refusing to
talk of either a "constituent assembly" or a "constitution," but
the "Parliamentary Council" which started meeting in September, 1948, to work on the drafting of the "Basic Law," was to
construct more than merely the transitional instrument described
in its preamble.

THE BASIC LAW. The members of the Parliamentary Council
could not easily shake off a deeply ingrained German bent toward
seeking to fit political realities to the Procrustean bed of legal
theory. But they could not ignore evidence that the traditional
operating concepts of the European nation-state were archaic,
that the most beautifully drafted constitutions could easily be
converted into useless scraps of paper, and that they had little
cause to base grandiose plans on an optimistic evaluation of man's
political potential. The party complexion of the Council—composed of equally large groups of CDU and SPD delegates, with
minor parties holding a balance of power—also discouraged
attempts to incorporate basic economic and social policy goals
within its framework. But, the name notwithstanding, the delegates did produce a complete constitution, which sought to draw
realistic consequences from specific historical experiences.[5]

Contributing causes of the Weimar failure, as the delegates
recognized, related to the inability of the legislature to surmount
internal party strife, the consequent weaknesses of cabinets and
the political executive and, finally, the disappointing function
of the president as a guardian of the Constitution. There was
some talk of foregoing the parliamentary system altogether, in
favor of a presidential system based on the separation of powers.
But the lack of European experience with this type of constitution, the unwillingness of all groups, in view of recent experiences, to concentrate as much power in a one-person executive
as the American model entails, and a decided distrust of the
voters' reliability, led them to discard this idea. Instead, the

[5] John F. Golay, *The Founding of the Federal Republic of Germany*
(Chicago, 1958), and U.S. Military Government, *Documents on the Creation
of the German Federal Constitution* (Washington, 1949).

delegates sought to create a "rationalized" variant of the parliamentary system which would meet the traditional problems of German politics.

As a result, the two institutions which had held greatest power under the Weimar Constitution, the popular branch of the legislature and the presidency, were both retained but their power was greatly reduced. The lower house, whose name was changed from Reichstag to *Bundestag,* was greatly weakened in its ability to overthrow cabinets. The presidency was shorn of most independent political power and almost reduced to the figurehead position of the British monarch. But the people were also deprived, through the abolition of the initiative and referendum, of those direct political powers which the optimistic drafters of Weimar had given them. By contrast, two traditional institutions gained in influence. One was the federal upper house called the *Bundesrat,* which, with Allied encouragement, was made much stronger than its pre-Hitler predecessor. Most importantly, it was the executive, especially the Chancellor's position, which was markedly strengthened. The constitutional basis on which Adenauer was later able to develop what many people have called a "Chancellor democracy" was in good part due to the drafters' conviction that the Weimar democracy might have been saved if some of its Chancellors had had greater power to impose their policies both on a divided legislature and on fellow cabinet members. The specific constitutional provisions will be examined in greater detail within the context of succeeding chapters, but it is important to become aware at this point of the redistribution of powers through which the Basic Law helped make the politics of Bonn so different from those of Weimar.

The dominant characteristic of the Basic Law consists of the grafting of multiple check and balance mechanisms onto a parliamentary structure. German parliamentarianism had always been heavily adulterated and it became more so. The delegates particularly liked the idea of the American Supreme Court, and they set about creating a Constitutional Court of their own which would assume the role of an arbiter of the Constitution. It was empowered to decide not only the constitutionality of legislation and administrative acts, but also basic questions of constitutional interpretation which were expected to develop both among the various parts of the federal government and between it and the Laender. By thus endowing a novel Constitutional Court with powers to discourage unconstitutional action and to adapt the constitution to changing circumstances, the

Basic Rules of the "Basic Law"

Article 20

(1) The Federal Republic of Germany is a democratic and social Federal state.

(2) All state authority emanates from the people. It shall be exercised by the people by means of elections and voting and by separate legislative, executive and judicial organs.

(3) Legislation shall be limited by the constitution, the executive and the administration of justice by legislation and the law.

Article 79

(1) The Basic Law may be amended only by a law which expressly alters or adds to the text of the Basic Law. [*Note: Special conditions are applicable for the implementation of certain kinds of treaties.*]

(2) Such a law shall require the affirmative vote of two-thirds of the members of the Bundestag and two-thirds of the votes of the Bundesrat.

(3) An amendment to this Basic Law affecting the division of the Federation into *Laender*, the participation in principle of the *Laender* in legislation, or the basic principles laid down in Articles 1 and 20 is inadmissible.

Article 73

The Federation shall have exclusive legislation on:
1. foreign affairs as well as defense, including both military service for males over 18 years and the protection of the civilian population.
2. citizenship of the Federation . . .
11. statistics for Federal purposes.

Article 74

Concurrent legislative powers extend to the following matters:
1. civil law, criminal law and execution of sentences, the system of judicature, the procedure of the courts, the legal profession, notaries and legal advice;
2. registration of births, deaths and marriages. . . .
23. railroads, other than Federal railroads, except mountain railroads.

---

drafters were confident that they had gone far to eliminate the internal contradictions which had plagued the Weimar system. They allowed very little room for "emergency powers" through which the Constitution could be hollowed out.

The challenge posed by the need to come to terms with the problems associated with the rise of nazism and the abolition of democratic rights was met by the Parliamentary Council in a piecemeal, but by no means ineffectual, manner. The prominence given civil rights is indicated by the conspicuous place accorded the Bill of Rights at the very beginning of the Basic Law, and also by the fact that its provisions are declared to be directly binding on all courts and authorities. Thus the rights of free speech, press, and assembly are strongly anchored, censorship is prohibited, and equality before the law and the equivalent of habeas corpus are guaranteed. German citizens have the right of carrying a constitutional plaint directly to the Constitutional Court. Guarantees of civil rights are reinforced with significant provisions for the general maintenance of the democratic order, particularly through provisions which permit the suppression of antidemocratic movements. Thus, "parties, which, according to their aims and the behavior of their members, seek to impair or abolish the free and democratic basic order" may be declared unconstitutional by the Constitutional Court.

The problem of the role of the Laender and of what kind of federal principles the Basic Law should express caused greater controversy, both among the Germans and the Allies. As regards the division of legislative powers between the Laender and the federal government, German traditions and preferences for a maximum degree of uniformity favored giving the federal government the lion's share of authority. Among the exclusive legislative powers which the federal government exercises are those which relate to the areas of foreign affairs, citizenship, etc.; the list of federal powers is very similar to that in Article 1, Section 8, of the United States Constitution. A more significant index of the greater legislative predominance of the German federal government is given by the provisions regarding concurrent powers. Here both constitutional provisions and German practice also leave to the federal legislature the lion's share of power in relation to such subjects as civil and criminal law, legislation relating to economic affairs, agriculture, forests and fisheries, housing, and many other areas which in other countries would usually be left to state or provincial legislation. The Laender's reserved powers were thus kept rather limited, but the Laender do retain the power to legislate in important areas like education, the police, radio and television, and on other subjects which are not listed as either exclusive or concurrent powers of the federal government.[6]

The "federalist" forces influencing the drafting of the Basic Law realized that the bulk of legislative power would remain with the central government, but were concerned nonetheless to reverse the long-term trend under which the Land governments had gradually become subsidiary and dependent units.

[6] Carl J. Friedrich and H. J. Spiro, "The Constitution of the German Federal Republic," in Litchfield, *op. cit.*, pp. 117–51.

To strengthen the position of the Laender in the area of administration, they successfully sought a return to the earlier German
practice under which the federal bureaucracy was largely con-
fined to policy-making, with the execution of federal legislation
on the lower echelons left to the administration of the Laender.
In this as in their endeavor to assure the Laender independent
tax sources, they were largely successful. But they also wanted to
assure the Laender an effective voice in the federal legislative
process; here the question was what type of second chamber to
create. The "centralists" were in favor of a Senate-type chamber,
whose members would be directly elected by the populations of
the various Laender, and who would presumably come to represent their parties more than their states. The "federalists," on the
other hand, succeeded in winning support for a second chamber
which was to be composed exclusively of the Land ministers
themselves, and this Bundesrat solution was finally adopted.

The Political Party System

The political party system has contributed much to the
achievement of political stability in the Federal Republic. Contrary to pessimistic expectations, the original parties licensed by
the Allies managed both to build and maintain independent
followings. Moreover, their number did not expand to the point
of inhibiting the functioning of parliamentary government, but
shrank in the course of the 1950's, with the result that Germany
moved closer toward a two-party system than any other continental country. Unlike their predecessors in Weimar Germany
or many of their contemporaries in other European countries,
the major German parties have avoided significant splits and
have maintained a remarkably stable following. For the first time
in German history the Federal Republic produced a party which
could win the votes of an absolute majority, while between them
the democratic parties have attracted the support of all but a
tiny minority of the German electorate. In sharp contrast to the
Weimar period, extremist parties have hardly counted, and small,
special interest parties have had little success in drawing support
away from the stable large parties.

THE CHRISTIAN DEMOCRATIC UNION (CDU). The key to an
understanding of the changed structure of the German party
system lies largely in an understanding of the character and
growth of the Christian Democratic Union. This party was
newly established in 1945 by Catholics who wanted to overcome

Political Parties

Article 21

(1) The political parties shall participate in forming the political will of the people. They can be freely formed. Their internal organization must conform to democratic principles. They must publicly account for the sources of their funds.

(2) Parties which, by reason of their aims or the behavior of their adherents, seek to impair or abolish the free and democratic basic order or to endanger the existence of the Federal Republic of Germany, are unconstitutional. The Federal Constitutional Court shall decide on the question of unconstitutionality.

(3) Details will be regulated by Federal legislation.

---

the limitations of the all-Catholic Center party of the pre-1933 era and by Protestants, conservatives, and liberals who had previously belonged to half a dozen right-of-center or middle-of-the-road parties. They now rallied to unite, partly because of a recognition of common values, but mainly from fear that they would be overwhelmed by the anticipated strength of the left-wing parties. They never attempted to work out fundamentals or details of their political program, and the party continued to retain quite different complexions in different parts of the country. In the industrial Ruhr, for instance, the CDU retains the loyalty of the Catholic workers by espousing social legislation and even, in the early days, the socialization of industry. In the north it is the party of the middle class and farmer groups largely indifferent to organized religion, while in the south it continues to present itself as the traditional party of Catholic orthodoxy. Many, including the Socialist leaders, expected that this alliance would soon fall apart, but they were proved wrong. What held the party together was neither its loose organization nor its largely negative anti-Socialist ideology, but strong personal leadership which turned the party's weaknesses into virtues. Konrad Adenauer, a pre-1933 mayor of Cologne who had never played a significant role in national politics, quickly emerged as the leader of the Christian Democrats, first in the British, and finally in all three Western zones. He proved himself an extremely skilled tactician who utilized the party's lack of attachment to organization, program, or ideology, to seize the opportunities which the rapidly shifting political situation opened up. In contrast to his great rival Kurt Schumacher, Adenauer never "fought City Hall" but accepted the consequences of the East-West split as inevitable and goaded his party to accept the facts, to get behind successful programs like Erhard's Social Market Policy, and to assume the responsibility of government.[7]

So adeptly did Adenauer play his cards that he found himself installed as Chancellor before the CDU had even formally elected a leader or set up a national organization. The position of leader fell naturally into his hands, but he became so preoccupied with governmental problems that he never got beyond developing the CDU into anything more than an instrument to lend his government stability and to execute policies which he considered desirable. Nevertheless his control of the government allowed him to hold his party together despite disagreements on many policies. He succeeded in identifying himself with Germany's reacceptance into the Western family of nations and with achievements in the area of German reconstruction. By appealing to the German's tendency to support established authority, he succeeded in developing a powerful popular following, both for himself as Chancellor and for the CDU as the party favoring constructive policies. This appeal allowed the CDU, together with its Bavarian branch, the Christian Social Union (CSU), to win the smashing electoral victories of 1953 and 1957, which resulted in successively larger majorities in the Bundestag, thus allowing Adenauer to diminish his reliance on minor party support.

In the course of time, the CDU outgrew its initial one-sided dependence on Erhard's economic policy as a magnet to draw non-Socialist voters, and developed a widespread net of alliances with all manner of interest groups. Competing successfully with the Free Democrats, it became the "chosen instrument" of the powerful leaders of German industry, won ,the loyalty of the middle class, artisan and farmer groups, and even broke into the traditional Socialist preserve of workers and social pensioners. Its program reflects its extremely wide following, and on the whole it has sought to distribute the fruits of German prosperity with reasonable equity. Its increasing dependence on Adenauer caused it to become predominantly committed to the Chancellor's foreign policy aims, particularly his commitment to Western defense and the integration of Western Europe. In its role as the Chancellor's party, the CDU became identified in the course of the 1950's with a policy of giving priority to the ties which bind the Federal Republic to the West, even at the cost of possibly

[7] Arnold J. Heidenheimer, *Adenauer and the CDU: The Rise of the Leader and the Integration of the Party* (The Hague, 1960), pp. 92–178.

hindering advances toward the achievement of German unification.

THE SOCIAL DEMOCRATIC PARTY (SPD). When Konrad Adenauer, as a septuagenarian, helped found the CDU in Cologne in 1945 he was seeking to check a party which was already well established when he himself was a youth in the Bismarckian era. In those days the growing Socialist-led working-class movement was a skeleton in the mental closet of the ruling classes, and middle-class mothers employed the names of SPD leaders like August Bebel and Karl Liebknecht to frighten children into obedience. Indeed the "better sort" of people had reason to fear those grim proletarian masses; the SPD was avowedly a working-class party pledged to the eradication of private property and the abolition of capitalist society. Though relegated under the Empire to the minor role of an "opposition of principle" which found no common ground between itself and the regime, it rallied increasing majorities of the working class to its banner until it became in the decade before 1914 by far the largest party in the Reichstag. Though the war experience and the subsequent split-off of its left wing into the Communist party halted a further increase in its voting support, the SPD remained throughout the Weimar period a strongly disciplined organization committed to evolutionary social change and the defense of democratic parliamentary institutions. During the Nazi period its leaders went into exile and concentration camps on behalf of their democratic convictions.

After 1945 the Socialists were supremely confident that as the party with the strongest anti-Nazi record, a long history of support of democracy and a strong party organization, they would become the party to lead Germany's reconstruction. Their expectations were frustrated. The shot-gun marriage between Communists and Socialists in the Soviet zone, which resulted in the formation of the Socialist Unity party (SED), and the subsequent division of Germany separated the Socialist leadership under the forceful Kurt Schumacher from those areas where they had traditionally enjoyed their strongest support. Next, the success of the CDU created a formidable rival for middle-class and even working-class support. But worst of all, the Socialists found the very strength of their organization and program an embarrassment. The loyalty of the workers maintained their image as a class party, and none of the roles in which Schumacher cast himself—as the champion of German national interests against Allied policies, as an opponent of economic liberalism and German rearmament, and finally even as an opponent of German participation in organizations like the Council of Europe and the European Coal and Steel Community—won the party any significant new share of middle-class votes. Thus, while the CDU succeeded in breaking out of the prewar Center party's traditional "Catholic ghetto," up to 1961 the SPD never succeeded in growing far beyond the industrial working-class districts.

Moreover, the successes of the Social Market Policy after Schumacher's death in 1952 put the party's functionaries and members under strong pressure to re-examine Socialist economic doctrine, and especially their commitment to the socialization of heavy industry and other fundamental branches of the economy. The party's last basic program, proclaimed in Heidelberg in 1925, had already replaced the orthodox Marxist formula of nationalization with a call for the placing of industry under the control of mixed boards, on which not only the state but also the unions and consumers would be represented.

After an extensive re-examination of industrial society and its own conscience, the SPD adopted a new program in 1959 at Bad Godesberg against only scattered left-wing opposition, which never once mentions Marx and accepts private ownership of the means of production as having "a claim to protection and support insofar as it does not hinder the building of a just social order." This dramatic reversal was accompanied by formulations which sought to make evident that the party had overcome its self-conception as a class party as well as the tradition of anticlericalism and doctrinal antimilitarism with which it had long been associated. In making it unmistakably clear that it was willing to join with all German groups in defending the Federal Republic against Communist threats, it sought desperately to overcome the stereotypes which CDU propaganda had perpetuated.[8] In subsequent discussion, party leaders sought to convince gray-haired members that the doctrines to which they had remained faithful for two generations had become outdated by economic and social change, and that the aims of the party could now be better achieved by preventing abuses within, rather than by abolishing, a system of free competition.

MINOR PARTIES. The decline of the minor parties proceeded inexorably. Whereas in 1950 almost a dozen political parties

---

[8] Lewis J. Edinger and Douglas A. Chalmers, "Overture or Swan Song: German Social Democracy Prepares for a New Decade," *Antioch Review,* XX. (1960), 163–75.

had fairly wide following and representation in the Bundestag, by 1960 only three managed to maintain themselves there. The first casualties of political rationalization and the "5 per cent clause" [9] were small regional parties. Some of these, like the Bavarian party (BP), the Center party in Rhineland-Westphalia, and the German party (DP) in Lower Saxony, were for a time aided by the CDU because they were useful in helping to establish majorities on the Land or national level, but they continually declined for lack of leadership and independent programs.[10] Others, like the early Reconstruction Association (WAV), with a base of support in Bavaria, and the Expellees party (BHE), with support in areas where the expellees were concentrated, were special interest parties whose following declined as their constituencies became absorbed into the prosperous German citizenry. Some of these have continued to maintain a measure of influence on the Land level, but this has not been the case with the extremist parties, like the neo-Nazi Socialist Reich party (SRP) [11] and the Communist party (KPD) which had lost most of their popular support by the time they were declared illegal in 1952 and 1956, respectively. Minor right-wing parties against which this penalty has not been invoked, like the German Reich party (DRP), have also steadily lost influence, as the minor nationalist revival which reached its high point in 1951 to 1952 continually ebbed in the face of official hostility and the present unwillingness of Germans to commit themselves to hoary causes. In attempts to preserve their power, leaders of the minor parties have frequently managed unlikely party mergers. Thus in 1961 two parties which had previously been supported by mutually quite hostile elements, the German party and the Expellees party, unified themselves into a new All-German party in a desperate attempt to hurdle the "5 per cent clause" in that year's federal elections.

The only party which by 1960 had still survived the deadly embraces of the Chancellor and CDU, and the SPD's eagerness to gobble-up odd remnants, were the Free Democrats (FDP). This party constitutes the remainder of what had once been the dominant political force of German liberalism. Its following had shrunk perceptibly during the Weimar Republic, and in 1945 many of its leaders joined either the Christian or Social

[9] See below, p. 75.

[10] Otto Kirchheimer, "Notes on West Germany," *WP*, VI (1954), 306–21.

[11] Otto Buesch and Peter Furth, *Rechtsradikalismus im Nachkriegsdeutschland* (Berlin, 1958).

1. *The changing party composition of the federal legislature*

Representation as per cent of Bundestag membership

Party	1949	1956	1960
CDU/CSU	35%	51%	55%
SPD	33	31	35
FDP	13	7*	8
DP	4	7*	2*
BHE	——	4	
Zentrum	2+	1—	
KPD	4		
BP	4		
WAV	3		
DRP	1		
SSW	1—		
Other	1—		

* After splits in parties.

2. *Size and structure of major party membership*

a) Approximate size of party membership

SPD	650,000
CDU	230,000

b) Denominational structure of CDU membership

Catholics	73%
Protestants	27%

c) Social composition of SPD and CDU membership

	SPD	CDU
Workers	45%	15%
Employees	17	18
Officials	5	9
Artisans		9
Businessmen	12	7
Professionals		7
Farmers	2	15
Pensioners, housewives, etc.	19	20

3. *Party organization and party finance*

a) No. of local party organizations

SPD	7,500
CDU	5,000

b) Normal Amount of party dues income

SPD	$1.6 million
CDU	$300,000

c) Expenditures in 1957 federal election campaign (approximate)

SPD	$2.2 million
CDU	$9.0 million

d) For comparison: estimated party spending in British campaign of 1955

Labour	$1.5 million
Conservative	$1.9 million

* Source: Max G. Lange, *et. al.*, *Parteien in der Bundesrepublik* (Villingen, 1955), pp. 205 ff.; U. W. Kitzinger, *German Electoral Politics* (London, 1960), pp. 202, 312; author's articles in *APSR*, LI, pp. 369-85, and *Revue francaise de science politique*, VII, pp. 626-45.

Democrats, who had come to espouse many of liberalism's fundamental principles. Nevertheless, enough liberals were sufficiently opposed to clericalism or economic planning to provide a respectable following for the FDP which, with support from some industrialists and portions of the Protestant middle class, has continued to attempt to shore-up its position as Germany's "third party." However it has continued to be plagued by feuding between its liberal South German and its nationalist North German factions, and has failed to throw up leaders of the calibre of its first chairman, Theodor Heuss, who resigned in 1949 to assume the federal presidency. FDP leaders frequently complained that the CDU had stolen most of its program, but this position drew sympathy from few except university professors. As late as 1956 the party proved strong enough to survive Chancellor Adenauer's successful effort to split its ranks, but it has been unable to check a slow but steady decline in its voting support. The question remains as to what will occur first: the CDU's loss of a majority, which would allow the FDP to play a balance of power position, or the FDP's failure to draw even 5 per cent of the votes, which would eliminate it from the Bundestag.[12]

PARTY LEADERS. The dominance which Chancellor Adenauer has exercised over West German politics since the death of Kurt Schumacher has handicapped the emergence of impressive personalities in both his own and the opposition parties. Schumacher's successor as leader of the Social Democrats and that party's candidate for the Chancellorship in the 1953 and 1957 elections, Erich Ollenhauer, showed himself a sort of German Clement Attlee, an honest balancing wheel between his party's factions but unable to exert charismatic charm on the voters. In 1960, after having changed their program and settled their intraparty differences in favor of a staunch pro-NATO course, the Social Democrats picked a new standard bearer in the person of Willy Brandt, the colorful young mayor of Berlin. A militant fighter, Brandt had opposed the Nazis as a member of the Norwegian underground and after his return to Berlin had, like his mentor, Ernst Reuter, taken an uncompromisingly anti-Communist position which differed from the more neutralist outlook of some of his party colleagues. Brandt is a powerful personality, but power within the SPD continues to remain dispersed. Herbert Wehner, who was once identified with the left wing of the

[12] Gerard Braunthal, "The Free Democratic Party in West German Politics," *WPQ*, XIII (June, 1960), 332–48.

party, remains very influential because of support among the party's functionaries. Parliamentarians like Carlo Schmid, Ollenhauer, and Fritz Erler are important figures in their own right, as are many of the Social Democratic leaders on the Land level. Policy differences within the party are likely to continue, but the SPD's tradition of party discipline makes it less dependent on the emergence of an all-powerful party leader, since majority decisions are likely to be more honored than in the CDU.

Among the CDU leaders the maneuvering for the leadership position has frequently been quite bitter. In seeking to display their strength, the rival pretenders have also exposed their weaknesses. Thus Ludwig Erhard, whose personal popularity is second only to that of Adenauer, has never convinced those who doubt his abilities as a statesman and party tactician. Other experts in the Adenauer cabinet, such as Heinrich von Brentano, the Foreign Minister, and Fritz Etzel, the Finance Minister, have failed to display the capacity to be all-around politicians who can project leadership to the masses. Though the dominance of Adenauer has prevented the CDU from elevating many other strong personalities to leadership, several have displayed toughness in fighting their way up. Among these are Eugen Gerstenmaier, the president of the Bundestag, who has on frequent occasions forcefully stood his ground not only against his party colleagues but even against Adenauer. Another important figure is Franz Josef Strauss, the ambitious Bavarian who has displayed both ruthlessness and tactical ability in achieving the positions of Federal Defense Minister and chairman of the CSU, the CDU's important Bavarian affiliate. The CDU will doubtless have difficulty in choosing a leader to replace Adenauer. The most likely short-term solution would be a deconcentration of power, with various roles of the party leadership being distributed.

PARTY ORGANIZATION AND FINANCE. The incompleteness of German evolution toward a real two party system is well brought out by the great difference not only between the parties' respective voting strengths during the Adenauer era, but between their internal structure and organization. That the SPD is called a "membership" party and the CDU a "voters" party implies more than the mathematical fact that in 1960 the average SPD Bundestag deputy was accountable to roughly five times as many party members as was his CDU colleague. In the SPD the members maintain the organization, and the organization channels decision-making democratically but also centralistically so that the party's national executive is both strengthened and limited by the articulate expressions of a mass membership. This kind of party organization, traditional with European socialist parties, imposes discipline on both members and leaders but also limits the leaders' freedom of action in making agreements with interest groups and in shifting party policies to meet changing situations. The CDU, though formally maintaining a similar structure, is organized quite differently. Its membership is much less active and less disciplined to make sacrifices, it does not attempt to maintain as ambitious a network of full-time party agents, and its various Land organizations are only loosely tied to a weak national party office which, like its American equivalents, assumes importance mainly during national election campaigns. Since it does little for the party, the CDU's predominantly middle-class membership is not able to make strong demands on the leadership, and there have been periods when the party's ineffectual national committee has failed to meet for as long as a year at a time. During such times Chancellor Adenauer made the effective decisions, which CDU party members had perforce to accept.

The difference in party structure not only causes different patterns of behavior among leaders, deputies, and members but results in the parties having different sorts of relationships with interest groups. The SPD, of course, gets considerable support from groups in the labor unions, and in the main it maintains its organization and fights its election campaigns with donations from labor and membership dues, which amount to about nine million marks a year. The CDU, by contrast, is not effectively able to collect dues from its more affluent membership and does not really try to do so; it receives funds with much less trouble from special "sponsors' associations" which collect funds systematically from industrial firms, banks, and commercial trade associations and distribute these among non-Socialist parties, the largest share going to the CDU.[13] While membership dues would barely keep its district agents from starvation, the national CDU has been able to spend what, by European standards (where until 1960 commercial television or radio played no substantial role), were extraordinarily large sums on massive advertising and public relations campaigns.

The problem of the inequality caused by the parties' vastly different supply of funds has caused considerable concern in Germany, where the Basic Law's stipulation that the parties be

[13] Arnold J. Heidenheimer, "German Party Finance: The CDU," *APSR*, LI (1957), 369–85.

given "equal" chances is interpreted quite strictly. As a result, the Constitutional Court has invalidated a tax law that had allowed businessmen to deduct political along with charitable contributions, on the grounds that the political spending pattern showed that this indirect use of public funds favored some parties more than others.[14] Subsequently, many Germans have advocated some form of direct state subsidy which would help the parties to fulfill their necessary functions and yet remain relatively independent of interest groups. A start in this direction has been made, insofar as the budgets of the federal and several of the Laender governments now include small appropriations to assist the parties in carrying on their "political education" work. At the same time, the draft of the Parties Law being discussed in 1960 provided that political parties must report the total amounts of donations received. This compromise provision, which freed the parties from having to declare who gave the money, failed to satisfy many critics. By 1961 the Parties Law, which is called for by the Basic Law in order to regulate the financing and internal organization of parties, still had not been passed, although various drafts had been under discussion for over ten years.[15]

Public Opinion and Elections

The fact that over 80 per cent of West German voters turned out in the elections of the 1950's, the vast majority to support democratic parties, might assure one as to the future of German democracy until one recalls that in the prosperous late 1920's observers drew similar conclusions, which were to be radically disproved in a few years' time. What does a comparison of election returns show, say, for the elections of 1928 and 1957? In both, the voting turnout was quite high, but it was considerably higher in 1957 (88 per cent versus 74 per cent). In both, the percentage of votes cast for democratic (or at least not antidemocratic) parties was quite high, but again higher in 1957 (95 per cent) than in 1928 (70–80 per cent). Finally, of course, the votes were distributed among far fewer parties in the 1957 election. It would thus appear that the degree of consensus on constitutional and broad political issues is much greater in the Federal

[14] See below, p. 145.
[15] Parteienrechtskommission des Bundesinnenministeriums, *Rechtliche Ordnung des Parteiwesens* (Frankfurt, 1957), and Carl J. Schneider, "Political Parties and the German Basic Law of 1949," *WPQ*, X (1957), 527–40.

Republic than it was even in the least troubled period of the Weimar Republic.

However, if one turns from election returns to public opinion polls for definite assurance that the voters will not, five years hence, entrust their fate to a totalitarian demagogue, the data do not lend themselves to the making of clear-cut judgments. Polls have shown that in the late 1950's anything from a third to a half of the population still expressed admiration for at least part of Hitler's program or showed strong signs of anti-Semitism. True, such inquiries have shown that only 5 to 10 per cent of the population are hard-core Nazis who would actively support a totalitarian revival, but on the other hand those who say that they would actively oppose such a development are also in the minority, though a larger one (about 25 per cent).[16] More than half of the respondents to such questions usually say that they wouldn't care, or that, though opposed, they would not do anything. Other more encouraging responses show a gradually increasing acceptance of democratic institutions. Advocates of a one-party system have gradually declined (from 22 per cent in 1951 to 14 per cent in 1955), while supporters of a multiparty system have increased (from 61 per cent to 74 per cent in the same period).[17]

The dominant characteristic of postwar West German political behavior, particularly after the situation became stabilized in the fifties, has been a striking weakening of the traditional German commitment to idea and value systems. Perhaps the best judges of German political attitudes are the flag manufacturers. In the Weimar period they did a brisk trade between purchasers who exhibited the republican colors and the conservatives who exhibited the monarchist black, white, and red banner. In the Nazi period every German household had to have a good sized swastika to display on proper occasions. However manufacturers now report that private demand for the official flag is almost nil. Instead, they make pennants advertising "Bockwuerste" for sausage stands. The excesses the Nazis committed in the name of ideology, the physical problems of survival, and, in the fifties, the opportunity for rapid material rehabilitation led in turn to a deemphasis on ideology and to an acceptance of existing political

[16] Karl W. Deutsch and Lewis J. Edinger, *Germany Rejoins the Powers: Mass Opinion, Interest Groups and Elites in Contemporary German Foreign Policy* (Stanford, 1959), pp. 40–43.

[17] Elizabeth Neumann, ed., *Jahrbuch der Öffentlichen Meinung, 1947–55* (Allensbach, 1956), p. 249.

instruments. In addition many Germans, faced successively with
Nazi and Communist systems, overcame historical lines of division
to discover that they actually agreed on more fundamentals than
they had previously realized. The fact that the major parties
produced strong leaders, who appealed to the popular imagination as few of their democratic predecessors had done, also
helped. Finally, the trend toward a stable two-party system may
be understood as the result of popular appreciation of a vastly
diminished German position in the world. Whereas earlier generations had felt that Germany, as a leading power, could well
afford and was perhaps even called upon to reflect within its
political system all varieties of political thought, postwar West
Germans seem to realize intuitively that they cannot afford this
luxury and that their voice in world affairs will only be heard if
expressed coherently through a limited number of responsible
parties.

This attitude did not become apparent immediately, for in
the early postwar years a good portion of the German electorate
displayed a tendency to revert to the pattern of voting behavior
they had displayed in the Weimar period. Had not Allied licensing policies limited the number of parties admitted, the host
of local and special interest group parties might have gotten
quickly out of control. Indeed as restrictions were liberalized,
their number increased rapidly and in 1950 there were no less
than twenty parties with reasonably significant following on the
Land or national level. In the 1949 federal elections, despite the
fact that some of the splinter parties were not allowed to compete, the party votes were so split that the initial installation
of the Adenauer cabinet can be attributed much less to a clean-
cut decision of the voters than to the enthusiasm and facility
with which the party leaders found allies among other politicians.
In the Land elections, which are held on varying dates so that
no more than two or three are held at the same time, the tendency toward a scattering of support among many parties continued to manifest itself throughout the 1950's, though on a
steadily decreasing scale. Subsequent federal elections, however,
set the trend under which, with the coming of prosperity and the
institutionalization of the Federal Republic, the vast majority
of Germans began to drift toward voting for the major government and opposition parties.

The nature of the federal electoral system has played a
significant role in this process. When the original federal election
law was passed in 1949 by the Parliamentary Council, the forces

favoring single-member districts and proportional representation were about evenly matched. The result was a complex political compromise. A new electoral law was passed in 1953, and yet another in 1956. Each time an intense struggle took place, and the resulting laws faced in several directions at once. Basically, the trend toward a two-party system would seem to justify the adoption of the single-member district, and had it wanted to push this system through the CDU could have done so after 1953. But in view of the voting pattern which had evolved, the adoption of such a system would not only have eliminated all the minor parties (several of which continued as coalition partners of the CDU), but would also have reduced the Socialist opposition to a tiny minority in a CDU-dominated Bundestag. Thus, influenced by the violent opposition of the other parties, by the German tendency to regard proportional representation as better because it reflects opinion more accurately, and by the fear of exposing the country to a situation closely approximating a one-party system, the CDU did not press the issue to its conclusion.

As a result, the German election law since 1956 has continued to be based on a modified and "personalized" variant of proportional representation. This is true even though half of the membership of the Bundestag is elected in 247 single-member constituencies, where the successful candidate is elected by a simple relative majority vote, much as he would be in the United States or Britain. For in addition to casting a vote for his local deputy, each voter casts a second ballot for a list submitted by the parties of his Land. The candidates from the Land lists are then chosen so as to give each qualified party a total number of seats proportional to the number of votes its lists poll throughout the Federal Republic.[18] The important word is "qualified," for a party which receives only 1 per cent of the total vote is *not* entitled to 1 per cent of the Bundestag membership. To shut out just such minor parties, the electoral law provides that only those parties which win either 5 per cent of the total federal second ballot vote or elect three deputies in direct constituency election can participate in the sharing of the distribution of seats according to the Land lists. It is this "5 per cent hurdle" which has gradually eliminated the minor parties which were originally able to enter under the more liberal provisions of the earlier versions of the law. In 1957 only the FDP succeeded in

[18] U. Kitzinger, "The West German Electoral Law," *Parliamentary Affairs*, XI (1958), 220–38.

passing the hurdle on its own; the German party, then a faithful satellite of the CDU, was enabled to get by the hurdle because in three constituencies the CDU told its voters to vote for German party candidates.

But despite the electoral law's attempt to emphasize the local element, German election campaigns have had a decidedly centralized focus. Thus in 1957, the CDU built its campaign solidly on Adenauer and a few of its other top leaders. Its surveys had shown that "over half the population 'revered Adenauer like a monarch,' demanded his statesmanship and authority at the head of the State, almost asked for the occasional paternal rebuke, and felt secure under his clear unwavering direction of affairs." [19] As a consequence, the entire Federal Republic was flooded with posters like one depicting him "in deep earnestness, sun-bronzed, fair-haired and with penetrating bright blue eyes that appeared to follow the voter." Beneath the portrait there was the simple slogan "No Experiments—Konrad Adenauer." This official CDU campaign was supplemented by many parallel campaigns, some of them paid for by Ludwig Erhard's supporters in industry, some of them run by organizations receiving subsidies from the federal treasury, all of them concentrating public attention on the Chancellor and his assistants. The SPD campaign, by contrast, "was not a campaign run by business tycoons, but one conducted by intellectuals and routine party officials." [20] Whereas the CDU based its propaganda on satisfaction with the status quo and on emotional appeal, the SPD tried to appeal to the rationality of the voter, attempting to convince him that with its changed policy emphasis it would do almost the same things as the CDU, only better. It sought to heighten appeal for its leader by building him up "as the kindly pipe-smoking husband of Martha Ollenhauer," but against the portrait of Adenauer he was no match.

An analysis of voting behavior for the federal elections of 1953 and 1957 shows, for some important population groups, a remarkable similarity with voting behavior in the 1920's. In the Weimar Republic close to two-thirds of all Catholics voted for the Center party, and thirty years later approximately the same proportion gave their votes to its successor, the CDU. Similarly, the Socialists were supported by a good majority of the working class, just as they were twenty years earlier. Catholics and workers represent at one and the same time the most politically cohe-

[19] U. Kitzinger, *German Electoral Politics* (London, 1960), p. 105.
[20] *Ibid.*, p. 131.

Voting behavior in West Germany

1. Sex, age, and religion as factors in voting behavior*

Party	Sex		Age			Religion	
	Men	Women	−34	35–54	55+	Catholic	Protestant
SPD	29%	21%	29%	23%	22%	18	30
CDU	42	52	48	44	53	61	36
Other	11	8	6	12	9	4	14
No response	18	19	17	21	16	17	20
	100%	100%	100%	100%	100%	100%	100%

* Party preferences of population groups as shown in 1957 polls.

2. Socioeconomic factors in voting behavior†

Occupation	SPD	CDU	Others	No preference
Professionals, businessmen	12%	55%	19%	14%
Employees, officials	24	45	11	20
Skilled workers	49	33	6	12
Semi- and unskilled workers	43	33	6	18
Farmers	10	55	24	11
Housewives	28	43	10	19

† Party preferences of social groups as shown in 1957 polls.

3. Regional factors in voting behavior‡

Land	CDU	SPD	FDP	BHE	DP	Other
Schleswig-Holstein	48%	31%	6%	8%	4%	3%
Hamburg	37	46	9	2	5	1
Dower Saxony	39	33	6	8	11	3
Bremen	30	46	6	2	14	2
Northrhine-Westphalia	54	34	6	3	2	2
Saar	54	32	8	5	1	1
Hessen	41	38	9	7	6	1
Rhineland-Palatinate	54	30	10	2	2	3
Baden-Wuerttemberg	53	26	14	5	1	1
Bavaria	57	25	5	7	1	4
Federal Republic	50%	32%	8%	5−%	3%	2%

‡ Party vote in the various *Laender* in the 1957 Federal election.

sive of the larger population groups and also the most important
political base for their respective parties. Catholic workers, subject to the pressures of overlapping membership, divided their
votes about equally between the CDU and SPD in 1953.

The CDU's success and the SPD's failure in breaking out of
their respective Weimar voting ghettos is best illustrated in an
analysis of the voting behavior of various other groups which in
the past supported neither Center party nor SPD. Protestant
white-collar employees, quite a sizable group, distributed their
vote better than two to one in favor of the CDU over the SPD,
although many still supported the FDP (Free Democrats). Catholic farmers voted CDU much more readily than Protestant farmers, but even the latter have in recent years relinquished an
earlier preference for the FDP in order to support the CDU,
which they prefer to the SPD by margins of better than five to
one. Protestant professionals and businessmen still tend to give
considerable support to the FDP, but again the CDU has attracted the loyalty of at least an equal number of them, while a
very small percentage have voted for the SPD. Although Protestant workers lean heavily toward the SPD, they do not balance
the Protestant middle-class groups leaning toward the CDU, so
that in 1957 the CDU even had a slight (45–40) edge among the
Protestants expressing choice between the two major parties,
while Catholic voters preferred it to the SPD by margins of almost four to one. Among socioeconomic groups, the CDU overshadowed the SPD in all nonworking-class categories and by
margins, moreover, ranging from two to one (employees, officials)
to five to one (farmers, professionals, entrepreneurs). By contrast
the margin with which working-class voters preferred the SPD
over the CDU was only about three to two.

Apart from its strong support from Catholics and middle-
class groups, the CDU's major asset has been the striking support
it has received from women. The latter tend toward more conservative parties almost universally, but the degree to which they
do so in West Germany is striking. While the CDU's vote among
men was only about 30 per cent greater than that for the SPD, its
support from women was almost double that cast for its major
rival. The Socialists found it almost impossible to break the
fascination which the Chancellor and his party seemed to hold
for women. Of the gains made by the SPD between the 1953 and
1957 elections, six-sevenths came from men, only one-seventh
from women. As regards age-differential voting behavior, the
West German example is characteristic of the phenomenon, re-

cently somewhat diminishing, that younger voters tend to support the more radical, older voters the more conservative, party. But the Socialists' satisfaction at exerting a somewhat above-average attraction on the younger voting groups has been diluted by the fact that the CDU has also proved quite attractive to those voting for the first or second time.

Groups and Political Behavior

INTEREST GROUPS. The foregoing analysis of voting behavior will already have led many readers to suspect that, as in other countries, political behavior in West Germany is shaped to a large extent by interest groups. But an analysis of West German interest group structure must take note of one circumstance which causes the situation to differ considerably from that of the United States: in Germany, many special interests are much older than the state, and some, like the Catholic church, even predate the time when Germans first began to feel conscious of their national identity. In the United States few groups or subcultures reject the main course of constitutional development. The vast majority of them, including even the major religious organizations, developed the bulk of their tradition only after the political institutions had already been established. But in Germany, Bavarian farmers or Catholic Rhinelanders or Hanseatic merchants remain very much aware that their traditions have far deeper historical and institutional roots than do those of the national political system.

A second category of German interest groups makes claims on the loyalty of members and seeks special treatment in public discussion because of factors related to the evolution of the German social system. That system, unlike the American, evolved from a feudal background and in the process of evolution created a tradition of loyalty to "estate" and social class which today still affects the function of some interest groups. A typical example of an antiquated estate claiming privileges for historical reasons were the East Elbian Junkers, who during the Weimar period demanded special subsidies essentially because their forefathers had captured East Prussia from the Poles in the twelfth century. Other old socioeconomic groups, like the civil servants and, to a lesser degree, artisans and farmers, continue to this day to make claims for special treatment based at least in part on rights accorded their estate during the feudal or preconstitutional periods. They compete with organizations based on social or class

position, like the trade unions, which also continue to appeal
both to the loyalty of their members and for recognition in the
political process not only because of the specific goals they seek
to achieve and the size of their membership, but because they
have played an historical role in opening up the full privileges of
citizenship for members of their class.

Both of the aforementioned kinds of group still object to
being placed on a level with an association of used car dealers or
a commercial fishermen's organization. Nevertheless, the newer
kinds of narrowly economic interest group set up to achieve pragmatic ends have become more numerous and more important as
Germany has disestablished vested privileges to become an industrial society much like the United States. Increasingly, these
newer associations with professional staffs, closely knit organizations, and experienced lobbyists rival the older groups in influence. At the same time, many of them have inherited from the
older groups the right to participate in the political process by
assuming a semipublic character, as administrators of certain
kinds of regulations. Thus German chambers of commerce, chambers of agriculture, and the professional organizations have much
greater power than most American equivalents, and are in a
position to make membership in related interest group organizations obligatory on all members. All of these factors serve to
strengthen the position of the interest groups to the point where
they at times emerge not only as powerful claimants on the political parties, but even as rivals, who through their representatives
in the legislature and their contacts in the administration will
work independently when the parties do not seem adequate instruments for achieving their ends.

The manner in which German interests function politically
can perhaps best be brought out through a brief examination
of the roles which two of the most important have played in
recent years. Though officially neutral, both the Catholic church
and the Trade Union Federation have made their sympathies
abundantly clear. When asked which groups tend toward which
parties, 83 per cent in a German poll associated Catholics with
the CDU, only 1 per cent with the SPD; similarly 77 per cent
associated the trade unions with the SPD, only 1 per cent with
the CDU.[21] During election campaigns Catholic organs give
fairly open support to the CDU. Thus the Government Press
Office reported in 1957 that, "The main theme for the month
of August in the Catholic Church press is the Bundestag election

[21] Divo Institut, *Umfragen 1957* (Frankfurt, 1958), p. 50.

of September 15th. Detailed reports highlight the great achievement of the present government in all domains." [22] In addition Catholic bishops send out pastoral letters which are read to a quarter of the German electorate on pre-election Sunday, with messages like: "Do your electoral duty! Vote only for men and women whose basic Christian principles are well known and whose public activity corresponds to these principles." The Bishop of Muenster was even more outspoken in 1957, declaring in a public address that, "You will already have felt that the SPD is not the only party to which we cannot give our approval," [23] thus seeming to warn Catholics away from the FDP as well.

As a result the CDU is usually extremely sensitive to the wishes of the Catholic church. Sometimes, however, it is not in a position to be a very good instrument of Catholic policy. Such a situation occurred in Lower Saxony in 1954 when a Socialist government fought to pass an education act which would improve public schools by integrating the separate Catholic and Protestant schools in the small towns. The Catholic church decided to fight to maintain the denominational principle, but the CDU could not represent its viewpoint forcefully enough, partly because it was weakly represented in the Land legislature, partly because many of the Protestants in its ranks did not agree with the Catholic position. As a result the church pursued its own public fight and Catholic groups organized monstrous rallies at which posters paired the profile of the Socialist minister-president with that of Hitler. When a subsequent election caused the defeat of the Socialists, the CDU demanded the replacement by a Catholic of the civil servant who had helped draft the law.[24] The new minister-president published a detailed analysis of the religious affiliation of the civil servants to assure Catholics that they were adequately represented, and several federal ministers have done the same. Such attempts on the part of interest groups to affect government personnel policies occur frequently, not merely on questions involving policy differences. Thus Catholic ministers have been successfully influenced against granting promotions to Catholic civil servants who have not had their children baptized as Catholics. On the whole, the Catholic church is far more effective and more outspoken on political issues than the

---

[22] Kitzinger, *German Electoral Politics*, p. 232.

[23] *Ibid.*, p. 226.

[24] Thomas Ellwein, *Klerikalismus in der Deutschen Politik* (Munich, 1956), pp. 183–212.

Protestant church hierarchy, which is more loosely organized and whose views are far more diverse.

The Catholic church's opposite number on the Socialist side, the German trade unions, were long admired by Labor in other countries for their strong leadership, militant ideological commitment, and success in organizing the bulk of the working class. Immediately after the war, when their re-establishment was given top priority by the Allies, prospects seemed very hopeful. For the first time in German history one trade union movement unified all organized workers (except for white-collar employees), in contrast to the pre-1933 situation when a dominant Socialist-inclined union movement had been rivalled by smaller Catholic and liberal movements. The high point of the unions' political success was the achievement of "codetermination" in heavy industry in 1951. But since that time the union movement has declined both organizationally and politically. Despite a vast increase in the work force, union membership has remained static since 1952. Organizationally, the central trade union headquarters increasingly lost authority to the individual member unions. In addition most of its aging leaders pursued extremely cautious policies, allowing their dread of inflation to outweigh their inclination toward militant action for the improvement of working conditions. Although wages and working conditions improved greatly, many workers associate this more with paternalistic management than with the militant policies of their own unions.

Ironically, the very achievement of a unified trade union movement handicapped the unions' political action, for an active pro-CDU minority successfully prevented the Socialist majority from using union facilities to give direct support to the SPD. In contrast to British practice, the trade unions are thus not affiliated to the party which claims to speak for the working class. Most organized German workers have nevertheless maintained their traditional loyalty to the SPD. But the older workers, once committed to a strongly Marxist program, have found adaptation difficult as their leaders have increasingly gone off in other political directions. And the labor history of the postwar period has not provided the dramatic episodes which might have solidified the attachment of the middle-aged workers to the unions. From their perspective, even the struggle for "codetermination" failed to result in any very noticeable changes. The unions have also been unfortunate in that during the difficult stage of transition from ideological to "bread-and-butter" unionism, they have lacked strong leaders who could arouse loyalty and respect.

Nevertheless, the unions continue to command a position of great potential influence in German politics. No less than 40 per cent of the members of the Third Bundestag were at least nominal union members. Three-quarters of these belonged to the SPD, while one-quarter were in the ranks of the CDU, where they formed the kernel of a left wing within the party. About 80 per cent belonged to unions affiliated to the Federation, the rest represented independent small white-collar unions. Of the total, about half were union-affiliated civil servants, who frequently tended to go their own way on matters affecting their special interests. However, on questions relating to the defense of fundamental democratic institutions and in their resistance to all forms of totalitarianism, the unions remain one of the strongest political assets West Germany possesses.[25]

There are of course many hundreds of other interest groups which operate within the German settings. Some of the more powerful ones are the Federation of German Industry, whose role in political finance has already been mentioned, the farmers' organization, the various expellees' groups and *Landsmannschaften*, and the artisans' organizations.[26] At least three hundred of them have offices in Bonn to keep in touch with political developments affecting their interest. The majority, representing industrial and trade associations, operate much like their American counterparts. If anything, however, their role in the political process is more controversial in West Germany than it is in the United States. The reason is that West German acceptance of the principles of a pluralistic democracy is still incomplete. Since many Germans developed their concepts of politics around hierarchical or monolithic models of the state, they are reluctant to concede that the public interest can be adequately defined through the free-wheeling competition of "selfish" pressure groups. There is still strong belief that interest groups should present their requests to the state "from the outside," that is, that they should not directly influence decision-making in the legislature and the administration. However, the organized interest groups are clearly triumphing over their critics. They are increasingly speaking up, as has a member of the executive board

[25] Wolfgang Hirsch-Weber, *Gewerkschaften in der Politik* (Cologne, 1959).

[26] Rupert Breitling, *Die Verbaende in der Bundesrepublik: Ihre Arten und Ihre Politischen Wirkungsweise* (Meisenheim, 1955).

of the Federation of German Industries, to assert that interest groups play a creative and not a negative role in the political process: "The interest associations, next to the parties, are the only channels through which the individual can assert his rights and interests against the state and the politicians. The interest associations are therefore not to be feared as a 'state within the state,' but should be regarded and nurtured as a creative force within the democratic system." [27]

THE PRESS AND COMMUNICATION MEDIA. The mass communication media are at one and the same time a channel through which parties and interest groups seek to influence public opinion and an independent force in their own right. In the Federal Republic the press in particular, but also radio and television, have emerged as quite significant political forces. In contrast to the Weimar period, most of the important newspapers are not closely tied either to specific parties or interest groups, but pursue fairly independent policies of their own.

If the democratic strength of any press is to be measured by important events at home and abroad, then the daily press in the Federal Republic today comes through the test satisfactorily. With few exceptions, the daily press has been outstanding in its condemnation of certain nationalistic tendencies . . . and of employment in public service of so called "Big Nazis." . . . Chancellor Adenauer does not enjoy a privileged press. Some newspapers, not only those in political opposition, are almost always critical of his decisions and policies, especially when these seem to aim at a too-great domination of public life. . . .[28]

The Occupation period's licensing policy not only gave important positions in the mass media to reliable democrats, but also decentralized the press, establishing all newspapers independently on the local level. The advantages of this system are that Germany has fewer powerful press chains than the United States and Britain, and the larger newspapers tend to have more individual character and editorial viewpoint. The disadvantages are that Germany does not have a powerful "prestige" paper such as *The New York Times* or *Le Monde* and also lacks, for the most part, a national newspaper that is distributed throughout the country. It does however have good regional newspapers, of which the *Sueddeutsche Zeitung* in Munich is the most lively, the *Frankfurter Allgemeine Zeitung* the most sound and the closest to big business, and the *Welt*, published in Hamburg and Essen, the

[27] Otto A. Friedrich, *Die Welt*, October 17, 1959.
[28] Emlyn Williams, "The West German Press," *Gazette* (Leiden), V (1959), 5–6.

most successful. None of these quality papers have circulations of much over a quarter of a million, and many other good papers do quite well with the sale of less than 100,000. However they are far more important in shaping political opinion than the apolitical tabloid press, which claims a circulation in the millions and thrives on sensationalism on the model of the British popular press. The total circulation of daily newspapers is about seventeen million, a very good showing when compared with Great Britain (thirteen million) or even all of Weimar Germany (fourteen million). Three-quarters of this circulation is distributed to subscribers, so that the pressure to produce sensational headlines is minimized for all but the tabloid papers.

Radio and television have traditionally been public monopolies in Germany, but these media have by no means been simply organs of government propaganda. Their relative independence is due to the fact that they are set up as independent public corporations on the Land and regional level and have been fairly well insulated from pressure by the federal government. As in most European countries, the mass communications directors do not consider themselves bound by the taste of the majority, but present cultural programs of a high level with the purpose of educating the public. The intellectuals in charge of these media are also conscious of a responsibility to educate the public politically, and hence they frequently present politically controversial programs. Despite a continuing increase in the number of television receivers in use (1959: 2.5 million), radio continues to be the most widespread medium, with some 15.6 million subscribers paying dues which provide the bulk of the funds on which the radio networks operate.

As it developed strength and power, the federal government has been sorely tempted to revert to the earlier practice of asserting direct pressure on the mass media. Many officials were at times extremely unhappy that they lacked the power, which the French government frequently exercised under both the Fourth and Fifth Republics, to order the seizure of newspaper issues which contained objectionable materials. Suggestions for the adoption of a federal press law to parallel those existing on the Laender level have at times been put forward, but have been resoundingly rejected. Other proposals have called for increasing the powers of the federal press and Information Office, a large organization which is located right across the street from the Bundestag and exerts a powerful public relations effect on behalf of the federal government and the majority parties. It has become known that accredited journalists have at times been paid from the Chancellor's secret funds to write "advisory" articles for government bureaus. If such revelations do not arouse great storms of protest, it may be in part because people remember that, in his time, Gustav Streseman not only influenced individual journalists but used Foreign Office funds to secretly buy up an important newspaper to create a sounding board for his policies. As regards radio and television, its lack of direct influence on these organs has always irked the federal government. Its attempt to establish a commercial second television network under its own auspices was rejected as unconstitutional in 1961, when the Laender successfully appealed to the Constitutional Court to maintain their authority in this area.[29]

SKELETONS IN THE CLOSET. In one very vital respect the political behavior pattern in the Federal Republic during the 1950's has been much more similar to corresponding patterns in the United States and Britain than to those of other large continental countries like France and Italy. In Germany, as in the Anglo-Saxon countries, the bulk of public political discussion and controversy has taken place within a relatively narrow sector of the political spectrum. Practically all political spokesmen or commentators, whether in the parties, the press, or even the interest groups, have made evident their acceptance of political democracy, the constitutional framework, and the fundamental structure of a free society. Even before the Communist party was outlawed in 1956, its size and influence had diminished to the point where its role was much closer to that played by the tiny British Communist party than to the Communist mass movements in France and Italy. Even more striking have been the absence of powerful Fascist or right-wing antidemocratic movements, like the neo-Fascist movement in Italy, and the Poujadist party and semi-Fascist cliques which played a significant role in preparing the downfall of the French Fourth Republic.

It is of course neither accident nor miracle that a visitor to Germany today would have to look hard to find an organization openly articulating Nazi values. The combating of the ideological remnants of nazism received high priority both from the Occupation powers and the German authorities. Ever since 1945, the Germans have been exposed to educational campaigns which sought to emphasize the true nature of the Nazi regime and the virtues of political democracy. The vast bulk of Germans and even the greatest proportion of former Nazi adherents have prob-

[29] See below, pp. 146–47.

ably been genuinely converted in the course of this process. In the case of many former Nazis, acceptance of at least the outward forms of the democratic system has been aided by the fact that the economic and social opportunities which were again opened up to them were strong inducements not to remain "unreconstructed." Since the government has been aware that suspicions of the continued existence of strong Nazi sentiment have been one of the main obstacles to re-establishing friendly relations with groups abroad, it has made great efforts to prevent any public utterances which might possibly be interpreted as pro-Nazi, anti-Semitic, or nationalist. Its efforts are supplemented by those of other groups: democratic organizations like the trade unions; interest groups anxious to avoid being branded as "pseudo-Nazi"; international organizations of various kinds; and finally, of course, the Communists in East Germany, who are eager for stray evidence of neo-Nazi activity which will fit into their propaganda attacks on the Federal Republic.

Beyond these predominantly informal control mechanisms, the government possesses great additional powers with which to crush determined campaigns by Nazis or totalitarian groups. It has sought to use these powers discreetly, but in 1952 it asked the Constitutional Court to outlaw the neo-Nazi Socialist Reich party, and this step had a marked effect in causing the decline of other neo-Nazi movements of smaller scope.[30] Those that continue to maintain some sort of shadowy existence through the publication of nationalist or anti-Semitic literature, the holding of guarded meetings, and contact with Fascist organizations in other countries are kept under close surveillance by the special police attached to the Offices for the Protection of the Constitution, which are maintained both on the federal and Land levels.

Greater difficulty is encountered in dealing with groups which have the backing of socially influential persons or considerable public backing, yet still issue statements and publications in which the role of the Hitler period is discussed rather uncritically. A situation of this sort achieved wide publicity in 1954 when a leading publisher of books apologizing for the Nazi regime became Education Minister of Lower Saxony. Critics asked how teachers could possibly be expected to treat National Socialism critically in class if students could answer back on the basis of books published by the Education Minister's private firm. In this instance, firm action by students and faculty at

[30] Kurt P. Tauber, "German Nationalists and European Union," *PSQ*, LXXIV (1959), 564–89.

the University of Goettingen led to protests which forced the Minister's resignation. Subsequently both the publisher and some of his totalitarian-minded authors were tried on charges of encouraging anticonstitutional activities and sentenced to jail terms of up to nine months.[31] On other occasions the activities of dubious groups have been impeded not only by government action, but by alert prodemocratic groups. Thus in 1960, trade union members found a legal and clever way of obstructing the meetings of the extreme nationalist German Reich party, some of whose members had become notorious for their anti-Semitic and antidemocratic statements. Union leaders simply gathered their followers from miles around, and by the time the nationalists began to drift toward the hall which they had rented for their meeting, every single place in it had already been taken by staunch and muscular unionists.

But however successfully open neo-Nazi manifestations are dealt with or, if publicized, condemned by articulate public opinion, it is evident that they constitute only that part of the iceberg visible above water. Twelve years' exposure to Nazi indoctrination is not easily eradicated. Evidence of this received world attention as a wave of anti-Semitic vandalism, which started in Cologne on Christmas Eve, 1959, quickly spread throughout Germany and to other countries as well. No fewer than 685 such incidents, mostly involving the smearing of anti-Semitic slogans, were officially noted in the Federal Republic. A good third of the cases successfully investigated were initiated by individuals with submerged Nazi and antidemocratic sentiments. More alarming was the revelation that about half of the cases involved youths below the age of nineteen who had not been directly exposed to the Nazi regime. Even though it was shown that the majority were motivated by simple teen-age rowdyism, serious questions were raised as to what German schools had been teaching about National Socialism and its heritage.

Subsequent investigation showed that both the authors of German textbooks and the majority of teachers had sinned, mainly by omission. Like the overwhelming majority of their fellow citizens, they found discussion of the Nazi period and the horrors which were committed in the name of Germany during this time extremely unpleasant. When pressed, teachers frequently said they did not feel justified in causing possible difficulties between pupils and the considerable number of parents

[31] For information regarding activities of neo-Nazi and nationalist groups, see the *Bulletin* of the Wiener Library (London).

who had gone along with the Nazis. In an attempt to avoid unpleasant recriminations, they had stressed the history of the
Middle Ages so that little time remained for twentieth century
history. But as a German historian has written, it was not just
the history teachers who were at fault; the whole society sought
refuge in silence. "In the time between 1933 and 1945, as it was
then so nicely put, we 'made history.' . . . Then we fell into a
deep depression which led us to the other extreme. We tried to
'climb out' of history, or at least we thought we could pull off
this trick . . . until the vandalism reminded us in front of
world opinion that we could not separate ourselves from our
history." [32]

The record of German political leaders in getting their followers to face the problem of the past has been extremely uneven.
They have frequently said the right things, but often not to the
people who needed to hear them most. In many concrete instances they have taken correct positions, as in assuming a large-
scale burden of financial reparation to Jewish and other victims
of Nazi persecution. But too many individuals who had been
deeply compromised through collaboration with the Nazi regime
were allowed to climb into positions of political responsibility,
while those who had emigrated during the Nazi period often
found themselves slandered. As regards the criminals who had
actually carried out dastardly work in the concentration and
extermination camps, the official machinery had worked only
fitfully at preparing prosecutions, until situations like that engen-
dered by the Eichmann trial of 1961 caused dusty files to be
pulled out of rusty cabinets. As Federal President Luebke said
at the time, an essential part of the German program of restitu-
tion must consist of the prosecution of murderers still in their
midst.

Bibliography

Occupation and Constitution

Almond, Gabriel A., ed., *The Struggle for Democracy in Germany* (Chapel
    Hill, 1949).
Balfour, Michael, and Mair, John, *Four-Power Control of Germany and
    Austria, 1945–46* (London, 1956).
Clay, Lucius D., *Decision in Germany* (Garden City, 1950).
Friedrich, Carl J., and Spiro, H. J., "The Constitution of the German Fed-
    eral Republic," in E. H. Litchfield, ed., *Governing Postwar Germany*
    (Ithaca, 1953), 117–51.

[32] Walter Goerlitz, *Die Welt,* February 3, 1960.

Golay, John F., *The Founding of the Federal Republic of Germany* (Chicago, 1958).

Grosser, Alfred, *Colossus Again: Western Germany from Defeat to Rearmament* (New York, 1955).

Kauper, Paul G., "The Constitutions of West Germany and the U. S.: A Comparative Study," *Michigan Law Review*, LVIII (1960), 1091–184.

Montgomery, John D., *Forced to Be Free: The Artificial Revolution in Germany and Japan* (Chicago, 1957).

Morgenthau, Hans, ed., *Germany and the Future of Europe* (Chicago, 1951).

Oppen, Beate Ruhm von, *Documents on Germany 1945–1955* (London, 1955).

U.S. Military Government, *Documents on the Creation of the German Federal Constitution* (Washington, 1949).

Zink, Harold, *The United States in Germany, 1944–55* (Princeton, 1957).

Political Parties

Bergstraesser, Ludwig, *Geschichte der Politischen Parteien in Deutschland*, 9th ed. (Munich, 1955).

Braunthal, Gerard, "The Free Democratic Party in West German Politics," *WPQ*, XIII (June, 1960).

Buesch, Otto, and Furth, Peter, *Rechtsradikalismus im Nachkriegsdeutschland* (Berlin, 1958).

Edinger, Lewis J., and Chalmers, Douglas A., "Overture or Swan Song: German Social Democracy Prepares for a New Decade," *Antioch Review*, XX (1960), 163–75.

Fogarty, Michael D., *Christian Democracy in Western Europe, 1820–1953* (London, 1957).

Heidenheimer, Arnold J., *Adenauer and the CDU: The Rise of the Leader and the Integration of the Party* (The Hague, 1960).

———, "German Party Finance: The CDU," *APSR*, LI (1957), 369–85.

———, "La Structure Confessionnelle, Sociale et Regionale de la CDU," *Revue Francaise de Science Politique*, VII (1957), 626–45.

Kirchheimer, Otto, "Notes on West Germany," *WP*, VI (1954), 306–21.

Lange, Max Gustav, *et al., Parteien in der Bundesrepublik* (Villingen, 1955).

Neumann, Sigmund, ed., "Germany," in *Modern Political Parties* (Chicago, 1956).

Parteienrechtskommission des Bundesinnenministeriums, *Rechtliche Ordnung des Parteiwesens* (Frankfurt, 1957).

Schneider, Carl J., "Political Parties and the German Basic Law of 1949," *WPQ*, X (1957), 527–40.

Tauber, Kurt P., "German Nationalists and European Union," *PSQ*, LXXIV (1959), 564–89.

Elections and Political Behavior

Divo Institut, *Umfragen 1957* (Frankfurt, 1958).

Faul, Erwin, ed., *Wahlen und Waehler in Westdeutschland* (Villingen, 1960).

Grosser, A., "Les Elections Allemandes: Le Plebiscite de 15 Septembre 1957," *Revue Francaise de Science Politique*, IX (1957), 839–64.

Hartenstein, Wolfgang, *et al.,* "Die Septemberdemokratie," *Neue Gesellschaft*, V (1958), 3–18.

Hirsch-Weber, Wolfgang, and Schuetz, Klaus, *Waehler und Gewaehlte* (Berlin, 1956).

Kitzinger, U., *German Electoral Politics* (London, 1960).

———, "The West German Electoral Law," *Parliamentary Affairs*, XI (1958), 220–38.

Neumann, Elizabeth, ed., *Jahrbuch der Öffentlichen Meinung, 1947–55* (Allensbach, 1956).

Pollock, James K., *et al.*, *German Democracy at Work* (Ann Arbor, 1955).

Interest Groups and the Press

Breitling, Rupert, *Die Verbaende in der Bundesrepublik: Ihre Arten und Ihre Politischen Wirkungsweise* (Meisenheim, 1955).

Deutsch, Karl W., and Edinger, Lewis J., *Germany Rejoins the Powers: Mass Opinion, Interest Groups and Elites in Contemporary German Foreign Policy* (Stanford, 1959).

Eschenburg, Theodor, *Herrschaft der Verbaende?* (Stuttgart, 1955).

Ellwein, Thomas, *Klerikalismus in der Deutschen Politik* (Munich, 1956).

Hirsch-Weber, Wolfgang, *Gewerkschaften in der Politik* (Cologne, 1959).

Jacobi, C., "The New German Press," *FA*, XXXII (1954), 323–30.

Speier, Hans, and Davison, W., ed., *West German Leadership and Foreign Policy* (Evanston, 1957).

Spiro, Herbert, *The Politics of German Codetermination* (Cambridge, 1958).

Williams, Emlyn, "The West German Press," *Gazette* (Leiden), V (1959), 1-10.

4 - The Executive

The Presidency

One of the greatest difficulties of political systems created by revolution in countries which have evolved from a hierarchical structure has always consisted of devising an adequate republican substitute for the figure of the monarch. Even if individual kings were loathed, the institution of the monarchy supplied a tremendously powerful symbol, which a large proportion of citizens needed in order to identify with the state. Many Germans after 1918, conditioned by generations of experience under an *Obrigkeitsstaat* (a state where authority derives from above), missed the security they had symbolically derived from the vestigial lord-vassal relationship. The Weimar Republic's difficulties with this problem were reflected in the fact that its first president, the Socialist Friedrich Ebert, had himself supported retention of the monarchy until just a year before he took office. Both he and his successor, Hindenburg, who remained a monarchist at heart

The Federal President

Article 54

(1) The Federal President shall be elected, without debate, by the Federal Convention. Every German who is eligible to vote in elections for the Bundestag and has reached the age of 40 years shall be eligible for election.

(2) The term of office of the Federal President shall be five years. Re-election for a consecutive term shall be admissible only once.

(3) The Federal Convention shall consist of the members of the Bundestag and an equal number of members elected by the popular representative assemblies of the *Laender* according to the principles of proportional representation.

Article 58

Orders and decrees of the Federal President shall require for their validity the counter-signature of the Federal Chancellor or the appropriate Federal Minister. This shall not apply to the appointment and dismissal of the Federal Chancellor, the dissolution of the Bundestag under Article 63 and the request under Article 69, paragraph 3.

---

even while in office, failed to institutionalize the Weimar presidency. Under the conditions that prevailed probably no individual could have done so, especially as the Constitution loaded down the incumbent with excessive powers which inevitably entangled him in partisan constitutional conflict. In 1949, the Parliamentary Council tried once again, and the office it created has turned out to fit relatively smoothly into the constitutional structure, while at the same time supplying, in the persons of its initial incumbents, likable uncle figures of whom most Germans grew both quite fond and reasonably respectful.

To secure this degree of acceptance, the presidency has been deprived of such important political powers as the power to appoint the Chancellor in times of crisis, the power to issue emergency decrees, and the power to serve as commander-in-chief of the armed forces. Most importantly, its incumbent is not expected to resolve conflicts between the cabinet and the legislature. Rather, his functions are mainly the routine ones of any head of state. He receives ambassadors, issues letters of appointment to officials, judges, and military officers, signs and proclaims treaties and laws, and possesses the power of pardon. But even these actions must be countersigned by a cabinet minister. In addition, he fulfills domestic political functions very similar to those of the British monarch. He proposes Chancellor candidates, appoints ministers on the Chancellor's recommendation, and can dissolve the Bundestag only under specifically outlined situations

involving a deadlock between it and the executive. Quite obviously, this job description is different from that appropriate to
counterpart offices in the United States or the French Fifth Republic.

The method of the president's election was also designed to
provide a figure who would be both fairly widely accepted, and
insulated from popular influence. The drafters of the Basic Law
definitely wanted to avoid the Weimar situation under which a
popularly elected president could both campaign for the office
and vie with the legislature in his claim to represent the people.
They thus provided for his indirect election through a special
electoral college made up of all the members of the Bundestag
and an equal number of representatives of the Land diets. This
Bundesversammlung elects the president for a period of five years
(compared to a seven-year tenure under Weimar), and an incumbent may be re-elected only once. In 1949, the position went
to a figure who very conveniently happened to be both the
leader of the third largest party and a story book image of "the
other Germany." Theodor Heuss, leader of the Free Democrats
(whose votes at that time also supplied the crucial margin for
Adenauer's election as Chancellor), was widely known not only
as a politician but as a writer of essays and belles-lettres. Originally a disciple of one of the most impressive liberals in modern German history, Friedrich Naumann, during the Weimar
period Heuss had been simultaneously a distinguished journalist,
a Democratic party member of the Reichstag, and a lecturer at
the Berlin Institute of Politics. With his Swabian humor, his
rejection of traditional pomposity, and his readiness to speak out
in words that were both enlightening and readily understand-
able, he quickly won affectionate esteem, and in 1954 his re-election was almost unanimous. Constitutionally, he set few precedents and on a few occasions retreated gracefully from incipient
conflicts with the Chancellor. When he left office in 1959 almost
the entire population of Bonn lined the streets to tender him a
tremendous ovation.

Not even a personality like Heuss could have achieved such
unreserved popularity, had he not made the office a purely
ceremonial one, leaving all political decisions to the Chancellor.
When the question of a successor to Heuss became acute in the
spring of 1959, Adenauer surprised the world by announcing his
intention of running for the office himself. He did so with the
avowed intention of supervising his successor as Chancellor and
keeping a steady hand on foreign policy. This implied a radical

change in the constitutional relationship between president and
Chancellor, for Adenauer would surely not have been a figurehead, and in fact he openly said that Heuss had not made all
he could of the office. But it developed that his acceptance of the
office was contingent on his being allowed to name his successor
as Chancellor. When prolonged wrangling failed to resolve the
conflict arising from the CDU parliamentary party's strong
preference for Ludwig Erhard and Adenauer's insistence on
Franz Etzel, he announced that he would remain Chancellor
after all.[1] As a result, the CDU-dominated *Bundesversammlung*
elected as Heuss' successor a candidate selected at the very last
minute, Heinrich Luebke, the incumbent Minister of Agriculture. Like Heuss the favored possessor of an impressive profile,
Luebke has adhered to his predecessor's interpretation of the
office. However, it may well be that the position of the presidency
will become more significant in situations where the Chancellor
is not as dominant as Adenauer has been.

The Chancellorship

In the light of increasing governmental control over immensely complex resources and weapons, students of government have become increasingly worried about how legislatures or
public opinion can hope to keep abreast of far-reaching executive action. But the Germans have perhaps been less troubled
than others, for their traditions have led the mass of them to
regard the supremacy of the executive as quite natural. Even
convinced democrats have reluctantly come to accept that the
German definition of democracy tends to mean "government for
the people" more than it does "government by the people." The
German penchant for order and their desire to be given at least a
sure sense of direction causes them to place a premium on an
individual who can keep firm control of the tiller. It is not only
because he unified Germany that Bismarck remains by far the
most admired historical German political figure. Despite reservations about his role in retarding progress toward parliamentarism and genuine political democracy, he is still widely regarded
as the ideal type of German executive.

If in 1948 an outside observer had accused the Parliamentary Council of drafting a Bismarckian constitution tailor-fit to

[1] Arnold J. Heidenheimer, *Adenauer and the CDU: The Rise of the
Leader and the Integration of the Party* (The Hague, 1960), pp. 221 ff.

the personality of its presiding officer and second oldest member (who had himself grown up in the Bismarckian era), he would probably have been ridiculed for letting historicism get the better of him. He would have been told that its members had no intention of writing a Bismarckian constitution; that, as presiding officer, Konrad Adenauer had relatively little influence on the important drafting—as distinguished from the polishing—work of the Council, and that it was still extremely problematical whether Adenauer would have a chance at the Chancellorship. The Council concentrated on remedying the faults of the Weimar Constitution. If in the process they created an extremely strong Chancellor, they did so by indirection, for having decided that the president should not have any significant executive powers, power had to be concentrated within the cabinet. As for the cabinet itself, the drafters, since they took the continuation of a multiparty system for granted, feared breakdowns of cohesion of the sort that had occurred under Weimar when ministers were frequently torn between their loyalty to cabinet policies and pressures from the various parties to which they belonged. It was largely to prevent the breakdown of cabinet authority during crises that the Basic Law endows the Chancellor with great powers to maintain executive stability against the legislature, and to impose cabinet cohesion on its ministers.

In effect, the legislature is allowed a clear-cut opportunity to accept or reject the government only once every four years, when it elects the Chancellor after each Bundestag election. Even then its powers of selection are limited. It must vote on the personality suggested by the president without prior discussion. (If it rejects him, it must vote again on another nominee. In both cases election must be by absolute majority; it is only after a two-week deadlock that the Bundestag may, with the president's approval, elect a Chancellor with only a relative majority). Once elected, the Chancellor has very strong powers. He does not have to ask the legislature either for a vote of confidence for his government program, or for approval of the list of ministers which he asks the president to appoint. (It is accepted that the president is pretty well bound to appoint the Chancellor's nominees.) His position is immensely strengthened by the fact that the Basic Law radically altered the traditional parliamentary practice that a Chancellor and his cabinet must resign if they lose a vote of confidence in the legislature. Instead, it provides that the Chancellor must resign after losing a vote of confidence *only if*

The Federal Government

Article 62

The Federal Government shall consist of the Federal Chancellor and the Federal Ministers.

Article 63

(1) The Federal Chancellor shall be elected, without debate, by the Bundestag on the proposal of the Federal President.

(2) The person obtaining the votes of the majority of the members of the Bundestag shall be elected. He shall be appointed by the Federal President.

(3) If the person nominated is not elected, the Bundestag may, within fourteen days after the ballot, elect a Federal Chancellor by more than one half of its members.

(4) If the Federal Chancellor is not elected within this time limit a new ballot shall take place immediately, in which the person who receives most votes shall be elected. If the person elected receives the votes of the majority of the members of the Bundestag the Federal President must, within 7 days after the election, appoint him. If the person elected does not obtain this majority the Federal President must, within seven days, either appoint him or dissolve the Bundestag.

Article 64

(1) The Federal Ministers shall be appointed and dismissed by the Federal President upon the proposal of the Federal Chancellor. . . .

Article 65

The Federal Chancellor shall determine and assume responsibility for general policy. Within the limits of this general policy, each Federal Minister shall direct his department individually and on his own responsibility. The Federal Government shall decide on differences of opinion between the Federal Ministers. . . .

Article 67

(1) The Bundestag may express its lack of confidence in the Federal Chancellor only by electing a successor with the majority of its members and submitting a request to the Federal President for the dismissal of the Federal Chancellor. The Federal President must comply with the request and appoint the person elected.

(2) There must be an interval of 48 hours between the motion and the election.

Article 68

(1) If a motion of the Federal Chancellor to receive a vote of confidence does not obtain the support of the majority of the members of the Bundestag, the Federal President may, upon the proposal of the Federal Chancellor, dissolve the Bundestag within 21 days. The right of dissolution shall lapse as soon as the Bundestag, with the majority of its members, elects another Federal Chancellor.

*the legislature at the very same time elects by majority vote some-
one to take his place.* The adoption of this "positive" no-confidence provision was intended to prevent the kinds of situation
in which mutually hostile parties combine to bring down a
ministry without being able to agree among themselves on what
is to take its place. In practice, its reinforcement of the position
of a Chancellor who is also leader of a majority party has made
his position virtually impregnable. For it means that as long as
he retains control of his party, the legislature is unable to enter
a no-confidence vote. On the other hand the Chancellor may, on
occasions of his choosing, ask the Bundestag to give him a vote
of confidence, but even if he loses he need not resign.

The Chancellor's powers over his fellow ministers are
equally impressive. The lack of an overt legislative role in their
appointment makes them so much more dependent on the Chancellor. This is reinforced by the fact that, in contrast to Weimar
practice, only the Chancellor, and not the individual minister, is
subject to parliamentary votes of confidence. These factors have
helped him to greatly increase the power potential of a position
whose description, curiously enough, is virtually the same in both
constitutions. Both provide that the Chancellor lays down the
main guide lines of policy. But the Weimar Chancellors found
that when they actually tried to impose policies, they ran into
such problems as the fact that the Defense Ministry considered
itself directly responsible only to the president; that the president could refuse to approve the reorganization of ministerial
jurisdiction or to accept the Chancellor's cabinet nominees; and
that party pressure effectively backed up their independent-
minded ministers. The frequent result was, in Eschenburg's
words, that "the person who was to lay down the main lines of
policy often became, in fact, the guardian of the policies of
others." [2] The emergence of a majority party in postwar Germany has produced a much different situation. As another leading German authority has put it, "although the Basic Law's description of the Chancellor's role is not signficantly different from
that of the Weimar Constitution, the Chancellor has in fact
ceased to be *primus inter pares* and has achieved a superior position reminiscent of that provided by the 1871 Constitution." [3]
The first incumbent of the position was to show just how far
that parallel could be carried.

[2] Theodor Eschenburg, "Die Richtlinien der Politik," *Die oeffentliche
Verwaltung,* VII (1954), 193.
[3] Theodor Maunz, *Deutsches Staatsrecht,* 9th ed. (Munich, 1959), p. 305.

Adenauer as Chancellor

When Konrad Adenauer was sworn in as the Federal Republic's first Chancellor in 1949, he had behind him a record as a public administrator and politician stretching over almost half a century. Most of this time he had served first as deputy mayor and then as Lord Mayor (1917 to 1933) of the Rhineland metropolis of Cologne. A typical Rhinelander, he felt himself much more akin to the culture and traditions of the Latin-influenced areas to the west than he did to the cold discipline of Prussia, and his aversion toward having to live in Berlin was one of the reasons why he never seriously competed for a top-level national political position in the Weimar period. In any case this self-willed, authoritarian figure could never have lasted long in the slot of a Weimar Chancellor, whose continuance in office was at most times dependent on his ability to wheedle and cajole his fellow ministers and party leaders. He was much more at home in the prestigious and powerful position which the Napoleonic reforms had bequeathed to the chief officers of the Rhineland cities. As Lord Mayor he was not only assured of a fixed term of office (twelve years), which was almost as long as the duration of the Weimar Republic, but he also possessed unchallenged control over the entire city administration, and tended to dominate the City Council, over whose sessions he presided. Although a member and local leader of the Center party, his prestige and power rested much more on his position as a high civil servant than on his party following. Moreover, in the "Cologne cabinet" there was no pretense at a relationship between nominally equal colleagues; the deputy mayors, though also elected and themselves experts of great experience, were bound by the city charter to reconcile their views to the decisions of the Lord Mayor.

By the time he became Chancellor he had suffered setbacks, but had always rebounded. The Nazis had deposed him in 1933, as they did all anti-Nazi high officials, and for the next twelve years Adenauer was limited to tending roses in the garden of his villa at Rhoendorf, just up-river from Bonn. He was briefly arrested a number of times, but since he had no ties to overt resistance groups, he was on the whole allowed to lead the quiet life of a pensioner. When the Americans took over Cologne in 1945 they reinstalled him as Mayor, but a few months later, after the city had been turned over to British administration, Adenauer was peremptorily dismissed by a visiting British general for failing to carry out British directives, among them one ordering the cutting down for firewood of the trees he had planted during his earlier tenure of office. But after a short lapse of time Adenauer was allowed to re-enter politics, and he quickly became the official leader of the CDU in the British zone and, after bitter competition, the dominant CDU party leader in all three Western zones.[4]

The recent experience at political in-fighting with both Allied officials and German politicians stood Adenauer in good stead when he was faced with the task not only of presiding over a multiparty cabinet, but of setting up an entirely new governmental structure in the university town of Bonn, which he had forced his followers to select as the capital site even though many had preferred Frankfurt. His experience and extensive contacts with other administrators helped him supervise the creation of the federal ministries, but for several years relationships with both the Allies, the legislature, and his own ministers proved very trying. While he was using subtle pressure to force the Allies to liberalize quickly the provisions of the Occupation Statute, the Socialist leader of the opposition, Schumacher, launched bitter attacks on his patriotic integrity, on one occasion causing a Bundestag uproar by labeling him "the Chancellor of the Allies." During the same time the minor parties, especially the Communists, allowed no consideration of parliamentary decorum to restrict the violence of their attacks, particularly after Adenauer agreed in 1950 to follow American suggestions for German rearmament. To make matters worse, it turned out that his fellow ministers had quite different conceptions of what cabinet discipline entailed. The results of cabinet discussions were all over Bonn in no time, and on Sundays the ministers roamed the countryside giving speeches in which they freely expressed their personal opinions, even if these were altogether contrary to those of the Chancellor and the rest of the cabinet.

Gradually, thanks to improving economic circumstances and generous Allied concessions, Adenauer got the situation under control, and as he did so he found time to give his ministers tutorials on the content of the Basic Law. These proved quite effective, especially as the polls were beginning to note the increase in Adenauer's personal popularity which was to prove so decisive in the overwhelming CDU victory of 1953. One by one, the ministers became convinced that the powers of the Chancellor were indeed a good deal greater than they had originally

[4] Heidenheimer, *op. cit.,* pp. 61 ff.

thought, and their attitudes toward Adenauer changed from virtual insubordination to what in many cases approached subservience. One minister, Gustav Heinemann (who later joined the SPD), resigned because he could not accept Adenauer's manner of committing Germany to rearmament. But for a decade he remained the curious exception who only proved the rule that Adenauer's ministers did not resign (and relinquish their pension rights) merely because of deep-seated differences of political view. A few ministers of independent mind were allowed a relatively free hand in their special areas, such as the Minister of Economics, Erhard, and the Minister for Finance (and later, Justice), Schaeffer. One other, Jakob Kaiser, was for special reasons allowed to make no secret of his dissatisfaction with Adenauer's foreign policy. But most accepted the subordinate positions which the Chancellor assigned them. A few difficult cases were dropped in the cabinet reshuffle which followed the 1953 elections. From that time on, except for the curious situation created by Adenauer's intentions regarding the presidency in 1959, there was no more talk of cabinet crisis. Indeed, in the areas of his main concern—working toward European unification, tightening the alliance with the United States, and maintaining an unrelentingly hostile front toward compromise with the Soviets—Adenauer acted mainly on the responsibility of his own conscience. His manner of policy implementation became known as "the policy of lonely decisions."

The Ministers

Parliamentary government developed with the acceptance of the convention that the executives in charge of government departments ceased being chosen on their merit as the king's civil servants, but were chosen because they enjoyed the confidence of party majorities in Parliament. In accordance with the rule that "the powers of the Crown must be exercised through ministers who are members of one or the other Houses of Parliament and who command the confidence of the House of Commons," [5] a clear line was drawn in Britain between politicians and civil servants. One could either enjoy the tenure and pension rights of a permanent civil servant, in which case one could not hope to become a minister, or one could go into Parliament with the hope of becoming a minister, but retain office for only so long

[5] Albert Dicey, *Law of the Constitution,* 10th ed. (London, 1960), p. 431.

as one's party remained in power. One could not switch back and forth between the two careers. In Imperial Germany, where parliamentary government was never fully established, this distinction was never drawn, and it has to this day not been clearly established. As a result, civil servants continue to be elected to Parliament (though since 1949 they have been obliged to take leave while holding office) and experts and nonparliamentarians continue to be appointed as ministers (though more rarely; there were four in Adenauer's first cabinet, one in the second, none in the third). The important point, however, is that ministers, whatever their background, are in an uncertain constitutional position between Parliament and the civil service.

The situation has changed very slowly from Bismarck's time, when practically all the "state secretaries" fulfilling ministerial roles were really civil servants responsible only to the Chancellor, who was himself the chief civil servant and only incidentally accountable to the Reichstag. In the Weimar period, though ministers were drawn predominantly from the ranks of parliamentarians, they were reluctant to relinquish the pension rights and other privileges arising from the fact that under public law they had much the same position as did civil servants. In 1930 a special law had to be passed to make it evident that ministers were not covered by *all* the civil service regulations. But the distinction between parliamentary ministers and civil servants still remains difficult for the German legal mind to grasp, and a constitutional law text published in 1954 has to devote a paragraph to informing law students that ministers do not *have* to be recruited from among civil servants.[6] Nevertheless, their salaries, as well as that of the Chancellor, remain tied to civil service scales. The former receive one and one-third times (presently about 1,200 dollars a month), the latter one and two-thirds times the salary of the top civil service bracket, plus expense allowances. As regards pension rights, postwar ministers could, until recently, become eligible only after ten years of government service or after reaching their fifty-fifth birthday. In 1960 the law was changed to make them eligible after four years' service.

However, Adenauer's manner of running his cabinet has served to perpetuate the ministers' unclear constitutional position and has gone a good way toward relegating them—parliamentary membership notwithstanding—to the status of the Bismarckian state secretary. His dominance has reduced ministers

---

[6] Fritz Munch, *Die Bundesregierung* (Frankfurt, 1954), p. 123.

to the position of expert supervisors of their departments, while depriving them of the responsibility for general policy-making which makes cabinet experience so worthwhile from the point of view of training future political leaders. It is evident even to someone who has never attended a cabinet meeting that the procedures employed there hardly encourage the participants' feeling of prestige and responsibility. In the first place, meetings are not exclusive. Not only ministers attend, but so also do the semipermanent state secretaries of their ministries, who as "political civil servants" are part fish and part fowl. The size of these meetings makes it impossible—Adenauer's predeliction for "lonely decisions" quite aside—for ministers to attain the degree of intimacy that their equivalents achieve in Britain, where the atmosphere is confidential, and minutes taken down only in outline are retained by the cabinet secretary only. In Germany, cabinet minutes circulate widely to all the ministries, so that a minister is hardly encouraged to speak his free mind even if he were not cowed by the Chancellor. Not a little of the weakness of the Adenauer cabinet procedure is revealed by the Cabinet Rules, which read as though they were adopted from a boarding-school manual. They include regulations such as the following:

#13   Each minister must inform the Chancellor if he intends to leave the capital for more than one day. Absences of longer than three days and visits abroad require the approval of the Chancellor. . . .

Before leaving the capital a minister must inform the Chancellor of the address at which he can be reached during his absence.

#22   Meetings begin promptly at the announced time. . . .

Meetings of the cabinet are confidential. Especially to be noted is that information about what individual ministers said, about voting results and about the contents of the minutes may not be revealed without the special authorization of the Chancellor.[7]

Documents such as these bear out reports that Adenauer's method of ruling the government of a major power has not changed considerably since the days when he was the terror of the office boys in the Cologne City Hall.

It should not be deduced from the foregoing that Adenauer has ruled completely autocratically, by ignoring the wishes of the political parties as regards cabinet appointments or by replacing ministers as readily as American corporations dismiss unsuccess-

[7] Hans Trossmann, *Der Zweite Deutsche Bundestag* (Bonn, 1954), pp. 367–76.

ful executives. Adenauer has not openly violated the politician's code just for the sake of arbitrariness. In 1953, when he was anxious to retain the support of the minor parties—even though the CDU had a majority—his negotiations with the party leaders held up the cabinet formation for several weeks. At the same time Adenauer was too deeply influenced by the civil service mentality to dismiss people just because they were not very competent or had become a political handicap. Once a minister was "broken in" to the Adenauer way of doing things, he had virtually achieved tenure, at least until eligible for a pension. But Adenauer's manner of emphasizing to the hilt his personal responsibility as Chancellor has inhibited the cabinet from growing into a body capable of making joint collective decisions; thus in Germany cabinet responsibility is still largely an unknown principle.

Provisions for Deadlocks and Emergencies

Adenauer's dominance over his party and cabinets together with the CDU's strong numerical position have all but shielded the Federal Republic from the kinds of crises the Weimar Republic experienced as a result of deadlock among differing branches of the government and other breakdowns in the decision-making machinery. The Constitutional Court, whose role is discussed in Chapter 7, has played an important part in arbitrating conflicts over constitutional powers between governmental organs. However, with a change in the constellation of political forces, it is quite possible that situations will develop which cannot be resolved by the normal techniques. The Basic Law includes special provisions for a number of such situations.

One of these (Art. 63) provides for the situation that arises when the president's nominee for the Chancellorship does not succeed in getting the requisite support of an absolute Bundestag majority. If another candidate can get the support of an absolute majority, he is elected. If, however, the Bundestag remains deadlocked for two weeks, another ballot is called for, and the president has the discretion of either appointing the candidate with the largest number of votes (even if short of a majority) or of dissolving the Bundestag. Provision for the use of the dissolution power is made in regard to one other kindred situation (Art. 68). If a Chancellor loses his political support in the Bundestag and is defeated on his own motion of confidence, he may within twenty-one days ask the president to dissolve the Bundestag and call new elections. Thus, while the opportunities for dissolving the Bundestag are limited, they do exist under these specified conditions.

The Basic Law also provides for a variety of techniques through which decisions of particular organs may be overridden or the abuse of power checked. Thus the president may be impeached by one-fourth of the members of either the Bundestag or Bundesrat "for willful violation of the Basic Law or any other Federal Law" (Art. 61). He may then be tried, and if found guilty, removed by the Constitutional Court. A Constitutional Court decision can of course also be overridden by amending the Constitution, which however requires an absolute two-thirds majority in both houses of the legislature (Art. 79). In conflicts between the federal government and the Laender relating to the manner in which the latter administer federal legislation or allegedly violate federal law, it is the Bundesrat which has the decisive voice (Arts. 37, 84). With its consent the federal government may send out commissioners to give direct instructions to the Laender bureaucracy.

Though normally not endowed with very significant political powers, both the presidency and the Bundesrat may have key roles to play in case of a prolonged deadlock between Chancellor and Bundestag. When the Bundestag refuses to pass a piece of legislation which the federal government declares to be "urgent" and when the powers of dissolution under Article 68 are not used, the president and the Bundesrat may, at the request of the cabinet, declare a so-called "state of legislative emergency" (Art. 81). In this situation the Bundestag can in effect be deprived of its legislative powers for a period of up to six months, during which time approval by the Bundesrat suffices to enact legislation.

The provisions of Article 81 had never been invoked up to 1961, and they are far more limited than those of the notorious Article 48 of the Weimar Constitution, which allowed the president to abrogate civil rights and pass legislation by decree. Indeed some Germans have felt that the Basic Law does not make sufficient provision for a general state of emergency, such as large-scale internal subversion or armed invasion. Such considerations led the government to introduce a draft constitutional amendment in 1960 which bore striking similarities to Article 48. It provided for the declaration of a state of emergency when "the free and democratic basic order" was imminently threatened. Admittedly, it left the initial power of declaring a state of emer-

gency to the Bundestag, but it provided that if obstacles prevented the Bundestag from coming to a decision, such power
might be lodged in the federal president, acting in conjunction
with the Chancellor. Once the state of emergency was declared,
the cabinet would have the power to legislate by decree, suspend
guarantees of free speech, assembly, association, and movement,
and take over the police forces of the Laender. The proposed
amendment was sharply attacked, particularly by the Social
Democrats, and since without their concurrence the cabinet
could not secure the necessary two-thirds Bundestag majority, it
was not passed.

Bibliography

Allemann, Fritz Rene, *Bonn ist nicht Weimar* (Cologne, 1956).
Altmann, Ruediger, *Das Erbe Adenauers* (Stuttgart, 1960).
Eschenburg, Theodor, *Staat und Gesellschaft in Deutschland* (Stuttgart, 1956).
Heidenheimer, Arnold J., *Adenauer and the CDU: The Rise of the Leader
     and the Integration of the Party* (The Hague, 1960).
Hermens, Ferdinand A., *The Representative Republic* (Notre Dame, 1958).
Hiscocks, Richard, *Democracy in Western Germany* (London, 1957).
Knight, Maxwell E., *The German Executive, 1890–1933* (Stanford, 1952).
Loewenstein, Karl, *Political Power and the Governmental Process* (Chicago,
     1956).
Maunz, Theodor, *Deutsches Staatsrecht*, 9th ed. (Munich, 1959).
Munch, Fritz, *Die Bundesregierung* (Frankfurt, 1954).
Speier, Hans, and Davison, W. P., eds., *West German Leadership and Foreign
     Policy* (Evanston, 1957).
Weymar, Paul, *Adenauer* (New York, 1957).

5 - The Legislature

Structure

The seat of the legislature of the Federal Republic is in a
series of white plaster buildings on the banks of the Rhine which,
before the war, served as a teachers' training college. Though its
location there is not inappropriate, most legislators would probably much prefer to work in the old Reichstag building in Berlin. That gutted structure is being hopefully rebuilt, but its

use has not been feasible because of the ambiguous status of West Berlin and because it lies within twenty yards of the Soviet sector. Most of the *Bundeshaus* in Bonn is used by the Bundestag and its members, while a smaller wing houses the Bundesrat.

Some information about the Bundestag chamber will help cast additional light on the peculiar character of German executive-Parliament relations. For the first twelve years the chamber has been arranged like the large lecture hall that it might have been, with deputies' seats and desks covering most of the space, except for a raised platform at the front where the ministers and their top civil service aides sit facing the parliamentarians. Members wishing to speak can not do so from their seats, but have to come to the platform, where they necessarily have to turn their backs on either their fellow parliamentarians or the members of the cabinet. Even the most brilliant orators are hard put to gain the attention of the entire house. The arrangement discourages a free give-and-take and leads speakers to prepare formal lectures. Deputies have called it the worst parliamentary chamber in the world. Many complained of the fact that the elevated position of the government bench suggested that the executive had a privileged position. Encouraged by Bundestag President Gerstenmaier, discussions were initiated in 1959 to renovate the chamber on the model of the British House of Commons, so that the majority and opposition parties would face each other.

But considerable difficulties were encountered. The members of the cabinet contended that (unlike British ministers) the Basic Law assigned them a special position quite distinct from their role as leaders of the majority party. This position was based on German practice going back to Bismarck and had been reinforced by a Constitutional Court decision in 1958. Also, the FDP and many members of the SPD feared that such a reconstruction would mean acceptance of a two-party system, which they feared. However, after prolonged negotiations a compromise was worked out. It was decided to redo the chamber so that the majority and opposition parties would face each other and so that members could speak from their seats, with the cabinet being assigned a special enclave on the majority party side of the house. This solution was adopted in 1961 with a narrow majority,[1] but even then implementation of the decision was postponed.

The importance of the Bundestag within the bicameral legislature is shown not only by its having, like other lower houses, a predominant influence on the budget, but also by the

[1] Bundestag *Stenographische Berichte*, III Wahlperiode, pp. 8301 ff.

fact that only certain enumerated kinds of legislation affecting prerogatives of the Laender must actually be passed by both houses. With regard to other legislation, the Bundestag's decision may be affected by the Bundesrat only through a "suspensive veto," which may be overridden by the lower house. Thus, though the Bundesrat has considerably greater powers than the contemporary House of Lords or the Reichsrat of the Weimar period, its legislative influence does not approach that of the United States Senate. Some idea of the relationship between the two houses may also be gained by knowledge of their size and the frequency of their plenary sessions. In 1960 the Bundestag was composed of 519 members, elected in accordance with the procedure outlined above (see p. 75), while the Bundesrat was composed of forty-one Land ministers, selected in the manner described below (see p. 120), who meet in plenary session only an hour or two twice a month.

While German legislatures had never been stable long enough to develop a really strong set of traditions and conventions, the problem of lack of parliamentary "know-how" became particularly acute after 1949. Only about 5 per cent of the members of the first Bundestag had had previous experience in the Reichstag, and although a good many had served in postwar Land legislatures (at that time hardly ideal training schools), the majority of the members were quite unknowing in parliamentary ways. The problem was well brought out by the difficulty in getting the members to understand the crucial significance of parliamentary immunity, and the criteria to be considered in allowing it to be removed. In 1950 one relevant case involved a notorious Bavarian deputy, frequently in trouble, who had charged outside the Bundestag that on his last stay in jail "he had been forced to eat excrement-covered bread kept in the lavatory." When the Bavarian Land government sought to enter a libel action, many deputies were inclined to lift his immunity on the ground that, as one put it: "The state stands over the parliament, and for this reason it is more important that an insult to the state be expiated than that the parliament be denied the service of one deputy." One of the few experienced parliamentarians, Bundestag Vice-President Carl Schmid, was forced to remind his colleagues what was at stake: "It is not a question of Herr Loritz, rather, the question revolves around this parliament. It is a question whether this parliament is ready to take itself seriously." [2]

[2] *Stenographische Berichte,* I Wahlperiode, p. 335.

The Bundestag

Article 38

(1) The deputies of the German Bundestag shall be elected by the people in universal, free, equal, direct and secret elections. They shall be representatives of the whole people, not bound to orders and instructions and subject only to their conscience.

Article 39

(1) The Bundestag shall be elected for a term of four years. Its legislative term shall end four years after its first meeting or on its dissolution. . . .

Article 43

(1) The Bundestag and its committees may demand the presence of any member of the Federal Government.

(2) The members of the Bundesrat and of the Federal Government as well as the persons commissioned by them shall have access to all meetings of the Bundestag and its committees. They must be heard at any time.

The Bundestag: Organization

Like the United States Congress, but unlike the House of Commons, the Bundestag has as its presiding officer an active party leader of the majority party. The office of Bundestag president is endowed with a good deal of formal dignity—the members rise when he enters the chamber—and its incumbents have in the main been men respected by their colleagues both for their outstanding intellectual capacities and their strong willpower. Both Hermann Ehlers, who died in 1954, and his successor, Eugen Gerstenmaier, were considered contenders for the leadership of the CDU after Adenauer's retirement. In the interim they were kept busy presiding over frequently unruly Bundestag sessions, supervising the modest legislative bureaucracy, and maintaining reasonably cordial relations between the legislature and the executive.

The internal machinery of the chamber is run in a fairly decentralized manner on the basis of rules which the Bundestag has inherited from the Reichstag. Most important decisions regarding committee assignments, the scheduling of debates, etc., are made on the basis of broad agreement by the party leaders. The instrument through which they function is called, not very appropriately, the "Council of Elders," and includes the president, the three vice-presidents (representing the three major parties), and a number of delegates sent by each of the parties in proportion to their Bundestag strength. One reason why this organ has worked relatively smoothly, despite the fact that the CDU has a majority with which to override the other parties, probably consists in the fact that the legislative leaders have been fairly united in wishing to avoid wrangling that would further reduce the prestige of the Bundestag vis-à-vis the executive.

The most important components of the Bundestag are undoubtedly the *Fraktionen,* the parliamentary parties with at least fifteen members. The tradition of party unity and discipline is strongly embedded in German tradition, and it is customary for the individual deputy to be very active within the party and its discussion groups. On most important matters party caucuses meet first to decide what the party position should be, and then appoint spokesmen to present their position in the plenary session. Work in the committees is less under direct party supervision, but most committee members, who owe their position to the fact that they were selected by their Fraktion, frequently carry out instructions from the party. The parties also tend to vote uniformly on roll-calls, though there is some difference between the behavior of the different party groups. The Socialists have inherited a strong informal tradition of party discipline, and their deputies very seldom fail to vote in accordance with the party position as determined by the party majority. The Christian Democrats, representing a far wider variety of interests within a much looser party framework, have always declared that they do not impose party discipline. But even their rules provide that a deputy who believes he cannot follow the party position must announce this fact beforehand, and on matters on which the leadership places high priority, such as most foreign policy issues, the Christian Democrats have in fact voted almost as much as a unit as the Socialists.

In Germany, as in Britain, there has been considerable criticism of the position to which such party dominance relegates the deputy:

Do not individual responsibility and conscience . . . wilt under the majority decisions of the parliament and the parties? Does not the real position of the deputy stand in crass contrast to the Constitution, according to which he is bound neither by instructions nor directives, but by his own conscience? Would it not suffice—so often one hears the sarcastic refrain—if the parties were represented by only one deputy apiece, empowered to cast a vote corresponding to the strength of the party? Would not this fully satisfy the functions of parliament? [3]

[3] Klemens Kremer, *Der Abgeordnete* (Munich, 1953), p. 10.

Essentially, the argument is between those who adhere to the nineteenth-century concept of the deputy as someone elected to help make national decisions on the sole basis of his personal judgment and those who believe that in an age of mass electorates democracy can only function rationally through cohesive parties that rely on party discipline to carry out election programs. In Germany, the "individual responsibility" argument has frequently been used by groups who wanted to impede the acceptance of parties as instruments of increasing democratization, and for a long time these succeeded in preventing parties from being officially recognized. Thus, the fact that as late as 1912 the Reichstag Rules of Procedure did not recognize the existence of parliamentary parties (it referred only to "sections") was a great impediment in a country as legalistic as Germany. During the Weimar period, parties were mentioned in the Reichstag Rules but not in the Constitution. Under the Basic Law, parties have finally been accorded the necessary constitutional legitimation (Art. 21), and so have the Fraktionen.

Despite the weight of the Fraktion leadership, there is considerably less uniformity of voting than there is in the House of Commons, where the parties almost always vote as a unit except in the rare instances when "the whips are off." One of the results of the lack of an organic tie between cabinet and majority party has been the fact that, except when pressure from the Chancellor is really strong, the majority party does not feel itself automatically bound by the wishes of the cabinet. Thus on many domestic matters the CDU Fraktion has frequently been at odds with the official government position, attacked its own ministers, and even introduced bills in direct competition with those introduced by the cabinet. Since in practice there is no such thing as a vote of confidence, the government's stability is not impaired if it fails to have its way, and the matter is usually argued out until a compromise is reached which is satisfactory to a Bundestag majority. On occasion it even happens that a cabinet bill is passed through the Bundestag with the support of the official opposition parties, and against the votes of a majority of the government party. This would be very puzzling to someone accustomed only to "pure" parliamentarism of the British type, but it is, of course, quite similar to what frequently happens under the American system of separation of powers. Nevertheless, the most common occurrence in the plenary sessions is still a fairly cohesive confrontation by the major parties.

THE COMMITTEES. Most of the Bundestag's real legislative

work is done in committees. Here, as in most other aspects of legislative procedure, the German example lies halfway between American and British practice. In Britain, the traditional cabinet dominance and the cabinet's fear that standing legislative committees would develop into dangerous competitors, both to the party leaders on questions of policy and to individual ministers as originators of legislation, caused the trend toward the development of specialized standing committees to be nipped in the bud. According to British practice, the parliamentarian is supposed to be a jack-of-all-trades and not an expert trying to compete with the civil servants, whom, as minister, he may one day have to direct on questions of broad policy, not detail. In the United States, under the separation of powers, no such inhibitions have prevented congressmen from attempting to become sufficiently expert to trip up the bureaucrats whenever possible. The committees have emerged as powerful centers, where interest groups frequently reject or rewrite bills submitted by the executive agencies. Germany combines the British deference toward executive initiative with something like the American tendency toward expertise. Thus the parties try to fill their committee places with experts, many of them ex-officials and interest group representatives who can compete with the civil servants in their own technical and legal language.

Comparative statistical evidence bears out the importance of committee and party meetings in the German legislative process. Thus in 1954 the British House of Commons, where committee and party meetings do not play a very large role, did the bulk of its work in 170 plenary sessions which totalled 1,408 hours. The same year the French National Assembly, which spent more time in committee meetings, met in plenary sessions 132 times for a total of 796 hours. The United States House of Representatives, which also did the bulk of its work in committee, held 123 plenary sessions that year for a total of 533 hours. The Bundestag, however, went furthest in concentrating work in committee and party meetings. Its plenary meetings, usually held on only two days a week when the Bundestag was in session, numbered only about fifty-five. However for every plenary session, the Bundestag that year held no less than twenty committee and nine party meetings.[4]

In the committees the parliamentarians are able to develop some sort of balance against the executive and to plan rational

[4] "Wie die Parlamente Tagen," *Das Parlament,* December 12, 1960, p. 11.

alternative solutions with which to structure the debate in the plenary session. However the executive's interest is always assured by the fact that ministers and their civil servants have a right to attend any committee sessions they like, while the ability of deputies to check deeply into facts and figures is hindered by the lack of a sizable committee staff or legislative reference service. Bundestag committee meetings are usually not public, so that they do not have the soothing "ritual" effect which their American equivalents have on competing publics. Often the chummy "togetherness" among parliamentary and civil servant experts hardly allows the outsider's common-sense point of view scope for expression, for the average Bundestag deputy will seldom dare to speak out against the profound judgment of his more expert party colleague.

There have been some areas where the executive has almost ignored Bundestag committees. This has been particularly true of foreign policy, where Adenauer has been very loath to discuss his "lonely decisions" with the large Foreign Affairs Committee. "Its participation in foreign policy does not extend to the point where the government need necessarily pay attention to comments or directions from the committee . . . Public opinion tends to over-estimate the committee's powers. It has no influence on personnel questions . . . and it would be quite in order for its members to hear of important diplomatic developments only through the newspapers." [5]

THE DEPUTY. The average German deputy is considerably more difficult to describe than his American equivalent. He might be a prominent businessman who was prevailed upon to go into politics when his local CDU was looking for candidates, or a man who had spent twenty years as a labor union secretary before being nominated by the SPD, or a teacher or journalist in either party, or a farmer sent by the farmers' organization into the CDU to look after their interests, or the executive secretary of a trade association, or an official who had entered the civil administration through political channels, or frequently a lawyer, doctor, or intellectual. The greater variety of types is due to the fact that in a traditionally class- and group-conscious country most interest groups want to be represented by "some of their own," and the parties take care to include candidates with all kinds of background and expertise. The CDU, for instance, will

[5] Werner Krauss, "Parlamentarische Kontrolle der Aussenpolitik," *Aussenpolitik*, VI (August, 1955), 526.

try to make sure that its Fraktion includes roughly as many workers and employees as businessmen and managers, while the SPD will try to include some farmers and artisans to balance its plentiful supply of trade unionists and intellectuals.

Some deputies are more active than others, but most will make ample use of their free railroad passes, commuting between their constituencies and Bonn. Heinrich Ritzel, an SPD deputy from a rural small-town constituency in Hessen, was perhaps one of the more active, judging from his report to his constituents for the year 1952. He told of having spoken thirty-three times in the course of the sixty plenary sessions which he attended and of having been present at 109 committee meetings and at thirty-six Fraktion meetings. In addition, he had made fifty-six political speeches outside of the Bundestag, attended eight meetings of the county council of which he was chairman, and had held office hours in his constituency on sixty-eight separate days.[6] Ritzel, who had served many years in local administration and had been briefly a member of the Reichstag, is clearly an old-line parliamentarian, probably satisfied with the position he achieved as chairman of the Committee on Rules, Credentials, and Immunity. Younger men who have entered politics not with the hope of making a parliamentary career but with using it as a steppingstone to positions of government responsibility have been somewhat more frustrated. Socialist deputies, of course, have served over a decade without hope of achieving government office, but even CDU members have not found advancement easy. The fact that the Germans do not have parliamentary assistant ministers, or parliamentary secretaries as they are called in England, severely limits the number of positions available. Thus, although Adenauer's cabinets have been quite large, only a relatively few CDU deputies have had a chance to become ministers. The rest have had difficulty enough becoming known to the leaders out of the mass of new faces which arrive in Bonn after each new Bundestag election.

When they get together informally in the Bundestag restaurant, most deputies tend to sit with their party colleagues, and personal friendships seldom cross party lines. But then each can find all kinds in his own Fraktion. The less intellectual CDU deputy with only a grade-school education would have found seventy-four others like him in the Second Bundestag. They would have been outnumbered by 110 university graduates, two-

[6] Heinrich Ritzel, *Einer von 402* (Frankfurt, 1953), pp. 59 ff.

fifths of whom had studied law, one-fifth economics, another fifth humanities, with a scattering of theologians, doctors and engineers. In the SPD, the relationships would have been reversed, with a majority of the deputies having concluded their formal education with grade school, while only about a fifth were university graduates. On the whole, the range of social backgrounds of Bundestag members is remarkably similar to that of the Weimar period Reichstag, another sign of the German tendency to return to earlier patterns, changes in labels notwithstanding.[7]

Only some German Bundestag deputies devote themselves as undividedly to their jobs as most American congressmen are obliged to. This vital group however includes the key party chairmen and secretaries, and the leading committee chairmen. Many other deputies also hold political or administrative positions—as mayors, chairmen of county councils, or board members of public authorities—which cause them to spend a good deal of time away from Bonn. This accumulation of offices is a peculiar German problem, arising in part because of traditions and also because those who achieved party status soon after the war had "inside" positions from which to ward off competitors for the best nominations. Finally, there are a fairly considerable number of deputies who manage to carry on private business and professional careers on a part-time basis.

As regards financial remuneration, most deputies are fairly well off due to increasingly wide acceptance of the idea that public service must be adequately paid for. This did not always exist. Bismarck ensured relatively brief Reichstag sessions by allowing the deputies no compensation of any sort. In 1906 a limited expense allowance was introduced, but the government still sought to provide an incentive for short sessions by providing that one-third of the annual sum be paid out only after the Reichstag had adjourned. A different kind of emphasis was inherent in the post-1949 practice of paying deputies according to the number of legislative and committee sessions they attended. This led to abuses, and in 1958 new rules were adopted under which deputies received monthly salaries of about 275 dollars, with an additional 125 dollars for living expenses, but minus 12 dollars for each unexcused absence.[8] Efforts to introduce a pension plan to provide for members of long service who have no other source

[7] Otto Kirchheimer, "The Composition of the German Bundestag," *WPQ*, III (1950), p. 599.

[8] Theodor Eschenburg, *Der Sold des Politikers* (Stuttgart, 1959).

Legislative Process

Article 76

(1) Bills shall be introduced in the Bundestag by the Federal Government, by members of the Bundestag or by the Bundesrat.

(2) Federal Government bills shall first be submitted to the Bundesrat. The Bundesrat is entitled to state its position on these bills within three weeks. . . .

Article 77

(1) Federal laws shall be passed by the Bundestag. After their adoption, they shall, without delay, be transmitted to the Bundesrat. . . .

(4) [In regard to bills where the Bundesrat has only a suspensory veto] Vetoes adopted by the majority of the votes of the Bundesrat . . . may be rejected by a decision of the majority of the Bundestag. Should the Bundesrat have adopted the veto by a majority of at least two-thirds . . . the rejection of the Bundestag shall require a majority of two-thirds. . . .

Article 81

(1) . . . the Federal President may, on the request of the Federal Government with the consent of the Bundesrat, declare a state of legislative emergency with respect to a bill, if the Bundestag rejects the bill although the Federal Government has declared it to be urgent. . . .

(2) If the Bundestag, after the state of legislative emergency has been declared, again rejects the bill or passes it in a version declared by the Federal Government to be unacceptable, the bill shall be deemed to have been passed insofar as the Bundesrat consents to it. . . .

---

of income were shattered in 1960 by the opposition of the CDU.

LEGISLATIVE AND CONTROL FUNCTIONS. It is well known that governmental processes do not dovetail with governmental institutions; that legislation is by no means the prerogative of the "legislative" branch or even necessarily the most important function. Like other parliamentary constitutions, the Basic Law allows the executive to compete with both houses of the legislature in introducing bills, and in fact most legislation originates with the ministries. The German legislator has more of an opportunity to toss bills into the hopper with some hope that they will become law than his British equivalent, who has to draw lots for such a chance, but even so he finds it hard to compete with the civil service bill drafters, who have all the authority and resources of the ministries at their disposal. Thus of the 483 laws passed in the four years of the Second Bundestag (1953 to 1957), seven originated in the Bundesrat, 126 were introduced by Bundestag members, while 350, or almost three-quarters, were submitted by the cabinet. In fact, so much do Germans identify the legislative functions with executive dominance that reports that the cabinet has sent a bill to the legislature are frequently headlined in German newspapers as, "Cabinet Decides To Pass Traffic Law," thus causing the unsophisticated reader to take passage by Parliament as almost a matter of course.

This in fact would be true in only a few areas. In most, especially where important interest groups have managed to rouse their followers both in and outside the majority party, cabinet bills do not always have an easy passage, as a few examples from the 1960 legislative session show. At the beginning of the year, Finance Minister Etzel announced that the budget could stand no more than a 4 per cent pay increase for government employees. The civil service organizations denounced this as altogether insufficient, and the opposition parties immediately announced they would press for a 9 per cent increase. In the Interior Committee, most of whose members possess civil service background, a majority, including the CDU chairman, altered the cabinet bill in line with the 9 per cent figure. But some weeks later in the plenary session, the same CDU committee chairman, having in the meantime consulted his party leaders, introduced a motion on behalf of the CDU calling for a 7 per cent increase, and this was finally passed. Another cabinet member, Transport Minister Seebohm, engaged in a battle royal with the Traffic Committee over the question of fixing a forty-five foot limit for trailer-trucks. By the time a forty-seven foot limit was finally agreed upon, Seebohm had threatened his resignation several times, denounced one of the committee members for taking a weak position on the recovery of the Oder-Neisse territories, and engaged in prolonged feuding with the trucking interests. During the same period the Labor Minister was having a difficult time with his bill to reform the medical insurance system, which called forth violent opposition from both the trade unions and the medical associations, and split the CDU so badly that even the Chancellor's personal intervention failed to bring about an acceptable compromise.

It would seem evident from this that in Germany the legislature serves as a forum for interest groups much as it does in the United States. The difference, perhaps, is that although they do have to make significant concessions, the ministers usually end up with a bill that is reasonably coherent, whereas in the United States bills are often gutted beyond recognition.

The strong position of the executive is also brought out by the fact that while the Bundestag was passing 483 laws, the ministries issued no less than 926 executive ordinances on the basis of authority granted them in previous legislation. On the whole, the German Bundestag's legislative function might well be described as that of a balance-wheel between the executive on the one side, and the parties and interest groups on the other. Whether the parties lead the struggle directly depends on the degree to which the issue at hand appeals to their ideology or program, as well as the degree to which they maintain cohesion and party discipline.

With regard to a second important parliamentary function, that of developing techniques to control the executive, the Bundestag has had more difficulty. Since the Bundestag cannot effectively threaten to overthrow the government, it has been dependent on developing institutional situations that place the ministers on the defensive by forcing them to account for their actions. An especially useful technique, which the House of Commons has perfected to a high degree, is the question hour. In Germany this institution has been very underdeveloped until recently. Until 1960 the rules provided for only one question hour per month, and deputies had to send written notice of their questions, which could deal only with clarification of facts, as long as two weeks in advance. At most, it resulted in cut-and-dried exchanges like the following:

Schneider (German Party): Is the Government aware that in the Oxford Atlas published by the Royal Geographical Society, the Soviet zone is shown as an independent state, the Oder-Neisse Line as a permanent boundary and the territory to the east as permanently Polish? Is the government prepared to approach the British government with a view to having this situation changed?

von Brentano (Foreign Minister): The German embassy has attempted, both through the Foreign Office and through direct contact with British map-makers, to bring about changes in British maps, but has not as yet succeeded. The Foreign Office declares that it cannot influence private map-makers, and the publishers say that they are guided by actually existing, and not by legal relationships . . . The director of the Geographical Service will be going to London this week in order to make practical proposals in an attempt to change the attitude of the British map-publishers. . . .[9]

[9] *Stenographische Berichte*, II Wahlperiode, p. 7782. The German arguments relating to the *de jure* status of the Oder-Neisse territories seem, however, not to have dissuaded the British map-makers from relating their atlases to *de facto* conditions. In December, 1960, the Foreign Minister again had to

Between the time he received word of the question and the day when he had to answer it, the minister had plenty of time to get action underway. Since 1960, however, the Bundestag has attempted to liven up question hours by introducing them at the beginning of each meeting, by allowing deputies to submit questions as late as the day before answers are expected, and by allowing supplementary questions to be asked from the floor.

Another effective way for Parliament to seek to force ministers to account for their policies is the full-scale debate. Bundestag procedure allows these to occur during discussions of the budgets of relevant ministries and through interpellations which may be introduced by thirty members. The latter method is the one most frequently employed. Usually the interpellation will be introduced by the party leaders—those of the majority as well as of the opposition—and the cabinet will agree to set a date for the debate, which frequently becomes quite heated. However Bundestag deputies are more adept at such parliamentary tactics as loud exclamations of dissent and stamping, than they are at the subtle maneuvering necessary to get a minister into a corner where he will have to admit unpleasant facts. Also the fact that they are obliged to express views previously agreed upon in some detail in the party meetings prevents debates from having a spontaneous character. An English observer, used to the atmosphere of the House of Commons, has written that "debating, in the true sense of the word, just does not occur in the Bundestag. The lack of color and life which this implies is enhanced by the almost invariable choice of the same speakers to represent the respective parties . . . The dullness of debates mirrors itself in the behavior of the members. Some read newspapers . . . others sign their names on dozens of documents which may relate to parliamentary business, but are more likely to be connected with family affairs." [10]

But the greatest weakness of the Bundestag has been its failure to educate the German public in democratic ground rules, especially its inability to project the real function of the parliamentary opposition. Unlike Britain, where the Leader of Her Majesty's Loyal Opposition possesses an official title and salary,

---

answer complaints, this time concerning a *London Times* atlas, about to come out in a German edition, which listed the Polish names of prewar East German cities.

[10] Terence Prittie, "The German Federal Parliament," *Parliamentary Affairs*, X (Spring, 1955), 235.

the leader of the major opposition party in the Bundestag is just another deputy. Unfortunately, the successive Socialist leaders have been unable to overcome this obstacle in order to project to the country at large the crucial need for institutionalized organs of criticism within a democratic system. The bitterness with which Kurt Schumacher attacked the government during the early years helped create barriers to the mutual tolerance necessary for an effective government-opposition relationship. On foreign policy particularly, the party leaders espoused such diametrically opposed views, that their followers for years talked past, not at, each other. Adenauer made tactical use of the situation by deriding the Socialists as sterile negativists who had no positive program. As Adenauer grew increasingly popular, the public was encouraged to see the Socialists as petty politicians who impeded the Chancellor's far-sighted policies and begrudged him personal recognition out of vindictiveness. As their position was weakened, Adenauer made ruthless use of his position of strength by excluding them from all significant consultations on foreign policy, thus engendering personal resentments and reducing still further the hope of creating a fruitful government-opposition relationship.

In an attempt to appear positive and responsible, the Socialists took to issuing statistics to prove that they had voted affirmatively almost as many times as the CDU. They worked out immensely complex foreign policy proposals in an effort to prove that they too were capable of constructive work. But this allowed Adenauer to turn the tables and subject the Socialists' plans to devastating criticism, which carried the overwhelming weight of his prestige as a statesman. Thus, as one of its leaders has written, the opposition found itself in an increasingly impossible situation, for it "was considered the more un-German the more vigorously it attacked, while its attempts to soften its criticisms were interpreted as signs of weakness and inability to provide leadership." [11]

The Bundesrat

The second chamber in Parliament is unique, in that it is the only chamber in the world which is in effect a continuous congress of state (Land) ministers who vote in accordance with the instructions of their governments. This throwback to an

[11] Adolf Arndt, "Die Entmachtung des Bundestags," *Neue Gesellschaft,* VI (November–December, 1959), 436.

The Bundesrat

Article 50

The *Laender* shall participate through the Bundesrat in the legislation and the administration of the Federation.

Article 51

(1) The Bundesrat shall consist of members of the Governments of the *Laender* which shall appoint and recall them. Other members of such Governments may act as substitutes.

(2) Each *Land* shall have at least three votes; *Laender* with more than two million inhabitants shall have four, *Laender* with more than six million inhabitants shall have five votes.

(3) Each *Land* may delegate as many members as it has votes. The votes of each *Land* may be cast only as a block vote and only by members present or their substitutes.

---

organizational form similar to that of the princes' chamber of Imperial Germany resulted from efforts to build up the Laender so as to prevent a return to the German tendency toward ultimate centralization of power in the national government. As presently constituted, the Bundesrat consists of forty-one members of Land cabinets, five each from the four Laender with populations of more than six million (Northrhine-Westphalia, Bavaria, Lower Saxony, Baden-Wuerttemberg) four each from the three Laender with between two and six million inhabitants, (Rhineland-Palatinate, Schleswig-Holstein, Hessen), and three each from the three small Laender with less than two million (the Saar, Hamburg, Bremen). In line with the legalist, single-will doctrine that it is unreasonable that a state should at one and the same time have two contradictory wills, the Land votes must be cast as a unit, which means that in cases where Land governments are based on coalitions (as most are), they are usually cast in line with the policy of the strongest Land party.

The Basic Law assigns the Bundesrat much greater legislative power than its Weimar predecessor possessed. Its approval is required for all constitutional amendments, and for all federal legislation affecting the administrative, taxation, and territorial interests of the Laender, rather a broad category. With regard to all other kinds of legislation it can enter a suspensive veto, which however can be overridden by an equivalent majority of the Bundestag. In addition to this impressive (by continental European standards) potential legislative authority, the Bundesrat approves federal government ordinances, shares in the election of judges to the Constitutional Court, and possesses considerable reserve powers in the case of serious conflict either between the executive and the Bundestag or the federal and Land governments.

The very nature of its make-up insures that the overwhelming share of Bundesrat work is done in committees. Almost all Bundesrat members are Land ministers for whom the Bundesrat role is a secondary one to which they attend in the course of brief visits to Bonn once or twice a month. By the time they arrive proposals have already been worked out in committees, and in 99 per cent of all cases where only one committee report is presented, this is adopted by the plenary session.[12] Obviously, the question of *who* writes the committee reports is more crucial here than in perhaps any other legislative chamber. The answer is that although Bundesrat members occasionally participate in committee sessions, the bulk of committee work is done by their alternates, who are not politicians but permanent Land civil servants. In view of the fact that the upper chamber has at most three weeks to consider legislation submitted by the government (and frequently much less), the Land ministers have extremely limited opportunity to form judgments other than those based on the recommendations of their civil service advisers. Indeed, a German law professor has written that, "In the committees . . . there is in process of growth a tight world of its own . . . in which the permanent civil service and changing delegates from the Land ministries are in their own metier, the world of a bureaucracy with its own laws." [13]

This curious intertwining of decision-making by politicians and administrators is in part explained by the development of German federalism. Unlike the American model, where both the national government and the states maintain not only their own areas of legislation but also independent and frequently overlapping administrative machinery, German federalism is characterized by the fact that the vast bulk of legislation issues from the federal government and is administered by the Land bureaucracies. State diets retain the power to legislate within their areas of jurisdiction, but the most important Land laws are issued in conformity with federal framework laws. By the same token, the federal government does not attempt to administer all its own

---

[12] Karlheinz Neunreither, "Politics and Bureaucracy in the West German Bundesrat," *APSR*, LIII (September, 1959), 716.

[13] Werner Weber, *Spannungen und Kraefte im westdeutschen Verfassungssystem* (Stuttgart, 1951), p. 91.

programs but delegates this duty to the Land administrations, whose work the small federal ministries only supervise. Seen within this traditional German context, the Bundesrat provides an ideal meeting-place where federal and Land officials can work out differences regarding federal legislation—as well as federal ordinances based on legislation—affecting their respective spheres of responsibility. Though it seems complex, this arrangement provides for a rational division of labor, while also introducing checks to unlimited power; the Bundesrat may be viewed as "providing a stage for the antagonism between the *Land* and the Federal bureaucracies, while at the same time forcing them to some kind of advantageous cooperation." [14]

But what has happened to the role of the Bundesrat as a political check on the powerful party leaders who control the Bundestag? Here painful political experience has shown that both the Land minister-presidents and the Bundesrat do not have the political strength to utilize fully their constitutional position in showdown fights with the national party leaders and the Bundestag. Because of the interplay of party politics, with both the CDU and SPD seeking to influence Land elections primarily to give themselves greater influence in Federal decision-making through the Bundesrat, the Land cabinets have at times been reduced almost to the status of the pawns of federal politics. In an effort to maintain at least some degree of independence, the Land ministers have on the whole discretely reduced their involvement in federal decision-making relating to the publicized, controversial big issues. The Bundesrat plenary sessions reflect this; their "atmosphere is sober, often dull, and not politically inspiring." [15]

In effect, the Bundesrat has sought to reinforce its delicate position by utilizing its constitutional powers only halfway and its legislative prerogatives largely under camouflage. It has sought to avoid being caught between the powerful party machines by, for instance, placing the elections of its presiding officer "above politics," rotating this honor according to a fixed scheme. On the whole, it adopted the coloration of the nonpartisan bureaucrats who are officially only its assistants. "A kind of exaltation of the administrative functions of the Bundesrat has taken place, while its political functions are more or less disparaged." [16] In line with bureaucratic aversion to public controversy, it has

[14] Neunreither, *op. cit.,* p. 726.
[15] *Ibid.,* p. 717.
[16] *Ibid.,* p. 728.

shunned frank conflict with the Bundestag (only one or two, usually minor, laws a year fail because of its negative vote) and instead seeks to get its way in the secret councils of the inter-chamber Conference Committee. The Bundesrat tends to call the Conference Committee into effect whenever it does not want to assent to a law, but even there the Land ministers argue less on the merits of the issue than on "grounds of administrative infeasibility." [17] Thus the Bundesrat "obscures its political inten-tions by cloaking them in recommendations of a technical char-acter so that they will be more readily endorsed by the relatively inexpert lower house. Staff members of Bundesrat Committees claim that this procedure is highly successful." [18] As best they can, the Land representatives try to protect the interests of the Land government against the increasing encroachment of the federal government, since they do not want to be relegated exclusively to the position of carrying out federal laws. At times the Laender even engage in some adroit horse-trading which angers the national party leaders. But this kind of Bundesrat action makes the headlines only very occasionally. On the whole, its policy of "obscuring political issues in administrative forms,"[19] has, in effect, turned it into a sort of federal-Land administrative council which is remote from the public (polls have shown that only one out of nine Germans know what the Bundesrat is) and insulated from the major political currents of the day.

Bibliography

Arndt, Adolf, "Die Entmachtung des Bundestags," *Neue Gesellschaft*, VI November–December, 1959), 431–38.

Dorr, Harold M., and Bretton, Henry L., "Legislation," in E. H. Litchfield, ed., *Governing Postwar Germany* (Ithaca, 1953).

Eschenburg, Theodor, *Der Sold des Politikers* (Stuttgart, 1959).

Glum, Friedrich, *Das Parlamentarische Regierungssystem in Deutschland, England, und Frankreich* (Munich, 1950).

Kirchheimer, Otto, "The Composition of the German Bundestag," *WPQ*, III (1950), 590–601.

———, "The Waning of Opposition in Parliamentary Regimes," *Social Research*, XXIV (1957), 127–56.

Kogon, Eugen, "Formen und Funktionen der Opposition," *Zeitschrift fuer Politik*, I (December, 1954), pp. 365–72.

Kremer, Klemens, *Der Abgeordnete* (Munich, 1953).

Loewenberg, Gerhard, "Parliamentarism in Western Germany: The Func-tioning of the Bundestag," *APSR*, LV (1961), 87–102.

[17] *Ibid.*, p. 722.
[18] *Ibid.*, p. 724.
[19] *Ibid.*, p. 728.

Markmann, Heinz, *Abstimmungsverhalten der Parteifraktionen in deutschen Parlamenten* (Meisenheim, 1955).

Neunreither, Karlheinz, "Politics and Bureaucracy in the West German Bundesrat," *APSR*, LIII (September, 1959), 713–31.

———, *Der Bundesrat* (Heidelberg, 1959).

Prittie, Terence, "The German Federal Parliament," *Parliamentary Affairs*, X (Spring, 1955), 235–39.

Weber, Werner, *Spannungen und Kraefte im westdeutschen Verfassungssystem* (Stuttgart, 1951).

6 - The Administrative Structure

German Officialdom

The shaping influence which any branch of government will have on political traditions will depend not only on its position of power vis-à-vis the other branches of government, but also on the degree to which it can influence patterns of behavior in everyday life. The average American is of course aware of the existence of bureaucrats in Washington and the state capitols, but, except during times of war and depression, his contacts with officialdom are apt to be limited. Many of the government employees whom he does encounter, such as the school principal, the county clerk, or the agricultural field agent, may themselves be only vaguely aware of their place in an official hierarchy outside of their local office. Whether for good or bad, this is a reflection of the fact that as a result of competitive, individualist values and great decentralization, American public servants have never gone very far toward creating an *esprit de corps* of their own. In Germany this situation has traditionally been very different. There, the administrative branch is the oldest of existing political institutions, and for a long time in Prussia its members even considered their experience and impartiality a sufficient substitute for a formal constitution.

It has been well remarked that "in dealing with the 'civil service' in Germany one is dealing with a concept which is vastly wider than that used by most other countries." [1] Under German law the employees of all public law institutions, communities,

---

[1] John Chapman, *The Profession of Government* (London, 1959), p. 67.

counties, and public facilities are all part of an integrated body
of public officials, a body that includes not only administrators
and government clerks, but also teachers, railroad conductors,
and the men who read the gasometers. All vie for the status
and security of the *Beamte,* the professional civil servant with
tenure. Also, the inhabitants of most German provincial towns
will more frequently be in contact with officials of the central
government bureaus, which, in contrast to American practice,
tend to be dispersed all over the country. Moreover, civil service
ranks and titles have for generations dominated German middle-
class society to such an extent that German businessmen used
to compete with each other in philanthropy and public spirited-
ness in the hope of being granted the honorary title of "Commercial Counsellor"—a title that would lift them onto a social
par with the higher officials. And civil service salaries remain
to this day an almost universal measuring rod, with everyone
from the Chancellor down receiving compensation pegged to
the pay of a specified Beamte rank.

The status of its officials, its interpenetration with society,
and its reputation of incorruptibility long allowed the German
administration to claim the position of a preferred instrument
for making political decisions. Many Germans, no matter how
opposed they might be on principle to the hierarchical traditions
of the administration, still cannot help feeling a greater confidence in its ability to make the correct, impartial decision than
in the ability of remote, party influenced parliamentarians. Thus,
whereas in the United States bureaucrats tend to seem more
remote than local politicians, in Germany the reverse is true.
German citizens are in close contact with the administrative
apparatus, not only because of the large number of services that
are traditionally state run (railroads, utilities, health services,
etc.), but also because most aspects of economic and social life
tend to be supervised by officials. This was particularly true of
the immediate postwar period, when official regulations covered
everything from the allocation of steel to the number of square
feet of living space allowed per family. The period of hardship
was not ideal for the Allied attempt to convert the administration into a bulwark of local democracy. The element of localized
decision-making which the Americans in particular tried to
develop was resisted by officials who believed that only a system
based on hierarchical coordination could provide rational and
equitable allocation of resources.

Federal and Land Functions

As a result, particularly after the creation of the Federal Republic, the German administrative system tended to reshape itself in order to conform to earlier patterns. The creation by the Allies of strong Laender bureaucracies did not deter this trend; even under the Empire effective, centralized control had been achieved without greatly expanding the size of the national administrative apparatus. Until the Nazi period, the bulk of administrative functions had remained with the Laender, and indeed a good part of the Land administration's tasks consisted of executing Reich laws. Both the national government and the Laender preferred a system under which the Reich exercised the bulk of legislative power, while the Laender retained control over administration. This allowed the greatest degree of uniformity in basic policy with a considerable amount of latitude in local application. The national administration consisted in part of ministries for the few areas in which the Reich had exclusive jurisdiction, but mainly of authorities who acted as top level planning and supervisory agencies in fields where actual administration was carried out by the Laender. Of course the national government set up norms to which the Land administrations had to conform concerning both internal structure and organization, and thus a maximum of uniformity was achieved.

Administration in the Federal Republic is set up in much the same way. The staff of most federal ministries is relatively small; only the Foreign Ministry, the Finance Ministry (in part), the post office, and the federal railroads possess their own administrative substructure. For the rest, administration of federal programs is carried out by the Laender either as a matter of traditional prerogative, or as a service rendered at the special request of the federal government. There are thus four different ways in which administration is carried out: (1) execution of federal laws by federal administration, for example, the railroads and the post office; (2) execution of Land laws by Land administration, for example, the police and education authorities; (3) execution of federal laws by Land administrations as a matter of right, for example, labor and social welfare offices; (4) execution of federal laws by Land administrations at the request of the federal government, for example, the agencies maintaining the Autobahnen and waterways. The over-all effect of this kind of arrangement is that though an overwhelming share of public expenditure is spent on programs based directly or indirectly on federal legislation, the greatest proportion of civil servants work for the Laender administrations. Thus, if one excludes the railroads and the post office, only about 10 per cent of public officials work for the federal government, about a third are in the employ of local government, and well over one half belong to the Land administrations.

How do the Germans avoid the kind of problems encountered by the United States in such areas as Southern state enforcement of federal voting guarantees or civil rights laws? The fact is that the federal administration has extensive control over Land administration of federal laws. Where the Laender administer federal laws, the federal government may issue binding administrative regulations, may demand the rectification of inadequacies, and may send agents to investigate cases. As a last resort, it may, with the approval of the Bundesrat, force the Laender to comply; the Basic Law provides that the federal government or its commissioner shall have the right to give orders to all Laender and their authorities.

These relationships give Germany a much more uniform kind of administrative system than someone acquainted with the American type of federalism might expect. The tendency toward uniformity leads the Laender officials to accept federal administrative regulations as a framework even when there is no obligation, that is, in relation to the administration of their own Land laws. Such regulations must have the approval of the Bundesrat, which however seldom opposes them. On the contrary, all the Land governments conceive it in their own interest to accept such federal regulations, so as to achieve the greatest amount of administrative homogeneity and to avoid haphazard differences between the Laender. After considering this development, some Germans have come to the conclusion that administrative rationalization has "led the *Laender* to derive their powers from the Federal Government and its laws, just as much as the counties and the cities derive theirs from the *Land* governments and their laws. They are as much subject to Federal supervision as the cities and the counties are to Land supervision." [2]

Finance and Taxes

Anyone surprised to find that the Basic Law includes a discussion of the beer tax should consider that in Germany the

[2] Heinz Kreutzer, "Bund und Laender in der Bundesrepublik Deutschland," in O. K. Flechtheim, ed., *Bund und Laender* (Berlin, 1959), p. 20.

Administration

Article 35

All Federal and *Land* authorities shall render each other mutual legal and official assistance.

Article 83

The *Laender* shall execute the Federal laws as matters of their own concern insofar as this Basic Law does not otherwise provide or permit.

Article 84

(1) If the *Laender* execute the Federal laws as their own concern they shall regulate the establishment of the authorities and the administrative procedure insofar as Federal laws consented to by the Bundesrat do not otherwise determine.

(2) The Federal Government may, with the approval of the Bundesrat, issue general administrative rules.

(3) The Federal Government shall exercise supervision to ensure that the *Laender* execute the Federal laws in accordance with applicable law. For this purpose the Federal Government may send commissioners to the highest *Land* authorities and, with their consent or, if this consent is refused, with the consent of the Bundesrat, also to the subordinate authorities.

Article 87

(1) The foreign service, the Federal finance administration, the Federal railways, the Federal postal services, the administration of Federal waterways and shipping . . . the administration of the Federal defense forces shall be conducted by a direct Federal administration with its own administrative substructure.

Article 106

(1) The yield of fiscal monopolies and receipts from the following taxes shall accrue to the Federation:

1. customs duties,
2. such excise taxes as do not accrue to the *Laender* in accordance with paragraph (2),
3. turnover tax. . . .

(2) Receipts from the following taxes shall accrue to the *Laender:*

1. property tax,
2. inheritance tax,
3. motor-vehicle tax . . .
4. taxes with localized application.

(3) Receipts from income tax and corporation tax shall accrue . . . to the Federation and the *Laender* in a ratio of 35 per cent to 65 per cent.

(4) . . . The requirements of the Federation and the *Laender* in respect of budget coverage shall be coordinated in such a way that a fair equalization is achieved, any overburdening of taxpayers precluded, and uniformity of living standards in the Federal territory ensured.

national government's share of taxes had not only increased steadily at the expense of the Laender and communities (from 40.3 per cent in 1913, to 67.6 per cent in 1928, to 78.5 per cent in 1937), but had reached a climax in the Nazi wartime experience, when no less than 95 per cent of taxes were collected by the national government. The authors of the Basic Law (and the Allies) were determined to halt this trend and not only took great pains to specifically allocate tax sources, but also sought to prevent overlapping revenue claims and to spell out responsibility for tax administration. The result is a "finance constitution," which is so well integrated that a German expert labeled this section of the Basic Law "as the specifically Prussian contribution to a constitutional liberal-democratic state, which otherwise bears more the hallmarks of Rhenish-Bavarian influences. It is surely no accident that the intellectual father of the finance constitution is a former Prussian finance minister." [3]

As a result, the Basic Law not only allocates exclusive tax powers, but also provides for the sharing of taxes utilized concurrently by both federal government and Laender. Thus the sources of the federal government's revenues include custom receipts (DH 2.6 billion), excise taxes like tobacco (DM 3.12 billion) and coffee (DM .5 billion), but most importantly a 4 per cent turnover tax on most business transactions (DM 13.16 billion) and corporation and income taxes (DM 6.1 billion). Federal and Land corporation and income taxes are administered uniformly with proceeds being divided in the ratio of thirty-five to sixty-five between the federal and Land governments. They provide the major source of Land revenue (DM 11.3 billion) and are supplemented with sources like the inheritance and beer taxes. Local government is dependent on the Laender for many services, such as education and police, but derives its own taxes from sources that include the real estate tax (DM 1.53 billion) and local business taxes (DM 5.55 billion).[4] Of total tax receipts, the federal government initially *collects* about 60 per cent, the Laender about 25 per cent, and the communities about 15 per cent. In the renegotiation of how the receipts shall be allocated among the various governments, the federal government has a potentially strong position.

[3] Karl M. Hettlage, "Die Finanzverfassung im Rahmen der Staatsverfassung," *Veroeffentlichungen der Vereinigung der deutschen Staatsrechtlehrer,* XIV (1956), 13.

[4] Amounts collected in 1958.

Most Germans were appalled at the suggestion that they follow the American practice of allowing the various governmental levels to administer concurrent tax powers independently. Hence, as hitherto, the federal and Land finance administrations are closely integrated for purposes of collecting income and corporation taxes. The chief Land finance officials who administer the collection of these taxes are chosen jointly by the federal and Land Finance ministries, while their salaries and the costs of maintaining the collection machinery are also shared. As the State Secretary of the Finance Ministry has put it:

Today we have one income tax, with two partial claimants, with a split administration active as a Land administration for the Land part, and as a Federal agent for the Federal part of the tax. This is curious enough. But if we had adopted the other method, we would have had two distinct income taxes collected by two claimants, as in the United States where 35 of the 48 states collect their own income taxes parallel to the Federal one. As to the retarded and economically dubious nature of such a double and unequal taxation of income I need not comment here . . ." [5]

Even with uniform tax rates, the richer and more industrialized Laender command much higher per capita revenue receipts than do the poorer ones. To the Germans, the limited way in which United States federal subsidies try to bridge the great gap between state tax resources in, say, New York and Mississippi, seems quite inadequate. Thus one of the major roles of the German federal government is to attempt to equalize the tax resources in the various areas. This is accomplished directly through the federal budget, insofar as it provides for welfare payments and subsidies to refugees, expellees, and war victims, who are cared for by the Land administrations. But in addition to this "vertical" equalization, the West Germans also have a "horizontal" equalization program, under which the richer Laender must contribute a certain proportion of their tax receipts for redistribution to the poorer ones. The table on page 131 shows how this worked out in 1955.

The result of this program, supplemented by others, is to provide throughout the Federal Republic something very close to uniformity in the matter of public services and administration, even on the Land and communal level.

[5] Hettlage, *op. cit.*, p. 24.

| | | Per capita Land tax income as per cent of federal average | |
Land	Subvention and/or contribution	Before horizontal equalization	After horizontal equalization
Northrhine-Westphalia	−DM 259.9 Mill	117.2	110.0
Baden-Wuerttemberg	− 105.5	110.8	104.8
Hessen	− .8	97.2	97.1
Bavaria	+ 82.0	83.5	87.1
Lower Saxony	+ 126.5	77.0	84.9
Rhineland-Palatinate	+ 71.6	74.7	83.6
Schleswig-Holstein	+ 174.0	62.3	93.7
Hamburg	− 81.3	171.5	152.7
Bremen	− 6.6	141.3	137.1
TOTAL	+ − 454.1 Mill		

The Civil Service

As mentioned previously, the core unit of the German civil service is the Beamte, a permanent professional civil servant who has achieved his position only after passing through rigorous training periods and examinations. Not all public servants are Beamten. Those who are simply public employees (*Angestellten*) may be ineligible for Beamten status because of the lowly function of their jobs, the temporary nature of their employment, or because they lack some of the specific qualifications which allow Beamten to claim lifetime tenure and pensions. Such pensions range from a minimum of 35 per cent of regular pay after ten years' service to 75 per cent of regular pay after thirty-five years' service. Within the public service as a whole there are four broad grades—the regular, middle, superior and higher services. For the middle and superior grades, which include everybody from secretaries, through inspectors, to supervisory officials, requirements include a training period of from one to three years, with subsequent examination. For the higher service, requirements include the completion of university studies (usually in law) passing of the *Staatsexamen,* and a three-year training period climaxed by the passing of a second broad state examination.

In return for security and high social status, the Beamte has traditionally been bound by a code of behavior whose premise is that, unlike other salary earners, he must as the representative of the state at all times exhibit exemplary behavior and self-sacrifice. Thus it was long widely accepted that those who entered into the Beamten status voluntarily limited their civil rights. The Beamte must be ready to take over nonpaid side work, change his place of residence, or work up to twelve hours above the regular weekly norm, which at forty-eight hours weekly is considerably higher than in most countries. In addition, he is bound not only to exercise correct and conscientious behavior on the job, but also to behave in private life so as to command the respect and confidence which his profession requires. The Beamten Law also enjoins him to look after the "reputation of members of his family," which in a commentary is held to include assuring "modest behavior by his spouse." The provision that he is allowed to accept gifts only with the permission of his superiors was ignored, in the course of the 1950's, by a fair number of federal officials who seemed to be under the impression that methods which prevailed in business life should also apply in the public service. A sizable number of prosecutions, particularly against members of the Finance, Defense, and Traffic ministries, but including also a case in the federal Chancellery, served to stem this minor wave of corruption. The German public did not react with as much indignation as it once might have, a reflection of the fact that the Beamte is no longer considered infallible. Many civil servants blame this loss of prestige on the fact that official salaries, especially in the higher grades, have failed to keep up with the general trend. In 1954 a civil service paper claimed that the buying power of the salary of a *Ministerialdirektor* was only half what it had been in 1910. Since then some considerable increases have been made in the salary scale.

The denazification and other reforms carried through by the Allies in the postwar period aroused a considerable amount of righteous indignation among dismissed officials, who held that their basic right to lifelong tenure had been arbitrarily violated. They claimed that the Allied action was illegal under German law and sought not only reinstatement but back pay. Of the fifty-three thousand civil servants removed in the Western zones, only about one thousand remained permanently excluded through German official action.[6] Most of the rest were gradually taken back into various official agencies, and the others enlisted the civil servants' associations to put great pressure on the Bundestag to enact legislation in their favor. They were known as the

[6] Taylor Cole, "The Democratization of the German Civil Service," *JP*, XIV (February, 1952), 7.

"131'ers," after the article of the Basic Law which provides that the status of civil servants who lost their jobs after 1945 was to be settled by law. There were basically two categories in the post-1945 group: (1) those dismissed because of Nazi activity and (2) those officials who had previously served in the Eastern sections of Germany now outside the Federal Republic's boundaries. The law which the Bundestag passed in 1951 neatly evaded the political problem involved by lumping the two groups together and giving their members priority in reinstatement to public positions as well as generous retirement options. A Constitutional Court decision of 1954, however, indirectly rapped the civil service over the knuckles. The Court found that the thorough nazification of the civil service had in effect turned the service into a tool of the Nazi regime. While recognizing that Article 131 bound the Federal Republic to provide some sort of care, it held that dismissed officials had no automatic right to reclaim positions in what was essentially a new postwar employment situation. However in practice few were denied a fresh start. In the Foreign Office, for instance, those officials who had been dismissed for anti-Nazi activities fared quite well after 1949. But on the other hand, of the majority who had retained their positions in the Hitler era, "only a few were actually rejected because of concessions they made to National Socialism." [7]

In addition to attempting to remove Nazis, the Allies had also sought to democratize the German civil service by breaking down its caste structure so as to allow the admission of "outsiders" who possessed qualifications other than the traditional legal training or long service on lower levels of administration. The Americans regarded the caste structure of the civil service as a fossilized remnant from the period of absolutism, whose strong *esprit de corps* perpetuated undemocratic and reactionary political values. They felt that the special status held by the Beamte led not only to dangerous claims of privilege against outside criticism, but also to internal administrative stratification which tended to perpetuate irrational methods of administration.

German reaction to this criticism was predominantly hostile. Beamten spokesmen argued that it was no accident that the Americans saw eye-to-eye on this problem with German Socialists. "American liberalism, with its trend toward a minimization of the state, has found common ground with Marxists who want to

[7] Samuel Wahrhaftig, "The Development of German Foreign Policy Institutions," in Hans Speier and W. P. Davison, eds., *West German Leadership and Foreign Policy* (Evanston, 1957), p. 32.

'socialize' the Beamtentum. Both want to do away with the remnants of class rule and to achieve a 'classless society.' " The Americans were said to be badly misguided in seeking to destroy in Germany what they themselves were trying to foster at home: a feeling of dedicated service among public employees. They were held to be ignorant in failing to realize that the legal prerequisite for German Beamten was made necessary by the continental type of legal system. "American officials do not seem to recognize that case law was abandoned in Germany in the 17th century. This may be deplorable, but adoption of the Roman law system requires for its application the legally trained civil servant." [8]

Only a minority of Germans, mainly "outsiders," agreed with a liberal Stuttgart lawyer who argued in reply that the German Beamte was still excessively concerned with carrying forward his former rulers' role as "carriers of the state's honor." He called for the abolition of the "marriage-like vow of fidelity through which the Beamte dedicates his entire service to the state," as well as for the abolition of distinctions between Beamten and other civil as well as private employees, and a de-emphasis of pension privileges. "The high premium placed on the generous pension forces the Beamte to make do with unsatisfactory or dishonorable working conditions, for no matter how much he disagrees with the legislator or his superiors he dare not leave his job, thereby forfeiting pension rights for which he has worked for years." [9] Such arguments, however, failed to prevail in the Bundestag, where strong Beamten organization influence caused the adoption of a new Beamten Law which embodied no really fundamental reforms. The traditional internal stratification, the difficulties facing entrance by noncareer applicants, and the emphasis on perpetuating the distinct character of the Beamtentum through pension and other privileges have been modified in only minor ways. One of the few concessions consists of the creation of Personnel Committees which check the qualifications of noncareer applicants and review complaints from individual civil servants. Intended to open up personnel policy-making to some degree, their make-up does not, however, indicate that the claims of nonprofessionals would meet with strong support. On the federal level, the Personnel Committee is made up of the

[8] Ernst Kern, "Berufsbeamtentum und Politik," *Archiv des oeffentlichen Rechts*, LXXVII, 108.

[9] Otto Kuester, "Zur Frage des Berufsbeamtentums," *Archiv des oeffentlichen Rechts*, LXXVII, 364.

president of the Government Accounting Office, the personnel chiefs of the Interior and Finance ministries, three representatives suggested by the two leading civil service organizations, and one appointee of the federal president. The federal Personnel Committee has only advisory powers, but its equivalents on the Land level sometimes make policy directly.

To some it appears that postwar reforms have left the German civil service fundamentally unchanged as an institution. Thus an English student of comparative administration wrote in 1959 that "the German public official's status is unique in western Europe" because the German respect for the expert causes him to be placed on a pedestal and idealized to a far greater extent than he is in other countries. Even in somewhat monarchic and Germanic countries like Sweden, Denmark, Austria, and Holland the public official may be "trusted, respected, and in some ways reluctantly admired," but unlike his German colleague he is "not assumed to have a monopoly on political wisdom nor to typify all that is best in the national character." [10]

Other observers, however, seem to note that the present-day German civil service has lost its dominant role and has ceased to develop political standards independent of the prevailing climate of opinion, as it used to do earlier. No longer an instrument which knows only one hierarchy of values, the civil service has had to accept the fact that political parties, interest groups, and other organizations will not tolerate being denied legitimate influence on official decision-making. Those who idealize the civil service as an aloof elite unbiased by party, class, or religion seem to be fighting a losing battle, as other hierarchies and bureaucracies effectively contest its pre-eminence. The postwar generation of officials seem to be quite aware of these changes and to have learned from recent experiences. They are less self-conscious and sure of themselves than were their predecessors. "Having gone through nazification and denazification, the 'new official' is unwilling to take risks. He will not be caught napping again; he does as directed and avoids responsibilities." Having accustomed himself to changed conditions, "the bureaucracy tends to bolster the present regime and type of government . . . whose orders and directives are therefore executed without much question."[11]

[10] Chapman, *op. cit.*, p. 310.
[11] John Herz, "Political Views of the West German Civil Service," in Hans Speier and W. P. Davison, eds., *West German Leadership and Foreign Policy* (Evanston, 1957), p. 100.

Bibliography

Brecht, Arnold, "Personnel Management," and Mott, Rodney L., "Public Finance," in E. H. Litchfield, ed., *Governing Postwar Germany* (Ithaca, 1953), pp. 263–93, 326–60.

Chapman, John, *The Profession of Government* (London, 1959).

Cole, Taylor, "The Democratization of the German Civil Service," *JP*, XIV (February, 1952), 3–18.

Eschenburg, Theodor, *Staat und Gesellschaft in Deutschland* (Stuttgart, 1956), pp. 760 ff.

Herz, John, "Political Views of the West German Civil Service," in Hans Speier and W. P. Davison, eds., *West German Leadership and Foreign Policy* (Evanston, 1957), pp. 96–135.

Kreutzer, Heinz, "Bund und Laender in der Bundesrepublik Deutschland," in O. K. Flechtheim, ed., *Bund und Laender* (Berlin, 1959), pp. 1–21.

Saintonge, R. A. Chaput de, *Public Administration in Germany* (London, 1961).

7 - The Judicial System and the Constitutional Court

Even more than other Continental peoples accustomed to a codified law structure, the Germans tend to see in the body of law a unified system which covers all possible contingencies arising out of the frailty of man in human interaction. While the citizens of more pragmatic political cultures, like those of the Anglo-Saxon countries, tend to utilize the machinery of law only after having exhausted less formal means of settling disputes, such as compromise and arbitration, the continental European, convinced of the rightness of his case, will go to court as a matter of course. He sees in the judge not a fallible fellow human seeking to decide between conflicting claims and precedents, but an expert trained to apply detailed code provisions and an aloof representative of an abstract justice.[1] Writers, social philosophers, and a surprisingly large number of average Germans have tended to agree with Hegel when he wrote: "How infinitely important, how divine it is, that the duties of

---

[1] Herbert Spiro, *Government by Constitution* (New York, 1958).

the state and the rights of the citizen, just as the rights of the state and the duties of the citizens, are legally determined."

The adoption of the modern German civil law code occurred at the end of the nineteenth century, a century later than in France. It was the fruit of stupendous labor by many legal scholars who paid intensive attention to problems of classification and arrangement. As a result the code, though more useful than the French in that the information it provides is more exhaustive, has a very elaborate and complicated structure.[2] Those who use it have to be thoroughly trained. In the course of their training, generations of German law students have been immersed in the ideological assumptions on which the code is built. Implicit is the premise that the written law is self-sufficient, and that the codes, together with the statutes through which they are implemented and amended, constitute a key capable of deciding all problems that come before the court. Judges are supposed not to seek answers outside the provisions of the written law. This orientation nurtured and accentuated a positivist tradition which had led German legal scholars to emphasize that the law is what the sovereign says it is. Since German jurisprudence has tended to emphasize that sovereignty rests with the state (in contrast to the French, who emphasized the role of the nation), justice and the interests of the state became difficult to dissociate.

For want of constitutional traditions or other expressions of community consensus, the Germans were more and more inclined to universalize the philosophical principles of law. This produced magnificent writers of jurisprudence, but it also encouraged super-positivist trends which tended to produce rules of constitutional law so "pure" that their relationship to the facts of social and political reality grew increasingly remote. Thus, in the upheaval preceding the advent of nazism, democratic legal philosophers found their theories inapplicable to the seemingly obvious political problems at hand. Later many judges and lawyers saw no incompatibility in remaining at their posts as long as the legal framework was left standing, even though hollowed out by the Nazis with the substitution of their own arbitrary decrees.

The Judiciary

German judges are very different from their American and British peers not only in their legal philosophy, but also in

2 Max Rheinstein, "Approach to German Law," *Indiana Law Journal*, XXXVI (1959), 546 ff.

their training, their professional standing, and the role they play in the decision-making process. In contrast to the Anglo-Saxon countries where judgeships are usually awarded to mature lawyers after successful careers in private practice, German judges get their practical training solely within the judicial administration. At the conclusion of their studies, German law students decide whether to go into the regular civil service, private practice, or the judiciary. If they decide for the latter they must be prepared to go through a prolonged period of preparatory service, examinations, and probationary service, similar to that expected for the highest grades of the civil service and stretching over a period of seven to eight years. Then, in their thirties, they are given lifetime appointments. They are then at the bottom of the judicial hierarchy as local judges with salaries of about three thousand dollars a year, and they can hope for eventual promotion to the highest regular judicial appointments on the Federal High Court, whose members are paid about eight thousand dollars.

Partly because of the very large numbers of judges required to staff the many different kinds of German courts (there are more than five hundred judges in the city of Hamburg alone), the average German judge has in no way the exalted position of his British colleague. He is, at all but the highest levels, very much like a civil servant, dependent upon the Justice Ministry for promotion within the hierarchy, and imbued with a spirit and tradition very much akin to that of the regular civil service. He has been characterized as seeking to clothe himself in anonymity, to hide his person behind his office, to insist that it is the "court" and not the "judge" which proclaims the verdict. Influenced by the traditional teaching that the judge should minimize his own role in the judicial process, he seeks conscientiously to apply the written law and does this with exacting objectivity. He "administers" the law; he does not "proclaim" or "find" it. However, in contrast to the Weimar period when many judges allowed their reactionary biases to distort equitable legislation, the administration of justice in the Federal Republic has left little ground for fundamental criticism, although not all courts have punished high ranking Nazis with sufficient severity.

German Court Structure

The West German court system differs from the American most significantly, in that (1) the regular courts are paralleled by an array of specialized and administrative courts; (2) questions of constitutional law are decided by still another series of courts; and (3) although there are both Land and federal courts, these are integrated into a single hierarchy. The Laender court systems include the lower courts and the middle echelon courts of appeal, while federal courts stand at the apex of both the regular and the various administrative and special court systems. Thus the regular courts have four levels, of which three are built into the Land system and the highest is on the federal level. At the lowest level, there is the district court (*Amtsgericht*) which has jurisdiction over the less important criminal and civil cases. The next highest court, the *Landgericht,* has original jurisdiction over more significant cases and acts in an appellate capacity for district court cases. The *Oberlandesgericht,* the highest regular court within the Land judiciary, is made up of separate senates for civil and criminal cases and has only an appellate judisdiction. Finally, the highest court of the regular court system is the High Federal Court (*Bundesgerichtshof*) at Karlsruhe, where close to one hundred judges adjudicate non-constitutional problems arising from the lower courts in all the Laender, and seek to preserve a uniform pattern of decision-making throughout the Federal Republic's regular court system. In addition to exercising wide appellate jurisdiction, the High Federal Court, whose members are named jointly by federal and Land authorities, exercises original jurisdiction in cases involving treason. The widespread Communist espionage activity and other consequences of the division of Germany cause them to be kept quite busy on this score.

In addition to the regular courts and the constitutional courts (discussed below), there are the special courts, which have been well developed on the continent to deal exclusively with controversies relating to administrative decisions, labor-management problems, and other enumerated areas. Most important are the *administrative courts.* These handle all manner of questions arising out of decisions made by administrative organs on both the Land and federal level. Individuals feeling ill served by administrative action can ask the court to review whether the regulations were properly applied in their case. Similarly, civil servants who feel that their rights to promotion, tenure, and pension have been violated may ask these courts to review the decisions of their superiors. Basically, the administrative courts are supposed to serve as a check on the bureaucracy, but since much German rule-making is based on administrative decree rather than on legislation, the administrative courts hear many kinds of controversy that would go before regular courts in other countries. Other kinds of special courts include the *labor courts,* which deal with questions related to collective bargaining agreements, working conditions, and the prerogatives of labor and management; the *social security courts,* which deal with cases arising out of the administration of welfare legislation; and the *finance courts,* which deal mainly with problems of tax law administration. All of these special court systems parallel the regular courts in that they have lower courts on the Land level with final appeal centered in a federal administrative court, federal labor court, etc.

It would seem that little is left to chance with regard to maintaining the uniformity of German court decisions, but the Germans remain concerned lest the regular and administrative courts should make decisions cutting across each other, though dealing with matters falling within different jurisdictions. This could happen, since on the administrative side the different court systems (on the federal level and in most of the Laender) are supervised by different ministries. Thus the regular courts are attached to the Justice ministries, the labor courts to the Labor ministries, the administrative courts to the Interior ministries, the finance courts to the Finance ministries. The Justice ministries have been struggling to persuade the other ministries to yield complete supervision of all the courts to them. If this does not occur the Germans have another way to ensure uniformity of legal decisions. The answer would be the creation of still another court, a Federal Supreme Court, which would coordinate the decisions of the High Federal Court, the Federal Administrative Court, and the other high special courts. Actually such a court is provided for in the Basic Law, and it will probably be set up eventually.

The Growth of Judicial Review

While the regular and special courts are all based on foundations well established before 1933, the Federal Constitutional Court with its sweeping powers of judicial review is only as old as the Basic Law, and its equivalents on the Laender level are also postwar innovations. In view of their traditional respect for legalistic forms of decision-making, one might have expected the Germans to have long ago created a judicial organ which would play a role analogous to that of the United States

Supreme Court, but until 1933 a number of factors impeded such a development. Some German lawyers and legal scholars, sharing as they did the continental code law tradition, believed a court to interpret the Constitution unnecessary, since they thought that a skillfully wrought body of constitutional and code law would suffice to settle all conflicts if administered by a trained regular judiciary. Others tended to deny that constitutional law had any special position, arguing that both Constitution and statute were manifestations of the will of the same legislative power.[3] Finally, democrats of the Weimar period were inclined to regard the judiciary as a reactionary clan, not only in Germany but the world over. This impression was, if anything, reinforced by their study of the role of the conservative United States Supreme Court in American politics in the period around the turn of the century. The drafter of the Weimar Constitution had said that his plans for introducing judicial review in 1919 had been opposed by the Social Democrats mainly because they were horrified by the "notorious practice of the U.S. Supreme Court." [4]

By 1949, the perspective of German democrats had undergone considerable change. For one thing, still looking at the American model, they saw from the record of the New Deal Court that progressive judges could deal with social problems in the spirit of the times. But more important was the imprint left by European experience. Not only in Germany, but also in other code law countries like Italy and Austria that had experienced totalitarian or authoritarian regimes, the old legalist belief that good laws would by themselves assure good government was seriously undermined. Recalling that Hitler had come to power without seriously violating the letter of the law, Germans now were more willing to experiment with techniques that would make the Constitution, the law, and the courts into more effective control mechanisms to preserve democratic systems. This entailed giving up the old positivist belief that the realm of law was sharply separated from the realm of politics. It also entailed a dismissal of the idea that sound law was virtually self-executing. Finally it entailed acceptance of the need for institutions which could (1) effectively supervise the judiciary's interpretation of constitutional norms; (2) interpret the Constitution flexibly and yet in line with the

[3] G. Dietze, "Judicial Review in Europe," *Michigan Law Review,* LV (1957), 564.
[4] *Ibid.,* p. 557.

liberal democratic spirit which gave birth to it; and (3) possess the power to enforce a consistent reading of the Constitution on the other branches of government. If the list of functions had ended here, then the powers of judicial review later vested in the Constitutional Court would have been no wider than those exercised by the United States Supreme Court. But the politicians who had observed the agonies of the Weimar system saw additional functions which had to be fulfilled. These included (1) a power which could prevent deadlocks between the various governmental organs by arbitrating their claims to jurisdiction; (2) a power which could exercise great discretion in preventing anticonstitutional forces from using constitutional rights to overthrow the system; and (3) a power which could grant quick and effective relief to individuals whose constitutional rights were infringed. All of these powers came to be concentrated in the Federal Constitutional Court.

The Federal Constitutional Court: Role and Powers

In their effort to prevent abuse of the powerful positions on the Constitutional Court, the West Germans devised a complex and revealing election procedure. Even though bestowing such vast constitutional powers on a court, the Germans showed their incomplete confidence in the political commitment of their judges by providing that only six of the original twenty-four places be filled from the ranks of professional federal judges. Other candidates were to be drawn from the ranks of legally trained candidates in the universities, the legal profession, the administration, and politics. This effort to prevent the development of a rigid "council of elders" was further reinforced by the provision that, except for the career judges (who are given lifetime appointments), most of the members of the court were to be appointed for a maximum period of eight years, with staggered terms to allow for the continued influx of new members.

No political organ is given as decisive a voice in the nomination process as that of the American president. The German procedure works as follows: initially the federal Ministry of Justice provides a list of (1) all federal judges who are eligible for elevation to the Court and (2) all other persons nominated for constitutional judgeships by the federal government, political parties, and Land governments. From these candidates, elections are then made, alternately by a Bundestag committee and by the Bundesrat. Elections require a two-thirds majority in the

Constitutional Court

Article 92

Judicial authority shall be invested in the judges; it shall be exercised by the Federal Constitutional Court, by the Supreme Federal Court, by the Federal courts provided for in this Basic Law and by the courts of the *Laender.*

Article 93

The Federal Constitutional Court shall decide:

1. on the interpretation of this Basic Law in the event of disputes concerning the extent of the rights and duties of Federal organs or of other participants endowed with independent rights by this Basic Law or by the Standing Orders (Rules of Procedure) of a Federal organ;

2. in cases of differences of opinion or doubts on the formal and material compatibility of Federal law or *Land* law with this Basic Law, or on the compatibility of *Land* law with other Federal law, at the request of the Federal Government, of a *Land* Government or of one-third of the members of the Bundestag;

3. in case of differences of opinion on the rights and duties of the Federation and the *Laender,* particularly in the execution of Federal law by the *Laender,* and in the exercise of Federal supervision;

4. on other public law disputes between the Federation and the *Laender,* between different *Laender* or within a *Land,* unless recourse to another court exists;

5. in all other cases provided for in this Basic Law.

Article 100

(1) If a court considers a law unconstitutional, the validity of which is relevant to its decision, proceedings must be stayed and, if a violation of a *Land* Constitution is involved, the decision of the *Land* court competent for constitutional disputes shall be obtained and, if a violation of this Basic Law is involved, the decision of the Federal Constitutional Court shall be obtained. This shall also apply if the violation of this Basic Law by *Land* law or the incompatibility of a *Land* law with a Federal law is involved.

Bundesrat and as much as a three-quarters majority in the Bundestag committee.

In contrast to American practice, the Court is not set up as single body, but is divided into two equally large senates which meet together in plenary session only when there are problems of deviating decisions. These occur rarely, primarily because the legislature sought to avoid overlapping by assigning each of the senates a distinct area of jurisdiction. However, due to political pressures and a misestimation of the number of different kinds of cases that would be forthcoming, the initial division of responsibility included in the 1951 law resulted in a gross imbalance in the workload of the two senates. Thus, after four years' operation, the First Senate had received 2,893 cases while the Second had received only 29. The figures somewhat exaggerate the imbalance, since the First Senate handled the bulk of minor constitutional complaints, but the distortion was still great. A partial redistribution was brought about by a 1956 Amendment Act, but by 1959 the First Senate still had a backlog of cases almost thirty times as large as the Second. Therefore, acting on powers granted it under the 1956 Amendment Act, the Court itself initiated a further redistribution which became effective in 1960. As a result, the First Senate is now virtually limited to dealing with most complaints of infringement of civil and constitutional rights, with the Second Senate responsible for most other kinds of cases. Some groups have expressed the desire that the Constitutional Court be reshaped into a one-chamber court, but there remain groups and parties opposed to such a step for fear of concentrating too much power in the hands of a Court majority. Political considerations have also caused considerable wavering with regard to the total size of the Court. The original number of twenty-four judges was felt to be excessive, and in its 1956 Amendment the legislature provided for a reduction to a sixteen-member group. But the deadline for fully implementing this change was subsequently postponed until 1963. In 1960 each senate consisted of ten members.

The multiple functions of the Constitutional Court, plus factors arising from its role within a code law system, make even a summary description of its jurisdiction complex. Perhaps one might start with its powers related to *judicial review of legislation*. Here the Germans distinguish between the Court's exercise of "concrete" and "abstract" review jurisdiction. "Concrete" review occurs when the Court is asked to rule on constitutional questions arising as aspects of an actual controversy being adjudicated in lower courts. Applicants for concrete judicial review of legislation are regular lower courts, which *must* submit problems of constitutionality that they encounter in the process of adjudication. Applicants for "abstract" judicial review may include organs of federal and Land governments contesting the constitutionality of legislation or the constitutional interpretations of other agencies even without reference to a particular case. In addition, "Everyman" may complain if he believes that enacted legislation (as distinct from the way in which laws are administered) directly infringes on his constitutional rights.[5]

[5] Ernst Friesenhahn, "Verfassungsgerichtbarkeit," in *Handwoerterbuch der Sozialwissenschaften,* XXIX (Stuttgart, 1960), 83–91.

A few examples may illustrate how these powers are used. A case involving abstract review of legislation was initiated by the Socialist Land government of Hessen in 1957, based on the allegation that a federal law which allowed contributions to political parties to be written off as tax deductible was unconstitutional because it violated the constitutionally guaranteed equality of political parties. Applying sociological jurisprudence, the Court found, on the basis of scholarly and empirical evidence, that some parties received much larger contributions than others from business groups favored by these provisions. It reasoned that enforcement of the provisions would indeed cause those parties close to business interests to be unduly favored and declared the applicable provisions of the tax laws to be unconstitutional because they violated the Constitution's equality clause.[6] In another case, the Land government of Baden in 1951 challenged federal legislation that was to merge several southwest German Laender into the new Land of Baden-Wuerttemberg. Baden argued that the Basic Law so fortified the position of the Laender that they could not be abolished without the majority approval of all relevant sectional groups, but the Court ruled that territorial reorganization could be carried out, even against the will of a majority of the population in one affected unit.[7] In another case, the 1956 Federal Electoral Law was challenged by a small party on the grounds that the provisions that only parties receiving 5 per cent of the total vote were eligible for Bundestag seats violated the equality principle. However, the Court held, in this and similar cases, that such provisions were justified even in the face of constitutional equality provisions because splinter parties prevented an "orderly handling of affairs," and that the legislature could legitimately discriminate against them in this manner.[8]

A second distinct function of the Court arises out of its constitutional power to *decide disputes concerning the extent of the rights and duties of the federal and Land organs, as well as parties functioning within them.* Many cases coming to the German Court under this heading would probably be dismissed as "political cases" if brought before the United States Supreme Court, but the German Constitutional Court must accept them, and is drawn directly into the area of partisan political conflict. Thus

[6] *Entscheidungen des Bundesverfassungsgerichts,* VIII (Tuebingen, 1952–60), 51 ff.

[7] Gerhard Leibholz, "The Federal Constitutional Court in Germany and the 'Southwest' Case," *APSR,* XLVI (1952), 723–31.

[8] Taylor Cole, "The West German Federal Constitutional Court: An Evaluation after Six Years," *JP,* XX (February, 1958), 294.

in 1958 when the Socialists were fighting against atomic rearmament, the federal government came to the Court with a plea to prevent the Socialist-dominated Land government of Hamburg from carrying through a popular referendum on the question at the Land level. In this case the Court, siding with the Adenauer government, ruled that the Hamburg action was unconstitutional since matters relating to questions of defense and foreign policy were exclusively the business of the federal government.[9] In another case decided in 1957, the federal government asked the Court to declare invalid a Lower Saxony education law which was in conflict with the provisions of the Concordat treaty signed between the Reich government and the Vatican in 1933. The Court said that the Concordat was still valid, but that this had no effect on the Lower Saxony situation since under the Basic Law educational policy fell within the reserved power of the Laender.[10]

But perhaps the most important decision shoring up Laender powers was handed down by the Court in 1961 in the Television case. The issues in this case were rather parallel to those in the famous American case of *McCulloch v. Maryland,* but it was decided the other way. It arose out of an effort by the federal government to break the Laender's control of radio and television by getting them to agree that a much needed second television program should be instituted by a federal network on a nation-wide basis. When prolonged negotiations proved of no avail, Chancellor Adenauer in 1960 singlehandedly chartered just such a network with instructions to begin operations the next year. When pressed, the federal government argued that it was merely building on its delegated power to "legislate on postal and telecommunications services" (Art. 73)—which up to then had meant merely technical services maintained by the federal Post Ministry—and that its entry into the field of programming was made necessary by the Laender's inability to fulfill supra-regional and national functions. Attacking this attempt to expand the federal government's functions by a *fait accompli,* the Socialist-led Laender carried the case to the Constitutional Court, which in its decision rapped the Chancellor sharply over the knuckles. It ruled that through his action the federal government had violated the Constitution in manifold ways, most importantly by ignoring the provisions of Article 30, which specified that state

[9] *Entscheidungen des Bundesverfassungsgerichts,* VIII, 124 ff.
[10] Cole, *op. cit.,* pp. 298–99.

functions not assigned to its jurisdiction remained automatically within the jurisdiction of the Laender.[11]

A third broad function of the Constitutional Court arises from its powers to *decide on petitions charging infringements of the constitutionally guaranteed basic rights of individuals.* These relate to the substantive and procedural guarantees of the Bill of Rights (Arts. 1–19) whose provisions are "binding as directly valid law on legislation, administration and judiciary" (Art. 1). In order to encourage Germans to feel that the Constitution was a close and living guarantor of civil rights, the German legislature went out of its way to allow citizens who feel their rights violated by actions (such as acts of legislation) against which there is no alternative route of appeal, to complain to the Constitutional Court directly. Their submission involves neither court costs nor even the participation of legal counsel—indeed, an ideal situation for Hans Everyman to bring his woes to the direct attention of the country's highest tribunal!

The legislators might have foreseen that in a country as legalist as Germany such generous provision would bring the Court a flood of complaints. Petitions have come in at the rate of over five hundred a year, and they have made up about 80 per cent of all items brought before the Court. Many complaints have been of a nuisance variety. Petitions have contended that police regulations relating to the closing of bars constituted infringements of the right of assembly, while prostitutes have argued that regulations against "loitering" conflicted with guarantees relating to the right to freedom of occupation and the right to choose one's place of work.[12] Serious complaints have also come in, and account for about half of all the Constitutional Court decisions. But the problem of weeding out serious from "freak" complaints has imposed a serious strain on the Court's work, especially since it does not have the United States Supreme Court's selective power based on a discretionary granting of writs of *certiorari.* Since 1956, however, the Court has been permitted to defend itself against the flood of constitutional complaints by the setting up in each senate of three-man committees which can by unanimous vote dismiss complaints unless decisions in the case will either help clarify a question of constitutional interpretation, or prevent the appellees from being exposed to a great and otherwise unavoidable disadvantage.

In still another role, the Court has the power to *deprive*

[11] *Entscheidungen des Bundesverfassungsgerichts,* XII.
[12] Cole, *op. cit.,* p. 288.

Basic Rights

Article 1

(1) The dignity of man shall be inviolable. To respect and protect it shall be the duty of all state authority.

(2) The German people therefore acknowledges inviolable and inalienable human rights as the basis of every human community, of peace and of justice in the world.

Article 3

(1) All men shall be equal before the law.

(2) Men and women shall have equal rights.

(3) No one may be prejudiced or privileged because of his sex, descent, race, language, homeland and origin, faith or his religious and political opinions.

Article 5

(1) Everyone shall have the right freely to express and to disseminate his opinion through speech, writing and illustration and, without hindrance, to instruct himself from generally accessible sources. Freedom of the press and freedom of reporting by radio and motion pictures shall be guaranteed. There shall be no censorship.

Article 8

(1) All Germans shall have the right, without prior notification or permission, to assemble peacefully and unarmed.

(2) For open air meetings this right may be restricted by legislation or on the basis of a law.

Article 14

(1) Property and the right of inheritance shall be guaranteed. The contents and limitations shall be determined by legislation.

(2) Property shall involve obligations. Its use shall simultaneously serve the general welfare.

---

groups and individuals of normal constitutional rights if they engage in enumerated kinds of antidemocratic and anticonstitutional behavior. This role of the Court as a kind of constitutional police-judge came into play in particular in two cases involving the outlawing of antidemocratic parties. The first of these arose as a consequence of the initial success achieved by extreme nationalist, neo-Nazi groups in the period immediately after the Allies' licensing requirements for the founding of political parties were dropped. The Socialist Reich party (SRP) included among its leaders men closely associated with the Nazi regime who copied Nazi agitation tactics in order to whip up antidemocratic sentiments among voters, particularly in sections of North Germany.

Organized in a conspiratorial manner, the SRP made startling gains, winning 11 per cent or more of the popular vote in some Land and communal elections in 1950 to 1951. After having gathered evidence of the party's internal make-up and its public slogans, the government presented to the Court a motion to outlaw the party as unconstitutional, in line with the applicable provisions of the Basic Law. The Court acceded to this motion in its decision of October, 1952.

The second case, involving the Communist party, was submitted by the government at the same time, but a decision was delayed for over four years. One difficulty encountered in this case was that while the relevant Basic Law clause had been clearly intended to hinder the growth of neo-Nazi parties, its application to a party like the Communists was not self-evident. Communist delegates had helped to write the Basic Law, and Communist ministers had served in West German Land governments as late as 1948. But with the increasing tension between the East and West German regimes, the Court found itself "unable to avoid rendering a decision in the face of continuing pressure from a government with its eye on both internal and foreign policies." Basing its decision on extensive materials seized in successive raids on Communist party headquarters, the Court decided that the Communists' campaign could, in the total perspective, be interpreted in only one way: "It is the result of a planned program of agitation which seeks to expose the constitutional system of the Federal Republic to slight and contempt . . . and to shake the people's confidence in the values it has created." In its decision of August, 1956, the Court thus added the Communists to the list of banned parties.[13]

The Constitutional Court has several other functions, including powers (1) to make decisions on constitutional questions arising out of election proceedings; (2) to decide whether parts of international law are binding on Germans; and (3) after impeachment by a legislative body, to try the federal president and federal and Land judges on charges of having violated the Constitution. It also had the power to give advisory opinions, but this was ended in 1956. The Laender constitutional courts adjudicate in questions relating to the Land Constitution in much the same way as the Federal Constitutional Court. But their powers

[13] Edward McWhinney, "The German Federal Constitutional Court and the Communist Party Decision," *Indiana Law Journal*, XXXII (1957), 295–312.

and significance are far more limited because decisions and
precedents on the federal level dominate decision-making procedures on the lower levels.

The Court and the Political System

Whenever a court is set up as a third branch of government,
there will be those who will question its right to make vigorous
use of its powers so as to overrule the political decisions of constitutional organs elected by the people. There is likely to be disagreement between those who argue on behalf of a policy of
"judicial restraint" and others who expound a doctrine of "judicial dynamism."

Some German constitutional law experts soon began to cry
alarm that the Court was using its powers with too much
abandon. In discussing the Court's decisions in 1954, one law professor took the Court sharply to task for allowing itself to express
opinions about historical developments under the Nazi regime.

> The great judicial art of moderation, the traditional judicial wisdom
> of saying only what is necessary for the decision of a particular case,
> seems not to stand in particularly high regard in our highest Court.
> Rather, there is a tendency toward elaboration and pedagogic explana-
> tion which is not suitable. . . . It is never the task of a court, not
> even of a constitutional court, to enunciate historical lessons which are
> not pertinent to the case, or which are at least not necessary. . . .
> The Constitutional Court should remain what it was created: our high-
> est Court, the protector of the Constitution. But it should not regard
> itself as *Praeceptor Germaniae*! [14]

Other critics attacked the Court's concept of its role as being one
of building up the Constitution by handing down opinions which
would form a substantial philosophical structure on which its
successors, as well as other political organs, should seek to
build. "The real task of a constitutional court is not . . . to set
up abstract rules for interpretation, but to bring concrete differences to a peaceful solution, and, by checking the validity of
norms, to secure general respect for the permanent constitution." [15]

Other criticism blames the Basic Law, rather than the judges,
for the Court's deep involvement in the making of so many

[14] Otto Bachof, "Beamte und Soldaten," *Oeffentliche Verwaltung*, VII
(1954), 226.

[15] Ulrich Scheuner, "Das Bundesverfassungsgericht und die Bindungskraft
seiner Entscheidungen," *Oeffentliche Verwaltung*, VII (1954), 647.

political decisions. The Court is seen as having to exercise "vast functions in the regularization of political dynamics far beyond the practice of most other constitutions. . . . In many instances in which, in other political civilizations, the compromise of conflicting interests is left to the natural dynamism of political forces (parties, state organs, public opinion), in Germany it is the judges who are called upon to decide. . . . One may well speak of a judicialization of political dynamics." [16] One deplorable effect of this "judicialization" is that the Court's wide powers have been a factor in retarding general acceptance of a body of political, as distinct from legalistic, "rules of the game." It will be seen from the kinds of cases brought to the Court, particularly under the second category enumerated above, that a political party or government organ can usually find a constitutional law "handle" through which to bring almost any political dispute to the Court. This means that in Germany a political party or a government organ that is defeated on a particular issue as a result of a parliamentary vote or even an election tends not to reconcile itself to this defeat. Rather, convinced of the rightness of its position, it will engage in prolonged legal proceedings before the Court, in the hope of perhaps overthrowing the earlier decision or at least deriving some political benefit from a Court ruling on a technical point. So much of the prestige of the British Parliament rests on the fact that a decision of Parliament is final and can be reversed only when the electors turn the opposition into the government party. In Germany, the legislature is frequently regarded not as the final arbiter whose decision can only be changed by the voters, but as a trial arena for arguments which may eventually be submitted to the Constitutional Court.

However, as Professor Taylor Cole wrote in 1958, "There does not appear to be any major pressure group in Germany which seeks to restrict the jurisdiction of the Court, and there are increasing evidences of growing popular support and appreciation of its work." [17] The Germans, as yet incompletely adjusted to the idea that in a pluralistic democracy decisions are made by groups and not by a fictional all-embracing state, welcome the presence of a strong reviewing power. Commenting that interest group pressure frequently causes laws to be more "ad-hoc commands in favor of a certain group than a well-balanced rule promoting the common weal," a member of the Court has written that it is

[16] Karl Loewenstein, "Justice," in E. H. Litchfield, ed., *Governing Postwar Germany* (Ithaca, 1953), p. 262.

[17] Cole, *op. cit.*, p. 305.

"quite natural" that the judiciary should be called upon to exert
a countervailing effect on behalf of "the individual and the
whole community." [18] This argument might seem quite alien to
an Englishman, but familiar and reasonable to an American.
Germans, like Americans, although for different reasons, favor
the idea of an arbiter who can curb irresponsibility on the part of
the political power-holders in the executive and the legislature.

Bibliography

Cole, Taylor, "The West German Federal Constitutional Court: An Evalua-
    tion after Six Years," *JP*, XX (February, 1958), 278–307.
Dietze, G., "America and Europe, Decline and Emergence of Judicial Re-
    view," *Virginia Law Review*, XLIV (1958), 1233 ff.
———, "Judicial Review in Europe," *Michigan Law Review*, LV (1957),
    539 ff.
Entscheidungen des Bundesverfassungsgerichts, 10 vols. (Tuebingen, 1952–60).
Friesenhahn, Ernst, "Verfassungsgerichtbarkeit," in *Handwoerterbuch der
    Sozialwissenschaften*, XXIX (Stuttgart, 1960), 83–91.
Kirchheimer, Otto, *Political Justice* (Princeton, 1961).
Leibholz, Gerhard, "The Federal Constitutional Court in Germany and the
    'Southwest' Case," *APSR*, XLVI (1952), 723-31.
Loewenstein, Karl, "The Bonn Constitution and the European Defense Com-
    munity Treaties," *Yale Law Journal*, LXIV (1955), 805–39.
———, "Justice," in E. H. Litchfield, ed., *Governing Postwar Germany*
    (Ithaca, 1953), pp. 236–62.
McWhinney, Edward, "The German Federal Constitutional Court and the
    Communist Party Decision," *Indiana Law Journal*, XXXII (1957), 295–
    312.
Rheinstein, Max, "Approach to German Law," *Indiana Law Journal*, XXXVI
    (1959), 546 ff.
Rupp, H. G., "Judicial Review in the Federal Republic of Germany," *Amer.
    Jl. of Comp. Law*, IX (1960), 29 ff.

[18] H. G. Rupp, "Judicial Review in the Federal Republic of Germany,"
Amer. Jl. of Comp. Law, IX (1960), 46.

8 - Land and Local Government

German Federalism

Many characteristics of the relationship between West German Laender and the federal government will seem unusual to a reader who thinks of federalism in terms of the American model. That the Laender pass much of their legislation in accordance with federal "framework laws," that the Land bureaucracy carries out both Land and federal administration, and that the Land ministers participate directly in the shaping of federal decisions through the Bundesrat—all these are indices of the very significant differences between the American and German varieties of federal structure. In fact it has frequently been asked whether the German arrangement can be really classified as "federal" at all. A leading British student of federalism, Professor K. C. Wheare, is among those who have answered the question in the negative. Following American practice, Wheare argues that the true principle of federalism is based on a division of power in which "the general and regional governments, are each, within a sphere, coordinate and independent." [1] In view of the aspects of German federal-Land relationships which have already been examined above,[2] he comes to the conclusion that the German system is not really federal, but constitutes instead a special example of a decentralized unitary state.

Critics have contended that Wheare's true federal model contains too much of an ethnocentric bias in favor of the example of the United States and other Anglo-Saxon countries. Thus one critic argues that: "The rigid requirement of the mutual independence of the executive and legislative institutions of both levels is at best a product of historical circumstances, and not an indispensable part of a general definition of federalism." The German arrangement, according to this point of view, is characterized by coexistence and voluntary cooperation leading to a

[1] K. C. Wheare, *Federal Government*, 3d ed. (London, 1953), p. 11.
[2] See above, pp. 119–23, 126–27.

Land and Local Government

Article 28

(1) The constitutional order in the *Laender* must conform to the principles of the republican, democratic and social government based on the rule of law within the meaning of the Basic Law. In the *Laender,* counties and communities, the people must have a representative assembly resulting from universal, free, equal and secret elections. . . .

Article 30

The exercise of the powers of the state and the performance of state functions shall be the concern of the *Laender,* insofar as this Basic Law does not otherwise prescribe or permit.

Article 31

Federal law shall supercede *Land* law.

Article 70

(1) The *Laender* shall have the power to legislate insofar as this Basic Law does not confer legislative powers on the Federation.

---

functional separation under which the federal government is assigned the bulk of legislative power while the states exercise most administrative powers. Hence the West German arrangement is seen as an example of "executive-legislative federalism." [3] Whatever the terms employed, the discussion of the merits of the American and German types of federalism continues unabated. A German politician who holds an office for which, from the American point of view, there is little justification, the federal Minister for Bundesrat Affairs, von Merkatz, in 1958 reaffirmed his faith in the native model. "I know on the basis of my own observations in the United States, that the system there is constantly criticized for its lack of any kind of systematic base. Our principle of the close interdependence of the Federal government and the Laender has developed historically and has throughout proved its worth." [4]

The origins of the German arrangement lie in the compromise through which the German Empire emerged under Prussian leadership. "It was painful enough for the non-Prussian states to see the symbols of political power move to Berlin; but they were considerably more apprehensive at the thought of Prussian administrators setting up offices of the national administration in their cities and towns. So they attempted to preserve their integrity by restricting the new national government as much as

[3] Peter H. Merkl, "Executive-Legislative Federalism in West Germany," *APSR,* LIII (1959), 732–41.
[4] Ossip K. Flechtheim, ed., *Bund und Laender* (Berlin, 1959), p. 51.

possible to the new political center, Berlin, and insisting that policy emanating from this center should be administered wherever possible by local officials." [5] The question of whether the individual states could prevent themselves from becoming overshadowed under this arrangement depended mainly on their ability to guard their tax revenues and to maintain a strong political position.

Under the Empire the states retained control over the bulk of direct taxes, but during the Weimar period the Reich took important state taxes over for its own use, and during periods of crisis the Laender were dependent on Reich funds to keep their administrations going. Politically, the problem of equilibrium was crucially affected by Prussian predominance in terms of power and population. The Prussian kings who inherited the Imperial mantle had tended to dominate the national scene, but at least they respected the formal rights of the lesser kings and princes. After 1918 the kings and princes were removed, but Prussia remained the German Land which had more population than all the rest of Germany put together. This fact, together with the strong centralist bias of the Weimar Constitution, tended to weaken the functioning of federal institutions during the interwar period. When Hitler abolished the Laender in 1934 their political significance had already all but disappeared.

The determination to break up Prussia was one of the few important points on which the Allies were in agreement in 1945. But in the formation of new Laender each of the occupying powers followed its own inclinations. In the south the Americans recreated Bavaria and combined smaller territories to form the Laender of Hessen and Wuerttemberg-Baden, both of which had some historical traditions. On the left bank of the Rhine the French combined the former Bavarian province of Palatinate with parts of Hessen and Rhenish Prussia to form Rhineland-Palatinate. The British combined other formerly Prussian areas to create the large and heavily industrialized state of Northrhine-Westphalia, while further to the north they shaped other ex-Prussian areas to make the Laender Lower Saxony and Schleswig-Holstein. Together with the two city-states of Hamburg and Bremen and (since 1956) the Saar, these constitute the Laender of the Federal Republic. The attachment of the population to their Laender varies considerably, growing less intense as one moves from south to north. Polls have shown that only one out

---

[5] Karlheinz Neunreither, "Federalism and the West German Bureaucracy," *Political Studies,* VII (1959), 235.

of four West Germans would be upset if the Laender were abolished. In 1954 to 1955 the people of Lower Saxony were four to
one in favor of dissolution, those of Northrhine-Westphalia two
to one, and those in Bavaria split one to one. If there are any
genuine state's rights advocates in Germany they tend to be the
Bavarians.

Land Governments

For the most part the structure of the Land governments
closely resembles that of the federal government. They are based
on the parliamentary system, and (except for Bavaria) they have
a unicameral legislature (*Landtage*). Elections to the Landtage are
made on the basis of varying Land election laws, all of which
however embody modifications of the principle of proportional
representation. The executive is composed of a minister-president
and a cabinet, but the powers of the former are considerably
more limited than are those of the Chancellor in Bonn. Land
cabinets usually are fairly small, and the ministers are appointed
by the minister-president on the advice of parties participating in
the government. Because the prime function of Land governments lies in administration rather than in policy-making, the
parties represented in the government tend to nominate leaders
with administrative experience for the cabinet positions. The
latters' salaries are pegged at a specific fraction, 70 per cent, of
the salaries of federal ministers. Since these in turn are fixed in
relation to prevailing civil service scales, the salaries of both civil
service and political decision-makers on both federal and Land
levels are closely linked.

Many Land ministries constitute positions of considerable
power, especially those relating to areas where the federal government plays a relatively small role. This holds true, for instance,
for the Land ministers of the interior, who set down policies for
the police, and the Land ministers of education and culture, who
are instrumental in handling perennial "hot" issues like those
dealing with the question of whether public schools should be
maintained on an integrated or denominational basis. Since the
Catholic church presses for the maintenance of separate public
schools for Catholic and Protestant, school controversies frequently break out, and Land ministers of education can quickly
become very well known indeed. However the bulk of the work
of other ministers tends to revolve around more prosaic problems.

of how to administer policies which are basically determined in Bonn.

Despite this fact Land politics have by no means been just a haven for those who can't succeed on the federal level. For one thing, the fact that the Laender existed for several years before the federal government caused the former to attract many of the most able politicians as well as some of the best civil servants. Many of these politicians stayed on at the Land capitals, and they, in turn, have been able to encourage the progress of potential younger successors by smoothing their way to prominence on the Land level. The concentration of talent has been particularly evident among Socialist Land politicians, since these have never even been given an opportunity to assume office on the federal level. Some of the ablest SPD politicians—such as Max Brauer and Wilhelm Kaisen, the Lord Mayors of Hamburg and Bremen, August Zinn, the minister-president of Hessen, Waldemar von Knoerringen, the leader of the Bavarian Socialists, and Willy Brandt, the mayor of Berlin—have made their names on the Land level. In fact, when the Socialists picked their "team" for the 1961 federal elections, about half its members were Land leaders. The ranks of Christian Democratic Land politicians have suffered somewhat more by the drift of talent to Bonn, but even here leadership has often been provided by men who have been active in Land politics ever since 1945, as by Hans Erhard in Bavaria and Peter Altmaier in Rhineland-Palatinate.

Land Politics

The nature of party politics on the Land level has in many ways been quite different from that on the federal level. The fact that parties with regional strong points have been able to hold out longer on the Land level has contributed toward perpetuating multiparty systems. At most times partisan conflict has also been much less intense, with the result that CDU and SPD politicians have frequently been found in coalition in Land cabinets. The voters, too, exhibit quite different forms of voting behavior in Land and federal elections. Finally, something of the character of the early Occupation period, when the Laender were fairly isolated political units, has been perpetuated. Many Land party leaders, especially in the CDU, have resisted pressure to integrate themselves into a uniform national party hierarchy, and have sought to make Land political alliances and policies that are based on local conditions, rather than on the desires of the party leaders on the federal level. When such personal motives have been linked to issues entailing the defense of vested Land interests, these politicians have at times been quite obstinate in fending off the claims of the federal leaders. Thus Lower Saxony fought a prolonged battle to prevent the federal government from laying sole title to the valuable Volkswagen works, which are located within its boundaries. Similarly, as mentioned above, many CDU Land politicians engaged in a drawn-out campaign to prevent the Adenauer government from establishing federally-controlled radio and television stations, since they felt this to be an encroachment on Land prerogatives. Though they did finally agree to this, the Constitutional Court did not, and television as well as radio remained under Laender control.

The fact that the smaller parties have played a larger role on the Land level has frequently had the effect of producing periods of postelection uncertainty as to who would form Land governments. Small parties have been in the position of the tail that wags the dog, and they have frequently taken their time in deciding which major party they would enter into coalition with. As a result, Land politics has been marred by many minor crises both at the time cabinets were formed and afterwards, when the parties backing them began to fall out among themselves. Many Land governments have been changed three, four, or more times while Chancellor Adenauer has continued his unbroken reign in Bonn. This brings out an interesting characteristic of German politics during the Adenauer period. The renowned stability of German politics has been largely a function of a polarization of German politicians into pro-Adenauer and anti-Adenauer alliances. Where, as on the Land level, the effect of the Chancellor has been more remote, this polarization has not occurred to the same degree, and consequently stability has been less in evidence.

If Adenauer has not dominated Land politics it is not because he has not tried to do so. When he first assumed power in Bonn he fought hard to force the more independent CDU Land ministers to toe the line by following Land policies parallel to his, especially by breaking previously existing coalitions with the Socialists. He got many of the weaker CDU Land leaders to fight Land elections (which are held, one or two at a time, at odd dates between federal elections) on federal issues, and sought to force the creation of Land ministries that were almost exact replicas of the Bonn cabinet as far as party make-up and policies were concerned.[6] For a while it appeared that the Laender would become coordinated to the point where German federalism would become a dead letter. But a number of factors have combined to halt this trend. One has been the decisions of the Constitutional Court, as in the television case. It should also be noted that smaller parties have fought back desperately. The FDP, when severely rebuffed in Bonn in 1955, retaliated by breaking up its coalition with the CDU in Northrhine-Westphalia and combining with the SPD to form an anti-Adenauer coalition on the Land level. The Socialists, who originally were extremely antifederalist in orientation, have in the course of time emerged as strong champions of Land rights, and have increasingly come to form alliances with the purpose of stopping federal encroachments. Finally, the German voters have displayed a curious immunity to the Chancellor's charm when voting for deputies to the Landtage. Despite his frequent personal campaigns on behalf of CDU candidates in Land elections, the voters have shown a distinct disinclination to vote for the Chancellor's candidates on the Land level; large numbers of those who have voted for the CDU in federal elections have persistently abstained from voting in Land contests. As a result there has not been (up to 1961) a single Land where the CDU has succeeded in winning as many votes for its Landtage candidates as it did for its Bundestag candidates in either the preceding or succeeding federal elections campaign. It would seem that the German voters are somehow quite acutely aware that the Chancellor's place is on the federal level, and that Land political campaigns should be fought about Land issues, however less dramatic these may be.

Local Government

Though many German cities can look back to periods of medieval splendor when they counted among the leading political powers in Germany, today (except for the city-states of Hamburg, Bremen, and West-Berlin) they owe their status to the Laender just as American cities owe theirs to the states. Because of the diversity of regional development there has been considerable variety in the kind of governmental forms adopted on the municipal level. The Rhineland cities, for instance, under Napoleonic influence developed a very centralized system (which

[6] Arnold J. Heidenheimer, "Federalism and the Party System: The Case of West Germany," *APSR*, LII (1958), 809–28.

might best be called the *dominant mayor* pattern) under which mayors elected by the city councils for terms of twelve years were unchallenged heads of the city administration while also serving as presiding officers of the city councils. Chancellor Adenauer held this kind of position as Buergermeister of Cologne from 1917 to 1933. In the Prussian areas of North Germany, by contrast, the municipal government was based on the *Magistrat* type, in which executive power lay in the hands of a plural board of magistrates elected by the council, who at the same time served as the upper house of a bicameral municipal legislature. In South Germany yet another system prevailed (the *council* type) under which the city council, made up both of elected members and the chief city administrators, was a unified organ responsible for both legislation and administration. All three of these systems included the figure of the Buergermeister, but he had much less power under the latter two systems. In their own way, the Nazis wrought uniformity through the German Municipal Government Act of 1935 which abolished all elections on the local level. Mayors and city councillors were appointed after consultation between local and national Nazi leaders and the Reich Ministry of Interior, and became agents of the Nazi party and the national government.

The postwar period was characterized by a tendency to return to the pre-Nazi system, modified however by an attempt on the part of the occupying powers to break up undue concentrations of communal power. The British, especially, sought to reduce or abolish the power of the mayor and magistrates by splitting the political and administrative functions of the chief local officials and vesting all executive and legislative power exclusively in the council (on the British model). They abolished the magistrate boards, reduced the mayor to the position of chairman of the city council, and centered administrative powers in a nonpolitical city manager (*Gemeindedirektor*) who was made responsible to the elected city council. This *council-manager* system has prevailed in Northrhine-Westphalia and Lower Saxony. Schleswig-Holstein, on the other hand, returned to a *Magistrat* system, but a weakened one under which this collegial executive is no longer also a second legislative chamber, while its members are subject to recall by the city council. Most cities in Hessen operate with the same system. The French also tried to get the Germans in their zone to abandon the dominant mayor form (even though it had been inspired by Napoleon), but they were less successful, and Rhineland-Palatinate reinstalled the dominant mayor system in 1948. Fewer problems were encountered in South Germany

where the Americans found the old council system to be acceptable in terms of distribution of powers. Thus in Bavaria and
Baden-Wuerttemberg, elected city councils combine legislative
with executive powers while a mayor, elected either by the council or the citizens, is the chief administrative officer responsible
to the council. This *council-mayor* system is distinguished from
the system prevalent in Northrhine-Westphalia and Lower Saxony by the fact that the mayor and not the city manager is
the main bearer of administrative responsibility. In addition to
these four types of West German city government, there is also
the system prevalent in Hamburg, Bremen, and West Berlin,
which combines the functions of municipal and Land governments. In these cities the council elects a collegial executive, the
Senate, which is headed by a governing mayor.

West German county government in rural and small town
areas varies in roughly the same manner as does city government,
that is, according to regional patterns. The leading organs here
are the county council (*Kreistag*) and the county director (*Landrat*). In some areas the Landrat is more politician than administrator, and in others he combines the two functions. The German tradition of interdependence, which inclines to squeeze
county directors into the state official hierarchy and to integrate
local administration into the Land system, tends to limit the
degree of self-determination that local government can achieve.
In any case, the cities are financially dependent on the Land
treasuries. The kind of equalization which operates horizontally
among the Laender, operates vertically among communities, with
the Land holding the purse-strings. The average German city is
dependent on Land subsidies of varying sorts to cover about a
fifth of its budget. In the early 1950's the cities were angry that the
Laender were not equitably sharing increases in tax revenues. As
a result of their pressure, the federal Parliament in 1956 amended
the Basic Law (Art. 106) to strengthen the communities' claims to
certain kinds of taxes, and to provide for some sort of fixed key
for the division of Land tax receipts between Land and municipal
treasuries.

The desire of local government advocates that cities and counties be placed on an equal level with the federal and Land governments by greater constitutional recognition of their role as a
"third power" in administration has, however, not been fulfilled.
Indeed, local government authorities have not yet succeeded in
getting many of the Laender to abolish what they regard as the
obsolescent middle-echelon district administrations. These sub-

sidiary Land government offices exist in all the Laender except the city-states and Schleswig-Holstein, and, among other duties, supervise communal police, education, and public health activities which are carried out with the support of Land funds. The communal politicians argue that these organs are undemocratic, since they are not directly responsible to any parliamentary organ, and are largely unnecessary in that their functions could be transferred to the Land ministries and communal governments. However the orthodox German view continues to differentiate between the higher claims of the "state" (the Land) and the communities. "The state has not become merely a 'holding corporation' for the communities and the communities have not taken over the role of the state. There has been a democratization of administration on all levels, insofar as free elections for the local and state legislatures are guaranteed . . . and in that these exercise a control over the administration. But the state is superior to the communities integrated within it, as its legislation, administration and legal system prove." [7]

Bibliography

Brecht, Arnold, *Federalism and Regionalism in Germany* (New York, 1945).

Flechtheim, Ossip K., ed., *Bund und Laender* (Berlin, 1959).

Heidenheimer, Arnold J., "Federalism and the Party System: The Case of West Germany," *APSR*, LII (1958), 809–28.

Merkl, Peter H., "Executive-Legislative Federalism in West Germany," *APSR*, LIII (1959), 732–41.

Neunreither, Karlheinz, "Federalism and the West German Bureaucracy," *Political Studies*, VII (1959) 232–45.

Newcomer, Mabel S., "Fiscal Relations of Central and Local Governments in Germany Under the Weimar Republic," *PSQ*, LI (1936), 185–214.

Peters, Hans, ed., *Handbuch der kommunalen Wissenschaft und Praxis*, 3 vols. (Berlin, 1956–59).

Wells, Roger H., *German Cities* (Princeton, 1932).

———, "Local Government" and "State Government" in E. H. Litchfield, ed., *Governing Postwar Germany* (Ithaca, 1953), pp. 57–83, 84–117.

Wheare, K. C., *Federal Government*, 3d ed. (London, 1953).

[7] Erich Becker in Hans Peters, ed., *Handbuch der kommunalen Wissenschaft und Praxis* (Berlin, 1956), I, 118.

PART III

COMMUNIST EAST GERMANY

9 - The Party and the State

The "Other Germany"

Most citizens of the Federal Republic find it difficult to "place" the political unit to their immediate East. Although the territory, as distinct from the regime, is accepted as German, there then arises the question of what to call it. Is it to be regarded as "East Germany," as common foreign parlance would have it, or would this not suggest German acceptance of the permanent loss of the Oder-Neisse territories now attached to Poland? Hence West German authorities always refer to "Central Germany" or the "Soviet zone" when talking about the Democratic Republic. Secondly—whether East or Central Germany—is the territory between the Elbe and Oder to be regarded as a state? Formally at least, West Germans refuse to so regard it since their government claims to speak for all Germans and considers itself the only legitimate government in Germany. By 1960 this position, judging by the standard of diplomatic recognition, was still supported with varying degrees of enthusiasm by almost all the non-Communist world. The German Democratic Republic, in turn, claims that it is at least as legitimate as the Bonn government, and is supported by all the Communist states. The resulting impasse epitomizes the lack of progress on the question of German unification during the decade from 1950 to 1960.

When examined from the point of view of formal milestones of political development, the two hostile German states seem at first sight to show some parallels. Both evolved from Occupation status in 1949, both achieved formal sovereign status in 1954 to 1955, and both have set up military forces which have become integrated with those of their respective power blocs. But though these parallels should not be lost sight of, they tend to obscure characteristics which indicate completely different patterns of

development. The sharply contrasting evolution of social and
economic structures in the two states has already been described
and analyzed (see Chapter 2). Their political systems are so different that meaningful comparison is difficult. Whereas the Federal Republic has revived and reinvigorated liberal democratic
political institutions to create a stable parliamentary regime on a
constitutional basis, East Germany has uprooted "bourgeois"
political institutions and developed instruments to facilitate increasingly totalitarian rule by a Communist party which seeks to
turn the rump-state into a proletarian dictatorship.

Camouflaged One-Party State

Like the other East European Communist-dominated states,
the German Democratic Republic (DDR) conceives of itself as a
"People's Democracy" at an intermediary stage of development
toward a genuinely socialist state on the Marxist-Leninist model.
Its rulers believe themselves to be some distance yet from the goal
since not all the means of production have been collectivized and
because remnants of nonworking class elements still exist. But
these elements have become increasingly insignificant. The East
German Communists claim legitimacy for their incomplete proletarian dictatorship by virtue of the numerical and political
dominance of workers and peasants. As the result of the elimination of "class enemies" and "reactionaries" and the pushing forward of collectivization, the Communists came to declare (in
1952) that they were beginning to lay the groundwork for a
"Socialist" order and later (in 1958) that this groundwork had
been completed. These progress reports were made in the context
of a theoretical Leninist timetable, but they serve also as rough
milestones of the institutionalization of totalitarian characteristics within the political system.

According to its official ideologists, the German Democratic
Republic is the first state in German history in which the working
class possesses power. "For the first time in the history of the
German people the talents and capacities of the broad masses can
develop freely. There has developed a powerful increase in the
awareness, initiative, activity and work-discipline of the workers,
farmers and other productive citizens." [1] Such bombastic language

[1] From 1957 DDR law relating to local government, cited in Bundesministerium fuer Gesamtdeutsche Fragen, *Unrecht als System: Teil III,
1954–58* (Bonn, 1958), p. 11.

betrays the debt which the East Germans owe to the ideologists of
Soviet communism, and indeed the Soviet influence has been
overwhelming. Not only did the political officers attached to
Soviet Occupation agencies facilitate the Communist rise to dominance, but the leading figures of the regime received extensive
training in Soviet party schools, and in times of crisis Soviet
advisers have stood by with advice (and sometimes orders), while
Soviet troops and tanks have been available to discourage dis-
senters. If Communist institutions have been imposed with
somewhat less brutality and in more disguised form than in some
of the other "people's democracies," this has been due less to
moderation on the part of the German or Russian Communists
than to the fact that the exposed geographical position of the
Democratic Republic limited the amount of pressure which could
be applied at any one time. This factor has also dictated the continued use of a constitution which formally provides for a multiparty parliamentary system and other democratic devices. But
even the continued existence of "non-Socialist" parties, which in
reality completely follow the Communist lead, does not disguise
the fact that the Democratic Republic is a totalitarian one-party
state. The ruling party calls itself—for reasons which will be
explained shortly—the Socialist Unity party (SED).

The Communists make no bones about the fact that the state
is essentially an instrument to advance the policy of the party.
Assuming as they do that the working class is the legitimate ruler
and that the SED executes policy on its behalf in line with
Marxist sociohistorical laws of political development, the Communists have little difficulty in convincing themselves that "the
decisions of the party constitute the highest scientific generaliza-
tions derivable from political practice." [2] They regard the fact
that their workers' and farmers' state is led by a Marxist-Leninist
party not as convenient fact but as irrevocable law. The SED
party statutes, adopted in 1954, recognize this manifest destiny
by declaring that the party is the force supervising not only all
other social and political organizations, but also dominating the
governmental apparatus of the state. In its instructional material
the party even tells its younger members that in the governmental
machinery "not even a single decision is taken without reference
to the guiding directions worked out by the party." [3] It is because

[2] A 1956 speech of SED Central Committee functionary, cited in Bundesministerium fuer Gesamtdeutsche Fragen, op. cit., p. 19.

[3] A 1956 collection of SED teaching materials, cited in Bundesministerium
fuer Gesamtdeutsche Fragen, op. cit., p. 15.

the SED regards itself as the center of state power and acts accordingly that an analysis of the functioning of the formal political organs of the Democratic Republic must necessarily be preceded by a study of the origins and organization of the party and the means at its disposal to maintain tight control over both society and state machinery.

The relationship between the party and the governmental apparatus is the most vital link in the totalitarian system, and it is not a simple one. The party does not merely make decisions and leave it to nonpolitical bureaucrats in the administration to carry them out, nor does the party apparatus as such try to run everything. Rather, the party exercises power indirectly in a number of ways. It sets the policies which the administration is to carry out, but it sends its *own* members—above all politically reliable and if possible technically qualified—into the administration to supervise their execution. Then, periodically, the work of the functionaries in the government machinery is reviewed and criticized by party organs to make sure that the decisions were really followed through in spirit as well as in letter. Moreover, since it is a totalitarian party which seeks to reshape the entire social structure according to its ideological dictates, the party must also make sure that its "line" is not only adhered to by important power-wielders, but permeates as much as possible into every nook and cranny of the social structure. To this end it manipulates a vast network of subsidiary social and political organizations whose efficiency must also be supervised. These vast responsibilities, as well as the even vaster ones involved in running a planned economy, must be met by a party whose cadre of active militants makes up perhaps as little as 1 per cent of the population.[4] To understand how the party developed sufficient power and discipline for this task and why it chose the pace and means that it did, it will be useful to review the party's postwar evolution and its changing role in what was originally the Soviet Occupation zone.

Post-1945 Politics in the Soviet Zone

The key to an understanding of political developments in East Germany lies in an understanding of the relationship between German Communists and the Kremlin. Paradoxically, while most of the leading German Communists spent the bulk of the war period in Soviet Russia, they were for the first three

[4] Ernst Richert, *Macht ohne Mandat* (Cologne, 1958), p. 148.

postwar years under specific instructions *not* to attempt to copy the Soviet example at home. Although installed in influential positions in the Soviet-occupied zone, the German Communists did not advocate either the radical abolition of private property, or the establishment of a one-party system, or any other innovation introduced during the early years of the Soviet Russian regime. Instead, there was talk of a specifically German road to socialism, which seemed to entail almost no demands for a class dictatorship, a relatively moderate amount of socialization of the economy, and a readiness to cooperate with other political parties. In an effort to attract a mass following, the Communists opened the party doors very wide. Even a knowledge of Marxism was not considered a prerequisite. "Who can expect honest anti-Fascists to be schooled in Marx and Lenin after twelve years of Fascist dictatorship," said the party strong-man, Walter Ulbricht.[5]

In contrast to the Soviets' plans to quickly transform the East European states into "peoples' democracies," they originally seemed to have no such intentions for their zone of Germany. In a sense, the Soviet Union did take seriously the plans for the eventual establishment of an all-German government, as vaguely laid down in the inter-Allied Potsdam agreement. Therefore they wanted in the Soviet zone not a separate, Communist state, but a beachhead from which to influence developments in all of Germany. They were excessively confident that under the conditions of general devastation large masses of Germans would embrace communism if it appeared in a reasonably attractive guise, and they were hopeful of being able to use their influence as an Occupation power and in the Allied Control Council to shape political development in an indirect rather than overt manner.

Hence the political system of the Soviet zone during the years from 1945 to 1947 displayed many characteristics of a democratic parliamentarianism resting on a plural party system. Democratic political institutions were established on the communal level, the newly created Laender were given legislatures based on open elections just as they were in the Western zones, and anti-Nazi politicians of almost all kinds were encouraged to take an active part in politics. Political parties were licensed earlier than in the other zones and given considerable encouragement, funds, and party newspapers. While the Communist party (KPD) was the first to be established in June, 1945, the Social Democrats (SPD), the Liberals (LDP), and the Christian Democrats (CDU) were

---

[5] Walter Ulbricht, *Die Entwicklung des deutschen volksdemokratischen Staates, 1954–1958* (Berlin, 1959), p. 34.

allowed to initiate formal activity shortly thereafter. The leaders
of the new parties were of course subject to screening by Soviet
political officers, but initially this process was little different from
that in the Western zones. The parties were also quite free to
spell out their programs.

Behind the scenes Communists were given key appointments
in the public administration and benefited in many other ways
from their close relationship with the Soviet Occupation power.
The KPD sought to portray itself as the leader of all anti-Fascist
forces. The widespread seizure of large-scale agricultural and industrial property was justified not on anticapitalist but on anti-
Fascist grounds, the argument being that the large landowners
and industrialists had as a class been allies of the Nazi regime.
The other political parties were expected to show support for the
measures pushed through the bloc of anti-Fascist parties, to which
all parties had to belong. At this time some of the more conservative politicians in the bourgeois parties began to leave the political arena, but the majority of non-Communist politicians, particularly in the SPD, agreed that these reforms were on balance a
positive step. Indeed at the beginning, many of the Socialist leaders were so convinced of the need for working-class solidarity
and so impressed by the Communists' new moderate program that
they urged that a fusion of the two parties be considered. But
the Communists rejected this proposal.

However, as the Communists realized that their hope of
emerging dominant from the first Soviet zone elections stood
little chance of realization, they radically changed their position
on the merger proposal. Toward the end of 1945 they called first
for the putting forward of joint Communist-Socialist candidates
in the forthcoming elections and then for a complete merger of
the two parties. Among Western zone Socialists, where Kurt Schumacher had already become dominant, this proposal was sharply
rejected, but in Berlin and particularly in the outlying areas of
the Soviet zone Socialist functionaries led by Otto Grotewohl,
chairman of the Socialist Central Committee in Berlin, were sym-
pathetic. In the prolonged intraparty struggle which ensued, the
antimerger Socialists succeeded in winning the overwhelming
support (12.4 per cent for merger, 82 per cent against) of party
members in West Berlin, and it became evident that even if they
forced a party merger in their zone, the Soviets could do so only
at the cost of increasing the solidarity and anti-Communist determination of the bulk of the Socialists in West Berlin and the
Western zones. After some hesitation, it was nevertheless decided

to go ahead, and in April, 1946, the pro-merger Socialists under Grotewohl merged with the Communists to form the new *Sozialistische Einheitspartei Deutschlands* (SED), under the joint party chairmanship of Grotewohl and the chairman of the KPD, Wilhelm Pieck.[6]

This step had many far-reaching consequences besides the one intended of providing a Communist-led party with mass backing and eliminating competition with another working-class party. It was the first important step toward the political division of Germany, for after the spring of 1946 the SPD could no longer operate as a recognized party in the Soviet zone, while the SED could not operate as such in the Western zones since the Western occupying powers refused to license it there. (There the Communists continued to operate independently under their KPD label until they were declared illegal in 1956.) Thus began the tendency toward a development of separate party systems for East and West.

Although operating in the Soviet zone alone, the SED, as a result of the merger and the special encouragement given to party joiners in the Soviet zone, became a real mass party whose membership (1.8 million in May, 1947) was not only far greater than that of all other Soviet zone parties, but larger than the combined membership of all parties operating in the Western zones. Initially the membership consisted about equally of former KPD and SPD adherents, and the party organization was built up on a principle of parity, with all organs presided over by two joint chairmen representing the two groups. It only gradually became apparent that tried-and-true Communists were being steered into the really important positions in the party as well as in the administrative apparatus.

The SED soon went all-out to woo the voters. During the 1946 election campaign, it competed with the CDU for the votes of Christians by calling for political partnership between Marxists and Christians, appealed to nationalist sentiment by asserting that it did not regard the Oder-Neisse border as final, and even welcomed the support of former nominal Nazis and fellow travellers by promising to assure them equal, unprejudiced treatment.[7] But although competing with only two much weaker and less well organized middle-class parties, the SED managed to win only 47.5 per cent of the votes against

[6] Carola Stern, *Portraet einer Bolschewistischen Partei* (Cologne, 1957), Chap. 1.

[7] Ulbricht, *op. cit.*, p. 74.

a combined total of 49.1 per cent for the CDU and LDP. Instead of achieving at least the appearance of an overwhelming democratic legitimation, the SED found itself tied to a parliamentary setting where the resistance of other parties could be broken only by means of pressure.

Nevertheless, outright force or frankly totalitarian instruments of persuasion were minimized as long as the Soviets still hoped to continue to influence events in the Western zones. Throughout 1947 the other Soviet zone parties continued to retain a considerable outward freedom, but were kept under control through their membership in the anti-Fascist bloc. There increasingly the CDU and LPD were placed under pressure to maintain unity by underwriting the SED's attacks on the Marshall Plan, the zonal merger of the Western zones, and their own Western party colleagues. As the anti-Fascist bloc was gradually transformed into an anti-Western caucus, those party leaders who would not play the Communists' game, like Jacob Kaiser and Ernest Lemmer in the CDU, were deposed from their party positions by the Soviet military government to be replaced by more pliable figures.

These developments at the beginning of 1948 quickly led to far-reaching changes in regard to the outward appearance of the SED, the character of the party system, and the structure of Soviet zone politics in general. The SED gave up its attempt to appear as a popular democratic mass party and adopted a rigidly Stalinist policy and different organizational forms. The emergence of the "new" SED meant that all other parties and social organizations, as well as the apparatus of the state, gradually became completely subsidiary organizations.

The SED from 1948

Starting in 1948 the SED quickly transformed itself, as well as the political structure of the Soviet zone, along lines which now closely resembled Communist practice elsewhere. It de-emphasized its attempt to become a mass party, and sought instead to transform itself into a highly disciplined, efficient mechanism, responding easily to direction from above and capable of controlling both state and economy. Many party members who had joined out of opportunism but lacked the qualities of "good Communists" were purged. New members were accepted only after undergoing prolonged periods of candidacy. The need to transform the SED into a "cadre party" was underscored by the adoption, starting with the 1949-1950 Two-Year Plan, of the principle of the fully planned economy. The consolidation and development of a vast economic bureaucracy which would coordinate and administer the planning mechanism called for large numbers of reliable, trained administrators, which only the SED could produce. Emphasis on ideological purity was accentuated. Those Communists who had earlier advocated a distinctly German road to socialism were forced to recant their heretical views, while Ulbricht and other Soviet-trained leaders emphasized the need for unhesitating acceptance of orthodox Leninist-Stalinist doctrine. The Soviet military administration also displayed its fear of "Western" ideas by decreeing in 1949 that all Germans (even long-time Communists) who had spent wartime exile in any Western country were to be removed from positions of responsibility in the party and the administration.[8]

At the same time, the SED established its position as the fountainhead of all political truth. In 1950, in discussing the resolutions of the SED party conference for the benefit of civil servants, Ulbricht dealt with the suggestion that these were after all *only* the resolutions of a party. "That is true. But it happens to be the conference of a party which is the spearhead of the German people, the only party which follows a progressive scientific doctrine. . . . Its resolutions constitute a document of the highest significance . . . with which all democratic forces must concern themselves." [9] And well they might, for no leaders of parties, trade unions, or women's organizations could afford to find themselves taking positions differing from those of the SED. All such groups were now united in a cover organization called the "National Front," where the policy of the SED was imposed on the rest. In 1949 free competitive elections ceased to be held, and instead the National Front set up unified lists which were submitted to the voters without an alternative choice. All the parties, as well as other kinds of organizations, were allotted specific quotas within the single list, with the SED's own candidates and SED members running on trade union and other "mass organization" tickets maintaining numerical preponderance. The two middle-class parties, CDU and LDP, though no longer able to run independent candidates and deprived of most of their original leaders, were distrusted by the regime as channels through which dissatisfaction might

---

[8] Stern, *op. cit.*, pp. 118, 127.
[9] Ulbricht, *op. cit.*, p. 212.

express itself. Their role was neutralized by the licensing of
two additional middle-class parties, the National Democratic
party (NDPD) and the German Peasants' party (DBD), whose
functionaries were tested pro-Communists, and which proceeded
to rival the two older parties in their efforts to "guide" the
nonworking-class, non-Socialist part of the electorate. In addition, the liquidation of organizations perpetuating loyalties no
longer convenient to the regime was brought about. Thus the
Victims of Nazi Injustice was ordered disbanded because the
fraternization of its Communist and non-Communist members
was no longer considered desirable. Similarly, neutralist groups
which the SED had previously encouraged in the hope of using
them to win sympathy in the Western zones were now denounced as vehicles of dangerous, disguised, "pro-imperialist"
doctrines.[10]

The most difficult testing period for the SED regime came
during the transition from the Stalin to the post-Stalin eras.
Throughout 1951 to 1952 the SED had to withstand very great
internal and external pressures. Internally, it was subject to
factional struggles in the top leadership and affected by the
various waves of purges which in other East European states
were decimating the old line Communist leadership. However
Walter Ulbricht's strong hand prevailed and the East German
Communists did not tear themselves apart as badly as their
equivalents in Poland and Hungary. At the same time, the SED
was feeling the tremendous resistance of the bulk of the population to the intensive controls through which the regime sought
to increase production, to contain living standards at their
low level, and to punish politically unreliable middle-class
elements. A consequence of this tough policy was the enormous
increase in the number of East Germans fleeing to the West
during the first part of 1953. In response to the uncertainty
caused by Stalin's death, the regime attempted to demonstrate
its control of the situation by depriving certain population
groups of ration cards while demanding a 10 per cent increase
in the work norms of industrial workers. These measures caused
great bitterness among wide sections of the population, and
after several weeks the leadership recognized that it had gone
too far. In early June SED spokesmen, including the minister-
president, Otto Grotewohl, declared that the government had
made errors, and promised remedial action.

However the anger, particularly of the workers, broke into

[10] *Ibid.*, pp. 213–15.

the open before the regime could make the necessary concessions. On June 16 construction workers in East Berlin launched spontaneous strikes against the norm increases, and the movement spread like wildfire throughout the rest of the city. Banners calling for a general strike and the release of political prisoners were raised among the demonstrators. On the following day, news of the demonstrations having been spread by radio stations in West Berlin, demonstrations began in most of the other East German cities. Events quickly got beyond the control of local police authorities as the crowds attacked and destroyed SED offices, set fire to official buildings, and stormed the jails and released political prisoners. The SED leadership, finding that its appeals for calm brought no response, was forced to call in Soviet tanks and troops to quell the riots. A state of emergency was declared in most areas and armed troops and police fired on the crowds, causing numerous deaths and casualties before it was possible to disperse them. Giving proof, as they did, of the desperate hostility of large sections of the East German population, while also setting the first example of a large-scale uprising in a Communist-controlled country, the events of June 17, 1953, won world-wide attention.[11] However, as in the subsequent Hungarian uprising, the West could give little effective aid, and order was restored.

Since 1953 the policy of the SED has been marked by short-term fluctuations in which periods of "liberalization" have alternated with stages of "toughness." Shortly after the uprising, the SED, in line with policies then being implemented in the Soviet Union, initiated reform programs which included the promise of an increased emphasis on consumer goods and a greater amount of freedom of expression to trade unions and other groups. Promises to increase the significance of the various legislative organs were among the many not implemented before a new change of course, in 1954, caused the regime to retract or modify many of the concessions it had earlier offered. In 1955, after Khrushchev's denunciation of Stalinist excesses before the Twentieth Soviet Party Congress, the SED once again adjusted to the more relaxed and liberal policies which quickly became the vogue throughout the Eastern bloc. It promised to improve living standards, ordered reforms in the administration, and for a time also allowed great leeway in internal ideological discussions. Encouraged by developments in Poland, young East German Communist intellectuals called for a radical revision of

[11] Stephan Brandt, *The East German Uprising* (New York, 1955).

party goals, which centered on the granting of greater freedom to all sectors of the population, as well as a thorough going reorganization of the party and its leadership. In 1956, however, the Hungarian uprising and the revulsion toward liberalization which it caused among top-level Communist leaders allowed the regime to tighten the reins once more, and to discourage revisionism within its ranks by sentencing its more provocative advocates to long terms in the penitentiary.[12]

SED Organizational Structure

Since becoming a "new type" cadre party in 1949, the SED has faithfully followed the organizational pattern of the Soviet Communist party. Party statutes notwithstanding, power and policy control is highly centralized in the Political Bureau, whose ten to fifteen members include the leaders of the party apparatus, the top-level figures in the government, the heads of the most important economic and security agencies, and heads of the mass organizations. As in the Soviet Union, the make-up of the Politburo frequently undergoes changes which reflect the changing power status of differing party cliques. During the period from 1947 to 1960, only five men consistently, or almost consistently, retained membership.[13] Two of these were ex-Social Democrats who held important "show" positions: Otto Grotewohl, the minister-president of the DDR, and Friedrich Ebert, the son of the first president of the Weimar Republic, who is mayor of East Berlin. The three others were all tried Communists who spent their wartime exile in the Soviet Union. Wilhelm Pieck, a cofounder of the KPD in 1918 and later Secretary of the Comintern, was a tried Stalinist who served in top-level prestige positions as cochairman of the SED and, until his death in 1960, president of the DDR. The other two were Walter Ulbricht, the most powerful man in party and regime, and one of his loyal adjutants, Herman Matern, who had in the past helped to destroy Ulbricht's intraparty rivals. Of the other Politburo members in recent years, only one was a premerger member of the SPD, and all were ardent Ulbricht supporters. Men like Fred Oelssner, Heinrich Rau, Karl Schirdewan, and Willi Stoph backed Ulbricht through all his twists and turns and were

[12] Melvin Croan and Carl J. Friedrich, "The East German Regime and Soviet Policy in Germany," *JP,* XX (1958), 44–63.

[13] For a full list of members up to 1957, see Stern, *op. cit.,* p. 326.

rewarded for their loyalty as well as their toughness with positions of power.

In theory, the dozen or so powerful members of the Politburo, augmented by a small number of colleagues in the party Secretariat and other key positions, implement policy on behalf of the approximately one and a half million members of the SED. But in practice, the ability of rank-and-file members to call their leaders to account is virtually nil. Organized in some fifty thousand local party organizations, the SED membership is limited by an institutional setting which encourages the carrying out of instructions from top-level party organs but makes effective criticism from the bottom up almost impossible. Though the SED strives to assert its popular legitimation by placing top constitutional importance on the decisions of the party convention, this body assembles only for show purposes every four years. The delegates are usually selected so that the convention resembles a cross section of the working masses, which the SED likes to think it represents. Workers and farm hands who have built up good production records are rewarded with delegate positions so that they can listen to the longwinded reports and exhortations of the party leaders. In contrast, for instance, to the pre-1933 Communist congresses where important issues of doctrine were often bitterly fought out, the SED party conventions are very mild affairs. Resolutions and policy statements submitted by the Politburo and the Secretariat are never criticized and always accepted unanimously.

Since the convention cannot even attempt to determine policy, it elects a smaller group of members to do so. This is the Central Committee, normally made up of some 100 to 150 members, and it is in its name that the policy-making apparatus of the SED actually functions. In theory it does this with the assistance of two important advisory bodies; on the one hand, the Politburo, which is authorized to conduct the work of the Central Committee between plenary sessions, and on the other hand, the Secretariat of the Central Committee, which maintains the bureaucratic apparatus through which the party exercises its manifold controls over all aspects of the party structure, the public administration, and society at large. In practice, however, these two organs do not advise the Central Committee, but prepare decisions which the Central Committee normally accepts and publicizes as official policy. In contrast with the party conference, Central Committee meetings are often the scene of fairly lively discussion, but usually over the means of implementing policy rather than over its merits. It also frequently happens that policies are quietly implemented by party functionaries months, and even years, before they are publicly announced as official by the Central Committee. Thus, in effect, the decisions of the Central Committee formalize acceptance of policies which members of the Politburo believe to be desirable and which party functionaries seem to think workable.

However, since the very nature of the totalitarian party lays emphasis on its ability to enforce decisions, the real core of SED power lies only in part in its decision-making organs; equally crucial are the organs that supervise policy execution. It is here that the Secretariat under the party's First Secretary, Walter Ulbricht, plays a key role. The Secretariat is the hub of the party's vast control mechanism, the instrument through which it supervises its own organization, the functioning of governmental organs, and the work of satellite groups. Its work is carried out under the direction of Ulbricht and six other secretaries, several of whom are simultaneously members of the Politburo. Each secretary supervises a number of Secretariat sections, which are in turn composed of anywhere from a dozen to several hundred indoctrinated and trained specialists. About half of the Secretariat sections parallel the formal governmental organs. Thus the Transport and Communications Section has the task of providing suggestions for, and control over, the Transportation and Post ministries. Similarly, the Agriculture Section watches the various state and mass organizations which execute policy in the agriculture sector. Other sections concern themselves with intraparty organization and the channelling of party resources. Thus the Top-Level Organs Section coordinates the work of lower-level party committees, gathers information about the important mass organizations, and acts as a kind of personnel office in selecting and assigning top-level party cadre to their proper jobs. Finally there are sections dealing with the problems of propaganda, agitation, science, and culture. The Press-Radio-Agitation Section guides the work of official party organs like *Neues Deutschland,* keeps a close eye on the rest of the East German press, and, in general, seeks to manipulate all mass communication media in line with party policy. The sections dealing with cultural, communications, and education problems are particularly important, in that here much of the work is done directly by the party, rather than indirectly through the state mechanism. Altogether the Secretariat comprises some twenty-five such sections with a total staff of about one thousand experts. The Central Secretariat, however, constitutes only part of the party bureaucracy. The general functions which it performs are duplicated in some sixteen regional secretariats, each of which also employs several hundred full-time functionaries, and on the county levels where secretariats normally include several dozen local workers. It is through this vast bureaucracy that the party carries out the manifold functions which it must fulfill in order to control all aspects of political, economic, and social activity.[14]

Control and Penetration: The Transmission Belt

Since the SED, as a genuinely totalitarian party, seeks not merely unchallenged political control but also the transformation of all East German society into its own ideological image, it requires a vast net of auxiliary organizations with which to penetrate all population groups. While the bulk of its own leaders man the crucial control towers, it relies largely on auxiliary organizations to function as transmission belts through which its slogans and exhortations are hammered mercilessly into the consciousness of East Germans. These are the various mass organizations, some led directly by SED functionaries, others by reliable fellow travelers. They include the organizational remnants of the old non-Socialist parties, the huge trade-union federation, the Democratic Federation of German Women, the Free German Youth, the German-Soviet Friendship Society, and sundry other groups. The vast majority of the East German population has been cajoled into membership of at least one of these organizations, and thus receives official propaganda specially filtered for its consumption. The leading mass organizations are united in the National Front which coordinates their activities. Each group, as well as the SED, sends four delegates to the National Front executive council, where decisions are made without dissent. "This means . . . that all questions put up for discussion and decision-making are considered until such time as a unanimous decision can be made," [15] that is to say, until the SED line is accepted without reservation.

One of the more public functions of the National Front consists in the setting up of the single candidate list for the People's Chamber and other "legislative" bodies (see below,

---

[14] Ibid., pp. 271–78.

[15] Deutsches Institut fuer Zeitgeschichte, Jahrbuch der Deutschen Demokratischen Republik, 1959 (Berlin, 1959), p. 59.

p. 186). But primarily it is a propaganda organ, as when the
National Council of the National Front meets to dedicate the
people to such things as the speeding-up of the economic plan
schedule, the campaign against West German nuclear armament,
or "great patriotic efforts on behalf of German unification."
Unlike the SED, the National Front is a very loosely organized
structure, without direct membership or statutes. Below the
national level, the National Front offices maintain informal but
tight liaison with the respective SED offices. The leading
officers of local National Front councils are in almost all cases
SED members, and effective control lies with the local SED
first secretary. But the National Front's most important function
lies at the lowest level, that of the apartment house or block.
There the NF claims to have some 350,000 voluntary, part-
time workers who fulfill important communal functions such as
the distribution of ration cards (until 1958), the gathering of
complaints about the functioning of administrative organs, and
the collection of pledges of one sort or another. The volunteers
thus serve not only as the local distribution point for the
"transmission belt," but also as a safety valve through which
the authorities hear of routine complaints. Some observers regard
the National Front block-warden system as a vast network of
neighborhood spies, but others disagree. "It displays aspects of
real Republicanism, in the original sense of the word—and on
a level where the individual doesn't even regard his task as
'political.' Observations lead to the conclusion that in allowing
people to carry out some sort of honorary community tasks,
however unimportant, the state in a certain sense wins them over
to its side." [16]

Individually, the mass organizations unified in the National
front fulfill more specialized functions. The most important
of these, the Free German Trade Union Federation with its
more than five million members, has been dominated by the
Communists since its founding in 1945, and its leader is
usually a member of the SED Politburo. According to *Neues
Deutschland,* the trade unions and the works councils which are
elected in the various factories are the "links in the chain
which the party must activate in order to raise the workers'
class consciousness, work morale and militancy to the highest
possible pitch." [17] The local union elections are not as rigged
as the general elections, and the SED Communists must make

[16] Richert, *op. cit.,* p. 120
[17] Stern, *op. cit.,* p. 258.

great efforts in order to get trusted functionaries elected to the key works council offices. The second largest mass organization, the Free German Youth, with some three million members, has vast responsibilities in indoctrinating and activating youth, particularly teen-agers, on behalf of the party program, while the women's organization carries out a similar task with its membership. The function of the mass organizations is seen most clearly in the case of the middle-class parties. Originally (at least in the case of the CDU and LDP) set up to articulate middle-class demands on the state, they now function solely to soften up the remaining middle-class elements to conform to the demands of the state. Thus during the year 1958, the parties were set the task of persuading artisans and peasants to join collectives and small businessmen to accept state partnership voluntarily. The DDR's 1959 *Yearbook* credits the CDU and LDP with having brought, respectively, 411 and 658 artisans to join collectives, and 397 and 433 entrepreneurs to accept state partnership. The NDPD was praised for similar achievements, while the DBD, the farmer's party, was recognized for persuading 13,000 of its members to join agricultural collectives in the course of 1958 (some two years before the final drive in this sector was undertaken).[18] Thus there is competition among political groups in East Germany, but only in the sense that there is competition among different Community Fund solicitation teams.

The Organs of Security and Legality

Just as it would be wrong to conceive of the DDR as a state based merely on repression, so it would be inadequate to describe it as a police state. The various police components, of course, play an indispensable role in buttressing the regime's stability, but their role is different from what it typically is in an unpopular Western dictatorship. This is especially true in regard to many aspects of social and political behavior where the line between conduct which is undesirable and that which is criminal constantly shifts, as legal decisions adapt to changing ideological lines and tactical situations. The complex security apparatus is thus as much charged with detecting situations which might culminate in actions that the state apparatus considers undesirable, as it is with apprehending Western agents

[18] Deutsches Institut fuer Zeitgeschichte, *op. cit.*, p. 62.

or East German citizens who are about to make illegal crossings of the zonal borders.

The most apparent component of the East German police apparatus is the People's Police, a uniformed, well armed, centrally directed force which exercises the more obvious control functions, such as the protection of strategic factories, the guarding of the zonal borders, and the dispersing of unruly crowds. It is the instrument of repression best known to the population, but although it too tries to maintain a network of informants, the bulk of the People's Police is made up of relatively apolitical youths serving in areas where they are not very familiar with the local population. A more important political police organ, particularly as regards the ferreting out of economic "criminals" and "saboteurs," comprises the civilian members of the Central Commission for State Control. They were in charge of gathering material for the frequent "show" trials through which the regime sought to reduce resistance to its various socialization and collectivization measures. But most important of all is the police apparatus of the Ministry for State Security. It is this force, with some 7,000 full-time agents and a network of an estimated 150,000 informants, which forms the core of East German political police and counterintelligence activities. It carries the responsibility for obstructing the development of groups that are hostile to the state, and of detecting and frustrating the infiltration attempts of Western agents. As the Russians have gradually pulled out, it is this body which has taken over many of the functions of the Soviet secret police, and has in the process copied many of the repressive and terror practices through which suspects are "softened up." However, unlike its Soviet equivalent, the Security police has never become a powerful force unto itself, but has remained subject to over-all party direction and closely linked to the official judicial administration.

In determining what kinds of action should be made liable to criminal prosecution, the police work closely with the public prosecutors, 99 per cent of whom are members of the SED. The more the regime seeks to mold opinion, the more chance there is that seemingly private acts, such as divorce, libel, and assault cases, might carry political overtones. As Kirchheimer has written, "in the eyes of the rulers, even the least significant and most ludicrous or banal run-in necessarily assumes a more sinister complexion. In every aimless individual reaction the exponents of governmental power are bound to look for traces of a repetitive, rebellious design." [19] In cases where it decides to intervene the prosecution can operate with such vague, general concepts as diversion, sabotage, and boycott. The regime is especially suspicious, of course, of any contact with persons in West Germany. Its legal commentators have made clear that persons establishing unauthorized contact with people in the West, even if they are of a purely private nature and are unrelated to any political activity, may be punished by prison terms of as much as three years. The catch-all boycott provisions may be applied against anybody who has had any contact with an illegal border-crosser. They have even been applied against a lady fortuneteller whose readings were said to have inspired her customers to leave the DDR.[20]

Assurance that the courts actually will hand down decisions which the police authorities desire requires close contact between prosecutors and judges and virtual negation of the concept of judicial independence. The latter is implicit in the Leninist view of law as merely an instrument of class rule, while judicial acquiescence is assured by the character of the judiciary and the ground rules of the judicial system. East German judges are predominantly men installed since 1945, and already in 1953 85 per cent of them were SED members. Judicial behavior is tightly supervised by the Ministry of Justice, and on the local level each court has a party unit. Frequently the court's clerks and administrative officers enjoy higher rank than the judges themselves, so that their influence within the party cell may be correspondingly greater when weak points in individual judges' decisions are discussed by the group.

The capstone of the East German court system is the High Court, which, staffed by the staunchest Communist jurists, transmits to the lower courts the directives of the Ministry of Justice, the attorney general, and other administrative agencies in the judicial area. The High Court sits as a court of original jurisdiction on whichever cases the attorney general thinks of sufficient political significance to submit to it. Decisions in such cases are clear signals to the lower judges. The Court also acts as an appellate tribunal for decisions in the district courts, but in addition the DDR, building on Soviet and Nazi practice, has introduced the institution of the extraordinary appeal. This opens a special route for reversing final court opinions, but

[19] Otto Kirchheimer, "The Administration of Justice and the Concept of Legality in East Germany," *Yale Law Journal*, LXVIII (1959), 719.
[20] *Ibid.*, p. 740.

one open only to the state. Under it, the attorney general may within one year bring any final judgment by a lower court or by a three-judge division of the High Court itself for review in a High Court plenary session. Invariably the High Court then follows the prosecutor's policy directives.

Bibliography

Brandt, Stephan, *The East Germany Uprising* (New York, 1955).

Croan, Melvin, and Friedrich, Carl J., "The East German Regime and Soviet Policy in Germany," *JP*, XX (1958), 44–63.

Doernberg, Stephan, "Die Gruendung der Sozialistischen Einheitspartei Deutschlands und Ihre Geschichtliche Bedeutung," *Zeitschrift fuer Geschichtswissenschaft*," IV (1956), 213–29.

Kirchheimer, Otto, "The Administration of Justice and the Concept of Legality in East Germany," *Yale Law Journal*, LXVIII (1959), 705–59.

Leonhard, Wolfgang, *Child of the Revolution* (Chicago, 1958).

Nettl, John P. *The Eastern Zone and Soviet Policy in Germany, 1945–50* (New York, 1951).

Richert, Ernst, *Macht ohne Mandat* (Cologne, 1958).

Schultz, Joachim, *Der Funktionaer in der Einheitspartei* (Cologne, 1957).

Sherman, George, "The Russian and the East German Party," *St. Antony's Papers*, No. 1 (1956), pp. 85–124.

Stern, Carola, *Portraet einer Bolschewistischen Partei* (Cologne, 1957).

Ulbricht, Walter, *Die Entwicklung des deutschen volksdemokratischen Staates, 1945–1958* (Berlin, 1959).

10 - Government and Administration

The Constitution

From what has been said in the foregoing chapter it is evident that the German Democratic Republic does not have a constitution in the Western sense, that is, one whose provisions regulate relations among the various power-holders in the political system. The SED cannot and does not recognize any power in the state other than itself, and its Leninist ideology would in any case prevent it from acknowledging the sanctity of any legalist framework. Nevertheless, like other Communist states, the DDR does have a quite elaborate Constitution, which among other

things guarantees a variety of civil rights, delineates the responsibilities of the various governmental organs and establishes the
privileges of the churches. Moreover the Constitution goes further
than other East European constitutions in providing, for instance,
for a system of proportional representation, which clearly could
only make sense in a plural party system with alternative choices
open to the voter. In fact, the entire document is basically cut to
the model of a parliamentary, multiparty system, and its most
influential model is not the Soviet Constitution of 1936, but the
Weimar Constitution of 1919, to which in many parts it bears a
much closer resemblance than does the West German Basic Law.

The explanation for the curious character of the Constitution
is that it was drafted not for the Democratic Republic as it has
developed during the 1950's, but during a period (1946 to 1947)
when the SED was still proceeding on the assumption that it
could come to power within the framework of an all-German
parliamentary system. At that time the Soviets were still taking
pains to keep the formal governmental structure in their zone
much like that in other parts of Germany. In addition to
relatively free parties, there were Laender (five) and Land
governments. While accepting many pre-Hitler institutions, the
SED Constitution-drafters did make some important changes.
They refused to accept the principle of separation of powers
and instead concentrated power in the legislative organ. They
also provided for the gradual reshaping of the traditional
German civil service and judiciary, and they gave the state
extra powers to socialize property. But private property was
definitely protected, could only be "abridged . . . on the basis
of laws . . . and against adequate compensation" (Art. 23),
small and medium-sized farmers were guaranteed the right to own
land privately (Art. 24), and the state was even enjoined "to
support farmers, artisans and business men in the development
of private initiative" (Art. 20). Other civil rights were guaranteed
with still greater forthrightness. Thus all citizens were guaranteed
the right to the free and public expression of their opinions
(Art. 9), were assured an equal and undiscriminatory claim to
education (Art. 35), and the trade unions' right to strike was
specifically sanctioned (Art. 14). Indeed some of the guarantees
given voluntary groups, such as the assurance that the churches
had the right to give religious instruction in public schools
through teachers of their own choosing, exceeds similar guarantees
in many liberal democratic constitutions in the West (for example,
the American).

The Constitution containing these guarantees was adopted in October, 1949, a month after the creation of the Federal Republic. At that time the Communists were still saying that they were ready to combine with the West Germans in a parliamentary regime, and the nature of the Constitution served to buttress this propaganda line. In actual practice, however, the Constitution was outdated before it was ever adopted. For in May, 1949, at the time of the elections to the People's Council which adopted the Constitution, the principle of a multiparty system had already been abandoned, and the uniform list system introduced. Many of the other principles of the Constitution, pertaining both to civil and political rights and the structure of the governmental organs, were also soon abandoned. The regime flouted its Constitution by openly refusing higher education to most children of middle-class parents, pressuring farmers to give up their property without even bothering to pass a coercive law, while the privileges of the churches were increasingly disregarded.

Many inconvenient governmental institutions were done away with even though they were provided for in the Constitution. Thus the Laender together with the Land diets were abolished by ordinary law in 1952, and for six years no Laender existed even though the Constitution provided for them. Finally in 1958, when it was decided also to abolish the upper chamber of the national legislature, the long overdue amendments were enacted. However, constitutional amendments (which technically are enacted by the legislature in much the same way as simple laws are) have been enacted with regard to only a few of the provisions where practice has clearly deviated from what the Constitution requires. Up to the end of 1960 only three amendments had been passed in over eleven years. The first, in 1955, provided the constitutional basis for the formal establishment of the East German armed forces; the second, in 1958, abolished the Laender and the upper house of the national legislature; the third, in 1960, replaced the president of the Republic by the State Council. Only in the last instance did the timing of the actual institutional change coincide with the constitutional change, and here both the person of Ulbricht and a position relevant to international relations were directly involved. In hosts of other instances the government has passed laws and decrees clearly in conflict with constitutional provisions, without the question of reconcilability ever being raised.

Legislative Organs

If the members of the East German assembly, the People's Chamber (*Volkskammer*), actually possessed the powers assigned to them by the Constitution, they would be among the most powerful parliamentarians in the world. They would possess great importance as members of the highest organ of the Republic and great confidence, because the Constitution says that they are "subject only to their conscience and may not be bound by instructions" (Art. 51). Their power would be evident from the fact that all the highest officers of both the executive and judiciary agencies would owe their office to election by the People's Chamber. The president of the Republic and the second chamber (since abolished) would be elected by it, while it would have sole voice in the election of members of the Supreme Court, as well as in the selection of the attorney general. The minister-president and his cabinet colleagues would only hold office subject to its approval and would have to follow policy outlines as laid down by the Chamber. All in all, judging from the Constitution, the DDR would be an extreme example of "assembly government," the type of parliamentary government in which the legislature holds the lion's share of power.

Needless to say, practice could hardly be more remote from legal letter. The People's Chamber is in fact an institution that operates mainly for ritualistic purposes, fulfilling its assigned duties with apparent enthusiasm but without conflicting discussion. It usually meets about eight times annually in order to ratify the nominations and to pass the bills which Communist leaders present to it. However, the Chamber and its members are by no means simple figureheads. They do fulfill fairly important functions within the political system as a whole, even if these are not the functions described in the Constitution. The Chamber does have a representative character, not for the purpose of real decision-making, but for the purpose of constituting itself as a reasonably accurate microcosm of a Communist society. This microcosm plays a symbolic role in the manner of certain institutions in constitutional regimes (for example, the British monarchy), and its assent to measures proposed by the executive is understood within such a framework. Individually, the members of this microcosm are expected to do their part to see that the portions of the macrocosm (society) which they represent follow the pattern of their "representatives." In this capacity, members of legislative bodies on the national, regional, and local level play an important role as auxiliary organs to the governmental and party executive in helping to gain popular acceptance of policies and programs.[1]

The emphasis on creating a People's Chamber which is widely representative can be seen in the nomination and electoral procedure. The chief role in the nomination process lies with the secretariats of the SED, the other "parties," and the mass organizations, which nominate candidates for the single joint list which is then run under the name of the National Front. The SED Secretariat selects the candidates for the SED part of the list, but indirectly it also has veto power over the nominations of the other organizations. In 1958 the quotas for the People's Chamber list called for one hundred SED representatives, forty-five each for the four non-Socialist "parties" and the Free Trade Union Federation, twenty-five each for the youth and women's organizations, fifteen for a farmers' organization, and ten for a group representing cultural and intellectual workers.[2] When the National Front has approved the nominations, the candidates are forced to undertake the rigorous task of making themselves known to their constituents. They must attend a myriad of meetings in factories, neighborhoods, and clubs. It is claimed that in 1954 candidates for elective office on the local as well as national level held almost a half million such meetings, attended by about fifteen million citizens. At one of these meetings the National Front candidate is then officially endorsed. Subsequently the entire list is approved in the elections, in which, characteristically, there is an overwhelming turnout (1958: 98.9 per cent of those eligible) and a virtually unanimous endorsement of the list candidates (1958: 99.87 per cent "yes" vote).[3]

This careful selection process results in the desired profile of the legislative body. It is almost a photographic image of the social structure of the East German population as seen through Communist lenses. According to official statements, the social structure is characterized by a working-class predominance, with workers and employees (the categories are defined very broadly) making up 78 per cent of the population. In the People's Chamber delegates of working-class or employee background

---

[1] Ernst Richert, *Macht ohne Mandat* (Cologne, 1958), p. 106.

[2] Deutsches Institut fuer Zeitgeschichte, *Jahrbuch der Deutschen Demokratischen Republik, 1959* (Berlin, 1959), p. 31.

[3] *Ibid.*, p 29.

made up 74 per cent after the 1958 elections; smaller social groups were represented proportionately. The make-up of the legislature also changed as a result of the increasing socialization of the means of production. Whereas private farmers and artisans had played a significant role earlier, by 1958 seventy members of agricultural and artisan collectives predominated over only five remaining representatives of private farmers and artisans.[4]

In its capacity as legislator, the People's Chamber's role has been limited mainly to giving passive approval to bills brought in from the outside, although frequently it is not even called upon to do that. When choosing between introducing new rules as laws via the legislative route, or simply introducing them as administrative ordinances, the East German executive much prefers the latter. Despite the enormous changes brought about in all aspects of East German life, the People's Chamber has in some years passed as few as ten new laws, and the over-all average is not much higher. During the six months of June through December, 1953, when radical changes in policy caused extensive changes in highly important rules, the People's Chamber passed only two laws, and these concerned themselves with hunting regulations and the protection of rare and useful plants.[5] In important areas like taxation there have been hundreds of administrative rule changes for every change officially imbedded in legislation. Since 1958 the decree-issuing power of the Council of Ministers and the Council of State has become so enlarged that rule changes via the People's Chamber have become even rarer.

Of the bills that are considered in the legislature, almost all originate with the executive, since neither the People's Chamber nor any of its parties—not even the SED—utilize their constitutional power to introduce bills. An apparently similar executive dominance in the initiation of legislation occurs also in some Western countries (Britain, for example), but the differences become evident when the subsequent discussion, criticism, and final vote are examined. In the People's Chamber about half the bills considered are passed without any discussion at all, and all are accepted by unanimous vote.[6] Charges that this reduces the legislative process to a farce would be answered with the argument that the unanimity of the legislature is

[4] *Ibid.*, p. 30.
[5] Richert, *op. cit.*, p. 31.
[6] *Loc. cit.*

merely proof of the constructive cooperation of all members of the National Front.

The most important function of the members of the legislature consists not of representing the people to the state, but of representing the state to the people. As one German writer put it: "In the deputy, the people have right at their front door a 'hunk of state' with whom they can talk . . . and who has official authority to extend help in case of need." [7] It is the deputy's task to make the vast and impersonal apparatus of the state seem less hostile and less remote. Even though many do not actually live in the districts they represent, they are expected to spend much of their time keeping office hours, speaking to the population on their work in the legislature, and taking up requests and grievances. At the same time they are expected to explain and popularize the laws and policies of the government, and to engender the population's acceptance or at least acquiescence. The SED's Central Committee has at various times emphasized the role of the legislature as a link between state and people, and the candidates are chosen with this in mind. As in America, great emphasis is placed on the legislator's ability to develop close links at the grass roots, and in practice it is his role as the link to his particular district which is most important. Other requirements, such as expertise in a particular area of legislative work, are much less important. Thus the Judiciary Committee of the People's Chamber has at times had as few as two lawyers among its members, a fact which well illustrates the negligible legislative role of the Chamber and its committees.

The regime's anxiety to maintain contact with the people, both for ideological reasons and in order to forestall possible trouble, can be seen from the very large number of persons holding some sort of elected position on the national, district, and local levels. It has been estimated that there are no less than 100,000 elected representatives, or about one for every hundred adult citizens. The local legislative organs have little opportunity to make policy, but they and the local councils have an important function as auxiliary organs for the executive, helping to plan and coordinate the manifold state activities on the local level. They play a particularly important role in helping to realize the objectives of the economic plans, especially since, starting in the late fifties, there has been an increasing attempt to

[7] *Ibid.*, p. 103

avoid overcentralization of the administration. The regional and local councils maintain auxiliary commissions, and these in turn have at their side teams of local citizens who serve as advisers on the solution of limited local problems. Thus the rigid bureaucracy of full-time state and party functionaries is supplemented and to an extent checked by a large army of part-time volunteers.

The local council machinery and the local mass organizations in theory compete with each other to carry to the people the policies and message of the top leadership of the state. If these organs actually work as they are supposed to, the average citizen should find himself so constantly saturated with government propaganda that he would gladly acquiesce, if only to achieve a brief moment of privacy.

The Executive

One of the peculiarities of most Communist regimes is that they generally seek to create the appearance of diversified decision-making, not only by bestowing great constitutional powers on the legislature but also by providing for a plural executive and head of state. In this, they differ both from totalitarian regimes of the right, and also from most constitutional political systems. Thus in West Germany, both the functions of the head of state and those of the head of the political executive are centered primarily in individuals. In East Germany, however, both of the major executive organs, the Council of State, which functions as the nominal head of state, and the Council of Ministers, which is in charge of the actual political and administrative work, strongly emphasize the collegial principle, at least in outward appearance.

Paradoxically, this tendency to emphasize collegial structure has increased in fairly direct proportion to the centralization of power in the hands of one man. Originally there was an individual head of state, the president of the Republic. In 1949 this position was given to Wilhelm Pieck, the "ex-Communist" cochairman of the SED, while the position of minister-president and chairman of the Council of Ministers went to Otto Grote-wohl, his "ex-Socialist" colleague. Ulbricht at that time was only a vice-chairman of the Council of Ministers. But increasingly he used his control over the SED party organization to win power at the expense of the other leaders. It soon became evident that the vice-chairman of the Council of Ministers had much more influence on its decisions than the chairman himself. Then, when Wilhelm Pieck died in 1960, the position of the presidency was constitutionally abolished in favor of a twenty-four man Council of State, similar to the U.S.S.R.'s Presidium of the Supreme Soviet. However the State Council has even greater rule-making powers than the Soviet body, and unlike the latter it is not an organ of the assembly. By having himself elected president of this body, Ulbricht succeeded in outdoing even Stalin by combining in his person the positions of head of state, vice-chairman of the Council of Ministers, and General Secretary of the SED.

The make-up of the East German equivalent of the cabinet has also changed frequently since 1949. The original cabinet was a very large and unwieldy body because the Constitution provided, firstly, that all parties with at least forty deputies in the People's Chamber be represented in the executive; secondly, that all ministers be automatically members; and thirdly, that many leading civil servants be included. In time, this large body came to be known as the Council of Ministers, meeting regularly under the chairmanship of the minister-president. Already in 1952 the Council of Ministers had been given legal authority "to change its own structure by independent decision whenever necessary to conform to the demands of economic planning." [8] This power was frequently taken advantage of, both to reorganize the ministries and to change the make-up of the Council of Ministers itself. One consequence was the creation of a kind of supercabinet, called the Presidium of the Council of Ministers, which in fact became the crucial executive decision-making body. Its size has varied from ten to sixteen, including the chairman, the vice-chairman, and the most important ministers. Two-thirds of its members have always come from the SED, but the "all-party" formula has been superficially adhered to by alloting each of the other parties one of the deputy chairmanships. The Presidium normally meets once a week and in general fulfills the important policy-making functions that in the Soviet Union are exercised by the body after which it is modelled. Attached to it is a secretariat to which are linked the State Planning Commission and the Central Commission for State Control. These top-level coordinating organs fulfill for the state apparatus roughly the same functions that the Central Secretariat fulfills for the party.

Within the Council of Ministers, the position of the minister-

[8] *Ibid.*, p. 36.

president, according to the Constitution, is much less dominant than that of the West German Chancellor. Although he is empowered to lay down the main lines of policy, he is supposed to take his lead from parliamentary decisions and must gain the approval of his fellow ministers. If Ulbricht had held this position it would doubtless have developed into a powerful one, despite the Constitution. But in the person of Grotewohl the position has yielded much power to Ulbricht's SED protégés. Ministers not coming from the inner circle of the SED have generally been assigned to positions which command little power but are much in the public eye. Thus the DDR's Foreign Minister has always been provided by one of the non-Socialist parties, a practice continued even after the first incumbent was sentenced to a longterm imprisonment for maintaining *sub rosa* ties with the West. Such ministries, however, invariably have staunch SED state secretaries to ensure that their chiefs do not dance out of line.

Because centralized economic planning is so dominant a preoccupation of the East German government, the administrative apparatus of the central government is divided fairly clearly between the "economic" ministries and the "political" ones. The latter include the ministries for Foreign Affairs, Interior, State Security, and Justice. As regards structure the political ministries have remained fairly stable, although reorganization took place as the result, for instance, of the official creation of the Ministry of National Defense in 1956. The political ministries have either no "line agencies" at all, or only those which function as its local branch offices. The "economic" ministries, on the other hand, such as the (former) Ministry of Machine Construction or the (former) Ministry of Raw Materials, are responsible for vast industrial enterprises which are mostly directly state owned and all state controlled. The attempt to find an administrative structure which would allow the ministries to exercise central coordination while avoiding excessive bureaucratic duplication has caused this area of the administration to be subject to frequent and radical reorganization. At some periods the individual ministries have been allowed to work fairly independently, exercising strong centralized control over local enterprises and subject only to the over-all supervision of the State Planning Commission. At other times there have been efforts to allow local enterprises greater initiative and to coordinate the central authorities into a kind of economic cabinet. After prolonged experimentation a radical administrative reorganization in 1958 abolished most of the economic ministries and transformed them into sections of the State Planning Commission.[9]

Planning and Administration

Even before this occurred, the State Planning Commission had been the crucial coordinating center for the work of the various ministries, allocating raw materials and setting top-level production quotas. Headed by a chairman who has always been an ex-officio deputy chairman of the Council of Ministers, the Commission relies on the work of about a thousand experts organized in divisions which parallel those of the various ministries or, since 1958, the relevant administrative sections of the Commission. The planning process is a laborious one and begins about a half year before a specific plan goes into effect. Originally the Planning Commission worked out tentative plans and production quotas; these were submitted to the ministries for suggestions, then re-examined by the Commission and transformed into all-inclusive production, investment, labor, and finance plans, which were in turn submitted for approval to the Central Committee of the SED and the Council of Ministers.

Many difficulties beset the regime in its attempts to transform the plans into actual achievements. A bureaucracy which after all consisted primarily of Prussians tended to follow instructions to the letter, resulting in wasteful duplication and excessive formalization of working routines. In an attempt to remedy the situation, ministries were forever being abolished or reconstructed. The area of machine construction was at some periods divided among as many as three ministries, at others combined as a subdivision of one ministry. Since 1958, the former heads of the production ministries have become section heads in the State Planning Commission and form part of a large collegial body which charts the Commission's course. In an attempt to experiment with decentralization, part of the ministries' former functions have been transferred to local authorities and to so-called Unions of Public Enterprise. As a result factory managers have been less bound by explicit directions from East Berlin, but their initiative is still kept under control through the system of "double subordination." [10] This provides for local production units to be subject to the control of both the over-all economic plan-

9 *Ibid.*, p. 170.
10 *Ibid.*, pp. 83 ff.

ning agency on the local level and to the more specialized technical section of the Planning Commission.

Apart from the low morale and lack of Socialist enthusiasm
of the population, the problem of administering the vast planned
economy has been perhaps the single most pressing internal
problem of the East German regime. A perusal of the speeches
Walter Ulbricht has given before East German administration
academies over the years shows frequent changes of policy. In
1949 he was calling on county and communal governments "not
to let themselves be carried away by talk of self-administration
which would disturb the fulfillment of the Plan." [11] The resultant
accumulation of tasks for the central ministries led to administrative methods which he described some years later by charting the
route of a directive for state-run enterprises from one ministry's
Labor Division:

The directive will go from the Labor Division to that deputy minister
who is responsible for this division, from him to the Minister, from the
Minister to the deputy Minister who is responsible for the Production
division, from him to the administrative head of this division, then on
to the deputy administrator until it finally reaches the head of the
Labor section of the relevant central administrative agency. . . . Cooperation between the many administrative desks at the central level
and the production enterprises is very inadequate and very complicated.
The result is that much paper is used up and that scientific-technical
work is not pushed forward as quickly as might otherwise be possible.[12]

By 1958 he was praising measures adopted once more to give
local government a more significant role in the economic planning process, in the hope that "the simpler the forms and methods through which direction is given to political, economic and
cultural activity, the better can the workers themselves participate
in the leadership of the state and the economy." [13]

The tradition of the German civil service as a tightly knit,
exclusive professional group, predominantly recruited from middle-class strata, was of course entirely unacceptable to the
Communists. They did not bother with halfway measures, but
virtually abolished the civil service in its traditional form. A
major bulwark of the system, the civil servant's claim to lifetime
tenure, was done away with, and under East German law a government employee may be dismissed at any time after being given

[11] Walter Ulbricht, *Die Entwicklung des deutschen Volksdemokratischen
Staates, 1945–1958* (Berlin, 1959), p. 175.

[12] *Ibid.*, p. 489.

[13] *Ibid.*, p. 543.

two weeks' notice. Great effort has been put into replacing the old line, politically unreliable, professional administrators with Communist functionaries. Various sectors of the government compete in seeking to demonstrate the working-class "purity" of their employees. Thus in 1957 two-thirds of the judges were said to be of working-class background, and only two out of 906 were listed as coming from the upper-middle class.[14] About the same time, the army announced that 85 per cent of its officers had working-class origins.[15] Claims for the administration were not quite as high, but in 1955 60 per cent of government employees were said to come from the working class.[16] In view of the limited administrative training facilities, most of the newcomers could be given only limited training. Some have been put through training programs of one year or longer, most have pursued part-time studies on the job, and many have had no training at all, although by 1960 about 70 per cent of government employees of the upper ranks were supposed to have had some kind of training course. The lack of uniformity or even similarity in educational background, together with the excessive importance placed on recruiting the sons and grandsons of workers and peasants, has had the over-all effect of depriving government employment of anything resembling professional standards. There is indeed a kind of rivalry for influence between the dual sets of functionaries in the party and state apparatus. But this rivalry carries few traces of an ideological nature, and at the very top level of the Politburo and the Council of Ministers the two networks tend to be joined in persons holding dual offices.

Bibliography

Albrecht, Guenter, ed., *Dokumente zur Staatsordnung der DDR* (Berlin, 1959).
Bundesministerium fuer Gesamtdeutsche Fragen, *SBZ von A-Z*, 5th ed. (Bonn, 1959).
——, *Die Wahlen in der Sowjetzone* (Bonn, 1956).
Deutsche Demokratische Republik, *Handbuch der Volkskammer der DDR*, 2d ed. (Berlin, 1957).
Drath, Martin, *Verfassungsrecht und Verfassungswirklichkeit in der sowjetischen Besatzungszone* (Bonn, 1954).
Glaser, Kurt, "Governments of Soviet Germany" in E. H. Litchfield, ed., *Governing Postwar Germany* (Ithaca, 1953), pp. 152–83.
Maunz, Theodor, *Deutsches Staatsrecht*, 9th ed. (Munich, 1959), Part II.

[14] *Ibid.*, p. 533.
[15] Deutsches Institut fuer Zeitgeschichte, *op. cit.*, p. 87.
[16] Richert, *op. cit.*, p. 158.

Polak, Karl, *Die Demokratie der Arbeiter und Bauernmacht* (Berlin, 1957).

Richert, Ernst, *Macht ohne Mandat* (Cologne, 1958).

——, "Zur Frage der Konsolidierung des Regimes der DDR," *Neue Gesellschaft*, VII (May-June, 1960), 216–22.

Ulbricht, Walter, *Die Entwicklung des deutschen Volksdemokratischen Staates, 1945–1958* (Berlin, 1959).

U.S. High Commission for Germany, *Soviet Zone Constitution and Electoral Law* (Washington, 1951).

PART IV
GERMANY:
PROBLEMS AND PROSPECTS

11 - Germany and the World Power Blocs

Berlin—A House Divided

Let us imagine the Grimm brothers, the famous German fairy tale authors, writing about Germany in the 1960's:

Once upon a time there was a rich and powerful farmer, who died after committing many dastardly acts and getting deeply into debt. Some of his land was seized by creditors, and the rest was contested by two sons, Konrad and Walter, each of whom claimed to be the rightful heir and was backed in his claim by different groups of neighbors. Lawyers were hired by the dozen, but the contest could not be effectively settled without launching the whole countryside into civil war. So each of the hostile brothers farmed those pieces of the family land which he had been tilling at the time of the father's death. Most of the farmers thought that Konrad's legal claims were superior, that he was a better sort of man besides being a better farmer, and indeed several of Walter's children cut their way through the barbed wire fences which had been put up across the middle of the farm to settle on their uncle's land. But in addition to having powerful friends of his own, Walter had one great advantage: the old family farmstead was located right in the middle of his land. At the time of the father's death an agreement allowed both the sons and the neighbors to share the house, and a temporary division of the farmstead's facilities were arranged on that basis, with Konrad and the neighbors guaranteed free access across Walter's land. As feeling grew more bitter, the parts of the house were all but barricaded from each other. In time Walter and his friends began to claim that the earlier agreement had lapsed and that the farmstead area formed an integral part of his land. He offered to let some of Konrad's children continue to live in "their" part of the house, but only on condition that Konrad and his friends recognize his

197

right to regulate admission to the house as a whole. This settlement was indignantly refused by Konrad and his friends, who insisted that the farmstead belonged to the legal heir to the farm, namely Konrad, and that awaiting a final settlement the old agreements regarding its use should remain in force.

The old farmstead is of course the prewar German capital, Berlin, which has literally remained a house divided for fifteen years. It has remained the center of conflict not only because of its symbolic significance for Germans, but because Germany is a miniature of a world divided between East and West. Berlin is both Germany in miniature and also the only large city in the world where the democratic and Communist forces meet head-on. (Vienna, once in a similar situation, escaped that fate with the signing of the Austrian peace treaty in 1955.) Although the two large power blocs also border each other in many other places, and have come into conflict in a number of them, including Korea, Indochina, Laos, and Quemoy and Matsu, Berlin has remained the Communists' favorite place for applying pressure not intended to lead to armed conflict. Its dubious distinction is explained by West Berlin's being completely surrounded by Communist-controlled territory, and by the fact that the instruments for such pressure, the East German Communists, are quite well disciplined and controlled, allowing a fairly fine check on the extent of particular provocations. In addition, the status of West Berlin, directly involving as it does West Germany as well as the major NATO powers, allows the Communists to subtly play on and seek to aggravate latent differences among the Western allies. Finally, Berlin, whatever its political status, is one of the major news centers of the world. If the East Germans block an access road to West Berlin or arrest an American journalist in East Berlin, the news will be halfway around the world in hours, if not minutes. Whenever the cold war settles down into a phase of psychological warfare, Berlin becomes the sensitized area for recording changes in tension.

The story of how Berlin developed this role begins with the wartime agreements of 1944 and 1945, when the victorious Allies agreed not only to divide Germany into four Occupation zones, but to run Berlin jointly, allocating to each of the four major powers a city sector for administration. The Western Allies maintain that neither the founding of the projected unified administration nor the subsequent development of the Federal Republic and the German Democratic Republic have affected their right to be in Berlin and to station troops there. They have expressed their intention to maintain the status quo until the signing of a German peace treaty. The Communists, on the other hand, have taken the position that the wartime agreements are to be interpreted only within the context of the larger framework of the inter-Allied plans for a united Germany. They maintain that the division of Germany and the establishment of the Federal Republic and the Democratic Republic have altered the situation radically, and that Berlin's status as a city-state under four-power control is antiquated.

In terms of the political struggle between the two regimes, West Berlin is of key strategic and symbolic significance. The West Germans regard West Berlin as a Land of the Federal Republic, and most of the Basic Law applies to the city. A lessening of the close ties between West Berlin and the Federal Republic would be a serious blow to the latter's status, and a setback for its supporters both in and outside of Germany. Furthermore, West Berlin serves as the contact point through which the West Germans keep in touch with their countrymen in the DDR, and encourage them to hold out against Communist oppression. The city's additional function as an escape hatch has cost the DDR dearly in population; in ten years close to one and a half million people have crossed over from East to West Berlin. Indeed some West Germans have said that if they can only hold onto Berlin and wait long enough, the "other Germany" will one day be a virtually unpopulated wasteland.

More realistic are some economic considerations relevant to the Berlin situation. As an ex-capital without hinterland, West Berlin has sought to encourage industry to replace the bureaucratic jobs which were once the mainstay of its economy. Great efforts have been made to build up its ability to support itself, even though most of its trade must move through DDR territory. During the Soviet blockade of 1948 to 1949, the city could only be fed because of an enormously expensive Allied airlift, in which over the course of a year 2.1 million tons of goods were flown in by 277,728 flights. Even in normal years, when it sells much of its industrial production to the West, Berlin can only be maintained by virtue of annual subsidies from the German federal government which run to 400 million dollars or 200 dollars per capita.[1]

West Berlin as a distinct political unit, rather than as a piece of land relatively free of Soviet rule, emerged in 1948. Up to that time a unified city administration had been maintained under

[1] Charles Robson, ed., *Berlin: Pivot of German Destiny* (Chapel Hill, 1960), pp. 134–55.

the supervision of the four-power Allied *Kommandatura*. However, early in that year, East Berlin became the center of the SED's campaign to coordinate political life throughout the Soviet zone. Then in June, 1948, the Soviets imposed a blockade on all land traffic into West Berlin in retaliation against the introduction there of the new West German currency. In November the city council and administration split into separate parts. During the airlift the West Berliners displayed great courage and endurance, and it was their toughness which finally forced the Soviets to back down and to cancel the blockade after eleven months.[2] After that the new Democratic Republic officially declared East Berlin to be its capital, while West Berlin concentrated on economic revival. Eventually the abnormality of relationships was accepted as normal, and throughout most of the 1950's life in the divided city continued with many minor, but few major, upsets. A series of strong Social Democratic leaders, Ernst Reuter, Otto Suhr, and Willy Brandt, provided excellent leadership in the position of Governing Mayor of West Berlin. There was little official contact between the two administrations, but those who cared to could usually travel freely throughout Berlin. While many streets lead to dead ends at the sector border, the main thoroughfares are kept open, and the subway and elevated trains have kept running.

Throughout this time the endless series of proposals and counterproposals about a German peace treaty got nowhere. The Federal Republic refused to enter into official dealings with the Democratic Republic and the Western powers refused to enter into any negotiations which would entail recognition of the latter regime. Instead they called on the Soviets to arrange for free elections through which citizens of both East and West Germany could choose their representatives for future negotiations. Although they had established diplomatic relations with the Federal Republic in 1955, the Soviets in their turn refused to make any concessions which might endanger the East German SED government, and continued to insist that the two German governments should negotiate together on a basis of equality. When the West refused to proceed on these terms, the Soviets began to talk of arranging a separate peace treaty between themselves and East Germany. Since November, 1958, the Soviets have sought to force the West into a complete renegotiation of the Berlin situation; they themselves proposed turning West Berlin into a demili-

[2] W. P. Davison, *The Berlin Blockade: A Study in Cold-War Politics* (Princeton, 1958).

tarized neutralized "free city" inside the DDR which would earn its keep by selling its manufactures to both East and West.[3] In June, 1961, Khrushchev again demanded that the West either renegotiate the status of West Berlin on these terms or sign an all-German peace treaty which would entail recognition of the DDR and surrender of hopes of unification. Were the West not to respond he threatened to conclude a peace treaty with the DDR alone, giving the latter control over Western access to West Berlin. Anticipating that the Communists would use the threat of blockade to seek to throttle the city, West Berlin had stockpiled imposing provisions to withstand a siege. The contest has continued in this context, with the Western powers attempting to avoid any action which would weaken the Federal Republic's position or make their entry to Berlin dependent on a DDR government which they do not recognize, while the Soviets have become more insistent on closing the Berlin loophole and seeking to force recognition of the DDR as a step in the strengthening of the Communist position in Germany and Europe.

The Revival of German Military Power

Because of Germany's size and her central position in Europe, the political orientation of any German government will always be a key factor in world politics. That is why both the Soviet Union and the Western Allies worked so hard to lay the groundwork for the emergence of the kind of German political system which would tend to ally Germany with their side. But one need only recall the two world wars to realize that Germany has been courted and feared even more for her military power. In 1945 the victorious Allies seemed determined that a revival of German military power should never recur, and they acted to wipe out all military organizations and to impress on the German people the close connection between German militarism and the disaster of 1945. But a demilitarized Germany was not in the cards. Within five years after Germany's unconditional surrender the very powers who had defeated and dissolved her armies were themselves seeking to encourage the re-establishment of German military contingents. The constitutions of both the Federal Republic and the Democratic Republic contained provisions forbidding large-scale rearmament; both soon had to be amended.

German rearmament was not the end result of isolated plan-

[3] Bruce L. R. Smith, "The Governance of Berlin," *International Conciliation* No. 525 (1959), pp. 189–90.

ning but came about as part of the increased tempo of the armaments race starting around 1948. The Soviet Union alarmed the
Western countries through the establishment of Communist regimes in Eastern Europe, the Communist take-over of Czechoslovakia, the Berlin blockade, and the development of large paramilitary organizations in East Germany. To meet anticipated
military threats to West Europe, the Western countries in 1949
formed the North Atlantic Treaty Organization. But the following year the near success of the Communist attempt to take over
South Korea by force raised further doubts as to the ability of the
democratic countries to meet localized Communist aggression. In
order to bolster Western military forces in Europe, American and
British spokesmen soon began to call for the formation of West
German contingents. To allay traditional and well founded
skepticism regarding the political effects of the re-establishment
of a German army, it was proposed that the German troops be
placed under a European army, with other countries doing likewise. The West German government strongly supported these
plans, and after some discussion the French cabinet overcame its
initial hesitation and agreed to the principles of the European
Defense Community (EDC), which would have established an
integrated European army including contingents from West Germany, France, Italy, Holland, Belgium, and Luxembourg. The
governments concerned signed the EDC treaty in 1952, and in
Germany a CDU-dominated Bundestag ratified it in 1953. However, successive French governments proved unable or unwilling
to make the plan acceptable to large enough sections of French
opinion, and in August, 1954, the treaty was defeated in the
French National Assembly.[4]

The defeat of EDC was a heavy blow both to advocates of a
supranational defense force and to friends of European federation. The Americans and Germans pressed for a solution, since
the treaties which were to give the Federal Republic full sovereignty were tied to the defense question and had been awaiting
ratification for over two years. In the autumn of 1954 Western
politicians undertook to devise an alternative solution. To allay
French fears the British agreed to enter into the defense arrangements, and committed themselves to maintain troops on the
continent within the framework of a loosely organized international coordinating body, the West European Union (WEU).
It was proposed that Germany be made both a member of WEU
and of NATO, and that German armed forces, though organized

[4] Daniel Lerner, ed., *France Defeats EDC* (New York, 1957).

on a national basis, be placed under the supreme command of these organizations. This formula was finally accepted by the French, the Germans, and all the other nations involved. In May, 1955, WEU was formally established, and the Federal Republic was admitted to NATO.

There were as yet no West German soldiers in uniform when five days after the Federal Republic's admission to NATO the states of the Communist bloc met in Warsaw and formed a counterpart pact, with reciprocal defense guarantees and a joint command for their combined military forces. In this way the effective control exercised through the top-level Communist leaders was augmented by a supranational military organization similar to NATO, whose existence underlined the polarization of the two hostile blocs. A Soviet general was named to command the forces of the Warsaw Pact countries, and a staff organization was established in Moscow. The DDR had not as yet given its "police" formations explicit military status, so although it became a member of the pact, no provision was made regarding its forces. This situation was rectified in January, 1956, with the official formation of the East German People's Army, and a few days later the Warsaw Pact countries announced the admission of East German contingents into the unified command. By 1959 an official East German source described the function of the armed services as "successfully fulfilling, at the side of the glorious Soviet army and of the other fraternal socialist armies, the duties assigned to us within the framework of the Warsaw Pact." [5]

Rearmament has caused both states considerable problems. In the East the main problem consisted of recruiting officers and personnel who could be trusted not to use their arms against the regime in case of a crisis. For this reason there has been no general draft, and instead an emphasis on requiring members of the Free German Youth, the SED, and other such groups to "volunteer" for military service. In this way a very sizable body of sixty-five thousand paramilitary "special police" had already been created by 1951, and their number was almost doubled in subsequent years. At the same time trusted Communists were given military training to prepare them for the very top military positions. Thus Willy Stoph, who joined the Communist party at the age of seventeen in 1931 and never saw military service, was given responsibility for the military build-up, first as Minister of the Interior, and from 1956 to 1960 as major general and Minister of

[5] Deutsches Institut fuer Zeitgeschichte, *Jahrbuch der Deutschen Demokratischen Republik, 1959* (Berlin, 1959), p. 86.

Defense. He was later replaced by Heinz Hoffmann, another tried Communist. The Communists have had some difficulty reconciling their military build-up with their traditional denunciation of German militarism and their self-description as champions of peace. The original paramilitary "police" were given uniforms which had no resemblance to those of the old pre-1945 Wehrmacht, but in color and cut closely resembled those of the Soviet army. In 1956, however, the decision was made to tie the People's Army to German traditions, and the new army uniforms closely resembled those of the Wehrmacht, despite the fact that the Communists had spent so much time in denouncing the latter as an ally of fascism.

In the Federal Republic, the problem of the reconcilability of old traditions and new roles also caused difficulty. Up to 1945 the ranks of the top-level German military men and those of genuine democrats had, for the most part, been mutually exclusive. "The German democrats had no military heroes in their tradition . . . and the German military had no democrats among their ancestry." [6] The character of West German society and the rapid build-up which was necessary after the long delays over EDC did not allow the training of a completely new military leadership and required the use of officers who had grown up in the antidemocratic Reichswehr and in the service of the Nazi state. In an attempt to prevent the re-emergence of a reactionary officers' corps and a tyrannical military tradition, the West Germans took extraordinary precautions to sift out politically unreliable candidates and to keep a democratic check on the armed forces. When recruitment for the higher offices began, all candidates for positions with the rank of colonel or above were subjected to close individual scrutiny by a special committee set up by the Bundestag. Many candidates were weeded out on political grounds. Then, building on a Swedish model, the Parliament provided for the creation of a parliamentary "military agent" whose job it would be to look into complaints from individual soldiers and to report to it periodically on the internal affairs of the military forces. However this institution has not established itself very well due to unfortunate staffing and the hostility of the Defense Ministry.

Still political problems remained. Most top-level officers had followed the German army rule of unquestioning obedience to the Nazi regime until the surrender, and many still felt resent-

<hr/>

[6] Emil Obermann, "Kraeftespiel um die Bundeswehr," *Neue Gesellschaft,* VI (1959), p. 96.

GERMANY AND THE WORLD POWER BLOCS

205

ment toward the treatment accorded some colleagues who were sentenced to long prison terms by the Allies for "crimes against humanity" or by West German courts for such offenses as shooting their own soldiers without due trial. High Bundeswehr officers have in fact been called as witnesses in cases which the federal government has brought against former fellow officers of the Wehrmacht, causing the former to be subject to conflicts of conscience. In addition, German officers remained divided in their attitude toward the military participants in the July 20 coup; some regarded these rebels against Hitler as traitors to country and army. For quite a while the Bundeswehr high command resisted demands that the participants of the July 20 attempt be given the recognition in military circles which they had won among civilians.[7] However, in 1959, the high officers of the Bundeswehr made the necessary gesture by laying an official wreath at the grave of those who had been executed fifteen years earlier.

Problems of tradition also bothered democratic opponents of German militarism. German Social Democrats had been particularly distrustful of the return to influence of an officers' caste, and the SPD was in the forefront of the political battle against rearmament for most of the 1950's. In turn the SPD rejected the European Defense Community treaties, the initial military laws, the introduction of required military service, and most other military legislation. They did so not on the grounds of pacifist principles but because they felt a German army would be politically dangerous and militarily unnecessary in view of the changing aspects of warfare. However once the army was established the SPD cooperated on measures to assure its democratic character, and in its 1959 program it rejected earlier antimilitarist attitudes to specifically endorse the principle of defense within the framework of NATO. The Socialists continue to oppose arming German soldiers with atomic weapons, but in preparing for the 1961 campaign they adopted a more flexible position on this point also. Thus, although there continue to be many differences over secondary aspects of the organization and aims of the West German army, political opinion in the Federal Republic has gradually consolidated in accepting, albeit unenthusiastically, the need for West German armed forces. With the strength of the East German forces estimated at 110,000, West German forces under Defense Minister Franz Josef Strauss were approaching their goal of 350,000 men in 1961. The build-up of

[7] Hans Speier, *German Rearmament and Atomic War* (Evanston, 1957).

a nuclear-armed force cannot fail to have political consequences. Reactions from Moscow and Eastern Europe have been bitter, and many in the West also have strong reservations.[8]

The Two German States in World Politics

A key to the understanding of the German problem lies in the fact that in the course of the 1950's both German states threw off the remnants of Occupation status, and, while they became sovereign in the legal sense, they became more closely tied than ever to the world power blocs led by their respective ex-occupiers. Although all countries in both the Western and Eastern camps have had to yield up considerable amounts of national control over their foreign policies, this has held especially true for the two German rump states on either side of the Iron Curtain. The DDR has developed the status of a province within the centrally ruled Communist state system. The Federal Republic was theoretically more free to choose between a number of alternative positions, but her leaders opted for integration with the West, thus making West Germany in effect a frontier canton of the Western alliance.

Both German states, of course, have foreign ministries and embassies (rather few in the case of East Germany), but very seldom have they undertaken important foreign policy initiatives independently of their major allies. A study of the two states' foreign relations is basically the story of their gradual rise and acceptance within their respective camps. For the DDR, the formalizing of pre-existent ties to the Communist states is, aside from some marginal wooing of neutral nations in Africa and Asia, the sum total of postwar diplomacy. West German diplomats have had a somewhat greater variety of experience, but the great bulk of the Federal Republic's foreign policy efforts have also been concentrated on forging a strong network of alliances, treaties, and other ties to the Atlantic powers, particularly to the United States. A second area within which the West Germans have been able to develop considerable independent initiative has been in the attempt to create regional political and economic institutions in Western Europe. Here the Federal Republic has, together with France, taken the lead in founding many supranational European institutions. The great bulk of West German foreign policy effort has thus gone into strengthening ties to two major countries, the United States and France. Questions involv-

[8] Gerald Freund, *Germany Between Two Worlds* (New York, 1961).

ing relations to other countries have had a far lower priority, although considerable effort has also gone into strengthening relations with other West European countries and laying the political groundwork for the development of West German economic relations with countries in South America, Asia, and Africa.

However, it is within the Atlantic alliance that the West Germans have regained political status and prestige. Under Konrad Adenauer's leadership the guidelines of policy have been to honor treaty commitments and to give diplomatic support to the leaders of the alliance in the expectation that they, in turn, would support West Germany in her efforts to bring about reunification on favorable terms.[9] Critics of the Adenauer policy have from the beginning argued that the Federal Republic's policy of alliance with the West was in fact making German unification impossible, but this position has always been rejected by the Chancellor, who believed that a Western policy of strength would induce the Soviets to ultimately yield up the DDR. Replying to neutralist critics after returning from his first visit to the United States in 1953, Adenauer said: "We Germans have in the past committed many foreign policy errors, but we would be committing the greatest error of all if we did not now seek to tie ourselves to the leading power of the world, a power which desires freedom and justice for all, including ourselves." [10]

In an effort to overcome traditional animosities and develop new ties to the major Atlantic powers, West Germany has devoted considerable effort to cultivating political and cultural groups in the United States, France, Britain, and other countries. Among large sections of the public in these countries the Federal Republic has won good will not only because of its democratic record domestically, but also for the steadfastness with which the West Germans have stuck to their commitments. In the United States during the Eisenhower-Dulles period German stock at times rose so high that there was speculation whether West Germany might not replace Great Britain as America's major and most reliable ally. Aware that of all the Western powers the British had the furthest to go in overcoming their distrust of Germany, the Federal Republic tried to discourage such speculation. In fact, West German diplomacy inside NATO has at times had to be delicate. This has been especially true when the French have tried to embarrass American leadership by dragging their

[9] Konrad Adenauer, "Germany: The New Partner," *Foreign Affairs,* XXXIII (1955), 177–83.

[10] From speech at 1953 CDU party convention.

feet on their NATO commitments. But in the final analysis the
West Germans have usually ended up supporting American
leadership. German-British relations have also at times been aggravated, mainly as the result of sharp economic competition and
of British suspicions that Adenauer was trying to freeze Britain
out of Europe.

A desire to participate in and speed up West European political and economic integration has indeed been one of the hallmarks of West German foreign policy. As the receivers of a bank-
rupt nation which had driven nationalism to its furthest extreme,
the postwar German leaders were acutely aware of the need to
forge a wider, supranational European political framework. Not
only did such an aim provide a favorable framework for German
political reconstruction, but for many West Germans the postwar opportunity was unique in that it favored turning Germany
from a country whose political imagination had always roamed
to the East into one which was bound by cultural and economic
ties to its Western neighbors. They therefore readily lent their
support to demands for the political unification of Western
Europe. Since the British and Scandinavians backed away from
proposals for integration, it was apparent that progress on this
front required above all an ending of the historical German-
French enmity and a policy of friendship with the smaller main-
land countries. To this end, the West Germans concentrated on
cooperating with "pro-European" political groups, particularly
in France, Italy, Holland, Belgium, and Luxembourg. The Germans gave strong support to the first concrete proposal for European integration—French Foreign Minister Robert Schumann's
plan for the integration of the West European iron and steel industry. This proposal subsequently led to the creation of the
European Coal and Steel Community.

It was hoped initially that Europeanization would be pushed
forward quickly, with supranational institutions in the area of
heavy industry followed by a merging of military forces under
supranational command and the creation of European political
institutions. These hopes were dashed by indecision in many
camps and by the French defeat of EDC in particular. However
the "Europeans" continued to fight for functional Europeanization, and in the late 1950's they succeeded in establishing the
European Common Market and a European Atomic Authority.
The West Germans have played a vital role in these institutions
and have provided much of the personnel to run the new European agencies. However, the unwillingness of the British and the

Scandinavians to enter into the new European economic organizations limited the scope of the movement, and led to the division
of Western Europe into two competing trade blocs—the Common
Market "Six" (West Germany, France, Benelux, and Italy) and
the European Free Trade Area "Seven" (Britain, the Scandina-
vian countries, Portugal, Austria, and Switzerland). Since Germany trades extensively with countries in both blocs, her leaders
have on occasion been split. Some German leaders have argued
that real political unification could only be achieved within the
"Six," that West Germany should therefore concentrate on Little
Europe, and place political aims over economic ones and alliance
with France over close friendship with Britain. Other Germans
however believe that Germany's economic interests transcend continental Europe, that she should claim a dominant place in the
Atlantic rather than in the "Little Europe" context, and that she
should cooperate more closely with Britain. Closer ties with
France or Britain, organic union on the continent or loose affiliation across the Atlantic, these have been the main alternatives of
German foreign policy as far as relations with its West European
friends are concerned.

With regard to policy toward the Communist bloc, West
Germany has been hemmed in by the physical barrier of the
DDR. Except for the establishment of diplomatic relations with
the Soviet Union in 1955, West Germany has adhered to the
"Hallstein doctrine" (named after the first State Secretary of the
Foreign Ministry who later became president of the European
Economic Community) that the Federal Republic would not
enter into relations with countries that recognize the DDR. Thus
up to 1960 Germany had no official contacts with any of the East
European countries except Yugoslavia, and when the latter recognized the DDR in 1958, West Germany withdrew its embassy
from Belgrade. One problem which has prevented the establishment of more cordial relations, particularly with Poland and
Czechoslovakia, has been the question of the areas in these countries formerly settled by Germans. In contrast to the DDR, which
in a 1950 treaty with Poland recognized as final the present Ger-
man-Polish boundary along the Oder and Neisse rivers, the
Federal Republic takes the position that the final disposition of
the areas east of this line can be settled only in the peace treaty.
In this it has the support of the West, but the Poles regard Bonn's
attitude as provocative and threatening. The activity of vocal and
frequently militant expellee groups who continuously agitate for
a reclaiming of the territories lost to the East have lent support

to those who doubt that West Germany will really live up to its promise to accept a peaceable solution to the issue. Expellee organizations from other territories, such as the Sudetenland area in Czechoslovakia, also press the West German government to fight for their right to return to their former homes. On several occasions pressure from these expellee groups has forced the West German Foreign Office to abandon attempts to establish better relations with the East European countries.[11]

The instruments through which both states conduct their foreign policies have frequently been unorthodox. During its first years of existence the Federal Republic did not have a foreign office or diplomatic corps, the vital negotiations with the Western powers being carried out largely by Chancellor Adenauer in personal discussions with the Allied High Commissioners. Later, Adenauer for quite some time combined the offices of Chancellor and Foreign Secretary, and continued to maintain tight control over foreign relations problems even after the appointment of Heinrich von Brentano as Foreign Minister in 1955. Adenauer's frequent visits to see the leaders of the Western powers have strengthened the emphasis on personal diplomacy and underscored the virtual merging of the most crucial domestic and foreign policy areas. For the DDR, foreign relations are also predominantly conducted outside regularly established diplomatic channels, the major decisions being made at the frequent meetings of Communist leaders of the Eastern bloc. The East German Foreign Ministry, which has traditionally been headed by a representative of one of the satellite parties (during the late fifties by Lothar Bolz of the Liberal party), is not very significant, especially since in 1960 it had no diplomatic representatives in countries outside the Soviet bloc, except for Yugoslavia. What contacts the East Germans maintain with neutral countries is largely through trade delegations without diplomatic status. Both states are also handicapped by the fact that they are not members of the United Nations, although here too the Federal Republic is ahead of its rival by virtue of its Observer's Mission at UN headquarters and its membership in organizations like UNESCO.

Its isolation and virtually complete dependence on Soviet policy allows the DDR little room for making even secondary foreign policy decisions. In contrast with other Soviet bloc countries like Poland, it has not been able to pursue diplomatic objectives which differ even in minor respects from those of the Soviet

[11] Elizabeth Wiskemann, *Germany's Eastern Neighbors* (London, 1956).

Union. Whereas the Federal Republic has been quite free to
shift its course between, for instance, support of British or
French policies within the European framework, the DDR has
not been able to play a corresponding role within the Communist
bloc. Its policies toward Yugoslavia or at times Poland have always completely followed the Moscow line. In its relations with
neutral nations, the DDR up to the end of 1960 was not successful
in establishing full diplomatic relations with even one country.
However it did greatly expand its network of foreign economic
contacts, particularly by offering exports to underdeveloped countries on very good terms. As a result, by 1959 it was maintaining
trade delegations in twenty-five non-Communist countries, among
them Burma, India, Indonesia, Guinea, as well as Sweden, France,
and Italy. However, only two countries, the United Arab Republic and Finland, maintained trade missions in East Berlin. By
contrast the Federal Republic maintained diplomatic (and, of
course, economic) relations with ninety-two countries.

West German–East German Relations

The ideological and diplomatic wall which the two German
governments have built up between themselves is imposing. Phys-
ically it finds its counterpart in the barricaded and tightly
guarded frontier which runs through the center of Germany.
Road blocks are thrown across highways and villages, farms are
cut in two, and there is even a place where the frontier barricades
run right through a house. On the East German side police patrol
constantly, and a thirty-foot-wide patch of ploughed ground runs
from the Czech border to the North Sea to record the footprints
of illegal border crossers. Nevertheless this formidable frontier
is not as insurmountable as it appears; there are ways of getting
across it, legally and illegally. Both governments want to maintain
contacts with the population across the way, and neither wants
to assume responsibility for preventing at least occasional meetings between relatives and friends. Beyond the level of family contacts, numerous associations—professional, cultural, economic—
still keep East Germans in contact with West Germans. Protestant
leaders travel from West to East to attend church meetings: doctors cross the frontier for medical conferences: theatre directors
occasionally move to accept new positions. Although most attention has been focussed on the large number of illegal border
crossers from East to West, there has at most times indeed been
a fairly sizable flow of people changing residence in both direc-

tions. Among their number are large numbers of political agents sent across the frontier by various organizations to engage in agitation, spying, and other activities calculated to undermine the political structure of the rival regime.

Spying is a mass industry in both West and East Germany, and announcements of the arrest of agents have become completely commonplace. West Germany estimated in 1960 that one thousand Communist agents entered its territory every month, and that sixteen thousand agents were continuously engaged in subversive activities. Both states may be unique in that for every politician working to support the regime there is an opposition agent working for its downfall. Agents have penetrated into all but the very highest positions of the East and West German governments and parties. In Bonn a number of deputies from various parties have been found to be working for the Communists for a variety of motives. In addition almost all the party organizations have been infiltrated by East German agents. In May, 1959, the West German government found out from an East German intelligence officer who had defected to the West that a network of about a dozen agents was reporting constantly on what went on in all the leading CDU offices. One of the persons involved had been active as secretary of CDU student organizations in Bonn and had later become executive secretary of an organization which, with the financial support of the federal government and West German industry, provided materials to help high school teachers prepare civics and political science lessons. Other agents have been discovered in much more sensitive positions in the Defense and Foreign ministries.

The job of apprehending agents is difficult for the police authorities in both East and West, especially for the latter, due to the protection of Western legal safeguards. In 1960 the West German attorney general announced that only about 10 per cent of indictments for treason actually resulted in convictions. At that time 130 persons were serving time in West German prisons on this charge, while thousands were in East German prisons. Desertions of trusted functionaries pose yet other problems. In the period from 1959 to 1960 some 9,000 SED members fled from the DDR to the Federal Republic, while many thousands of administrators and policemen have done likewise. In general this sort of movement favors the Federal Republic, although it does work both ways. Thus between 1956 and 1960, according to West German sources, some 5,000 members of the East German army fled to the West, while 161 members of the Bundeswehr went in the other direction. In both states there are sizable groups with pronounced political sympathies with the other side. Not all the 70,000 West Germans who were members of the Communist party up to the time of its official dissolution in 1956 could be placed in jail or kept under constant surveillance. It is estimated that about half continue to be active in underground agitational activities, particularly in the trade unions. In arguing for causes like German unification and world-wide disarmament, the Communists have also been able to sponsor large numbers of "front organizations" which attract non-Communist support. The question of how to contend with these groups without, on the one hand, infringing on the constitutional right of freedom of expression and, on the other, causing retaliatory moves in the DDR, poses a constant problem for West German authorities. Their consolation lies partly in the knowledge that their opposite numbers in East Germany must work equally hard for their salaries, for ardent anti-Communist groups have continued to maintain well organized underground organizations in the DDR.

Aside from attempted subversion, the two German governments engage in a costly and unceasing campaign of propaganda against each other. This propaganda is aimed both at the German population in the two states and at publics in foreign countries. A favorite medium for reaching the former are the air waves, for all parts of both states are of course easily within range of powerful transmitters located across the frontier. The East German radio carries programs featuring speakers whose regional accents correspond to those of their West German listeners, and vice-versa. The circulation of printed propaganda is more difficult since newspapers are not allowed to cross the frontier, and other periodicals are severely restricted. However masses of propaganda are printed and smuggled in both directions in manifold ways. Communist underground groups in West Germany distribute leaflets and publications in the factories; soldiers in the Bundeswehr receive brochures in the mail which combine barracks-type cartoons with bitter attacks on their officers and political leaders; special material is put out for West German pacifists and other critics of the government's policy. In 1960, an estimated twelve million pieces of illegal Communist literature were distributed each month.

In the Federal Republic the job of keeping track of developments in the DDR and of publicizing them appropriately lies in the hands of the Ministry of All-German Affairs. This ministry was set up in 1949 to point up the fact that the Federal Republic conceived of itself as representing all Germany, and it has attempted to act in a sense as the representative of the East German population, much as the ministries of Labor and Agriculture represent the interests of workers and farmers within the government. The curious position of this ministry is pointed up by the fact that the two politicians who have headed it, Jakob Kaiser and Ernst Lemmer, were themselves leaders of the East German CDU active in Soviet zone politics until the end of 1947, and at times were in close contact with the SED leaders to whom they are now bitterly opposed. Despite the fact that the East Germans have constantly denounced him as the "Espionage Minister," Lemmer felt secure enough in February, 1960, to attend an East Berlin church service which opened the meeting of the synod of the Protestant church. His visit was cheered by many East Berliners, and although it was denounced as a provocation by the East Berlin authorities, nothing happened to him. The degree to which West German leaders will continue to be able to make such demonstrations on behalf of the "all-German" cause, while also discomfiting their East German competitors, will remain dependent on their popularity and confidence as well as on the power relationship of the two world blocs between which their nation is divided.

Bibliography

Adenauer, Konrad, "Germany: The New Partner," *Foreign Affairs*, XXXIII (1955), 177–83.

Bundesgerichthof, *Hochverrat und Staatsgefaehrdung: Urteile des Bundesgerichthofes* (Karlsruhe, 1957).

Craig, G. A., "NATO and the New German Army," in W. Kaufman, ed., *Military Policy and National Security* (Princeton, 1956).

Davison, W. P., *The Berlin Blockade: A Study in Cold-war Politics* (Princeton, 1958).

Deutsch, Karl, and Edinger, Lewis, *Germany Rejoins the Powers* (Stanford, 1959).

Erler, Fritz, "The Struggle for German Unification," *Foreign Affairs*, XXXIV (1956), 380–93.

Freund, Gerald, *Germany between Two Worlds* (New York, 1961).

Grewe, Wilhelm G., *Deutsche Aussenpolitik der Nachkriegszeit* (Stuttgart, 1960).

Haas, Ernst B., *The Uniting of Europe: Political, Social and Economic Forces, 1950–1957* (Stanford, 1958).

Kapp, Fritz, *Chronik der Wiederbewaffnung in Deutschland* (Cologne, 1958).

Kissinger, Henry A., "The Search for Stability," *Foreign Affairs*, XXXVII (1959), 537–60.

McInnis, Edgar, *et al.*, *The Shaping of Postwar Germany* (New York, 1960).

Obermann, Emil, "Kraeftespiel um die Bundeswehr," *Neue Gesellschaft,* VI 1959), 88 ff.

——, *Soldaten, Bürger, Militaristen: Militaer und Demokratie in Deutschland* (Stuttgart, 1958).

Prittie, Terence, *Germany Divided: The Legacy of the Nazi Era* (Boston, 1960).

Robson, Charles, ed., *Berlin: Pivot of German Destiny* (Chapel Hill, 1960).

Siegler, Heinrich, *Dokumentation zur Deutschlandfrage* (Bonn, 1959).

Smith, Bruce L. R., "The Governance of Berlin," *International Conciliation* (1959), pp. 171–230.

Speier, Hans, *German Rearmament and Atomic War* (Evanston, 1957).

——, and Davison, W. P., *West German Leadership and Foreign Policy* (Evanston, 1957).

U.S. Senate Committee on Foreign Relations, *Documents on Germany, 1944–1959* (Washington, 1959).

Wiskemann, Elizabeth, *Germany's Eastern Neighbors* (London, 1956).

12 - German Politics: An Overview

Rules and Style of the Game

In their continuing propaganda battle West and East Germany frequently accuse each other of being mere "puppet states," the one of the "Western imperialists," the other of the "Communist imperialists." When one cuts through the semantics, it is indeed clear that both political systems have been powerfully shaped by outside influences and that both are tied by commitments to outside powers. Both are, to a very considerable extent, controlled in the sense that domestic political forces are allowed only limited degrees of free play. The essential distinction between the two states is, however, not how much leeway each does allow (this is, of course, much greater in West Germany) but is related to who exercises what kinds of controls. As to the DDR, the Soviet Union's control is so obvious that it needs no elaboration; no one doubts that if one day Moscow were to disavow the East German regime, the latter would collapse within hours. By contrast, if the United States and NATO were to completely renounce the Federal Republic, the West Germans could hold out on their own for an indefinite period.

The question of "controls" with reference to the West German system is more complex. The re-establishment of democracy in West Germany has clearly not been the result of a natural or spontaneous development, but rather the outcome of a closely controlled experiment. By their programs of denazification, the licensing of political parties, and pressure for legal and constitutional reform, the Western Allies did lay the groundwork for democratic institutions with a reasonable life expectancy. But in contrast to East Germany the controls involved have been based only in part on the occupation powers' direct and indirect powers. From a very early point, sometimes before the Allies were ready to let them, West German political leaders assumed responsibility for protecting the frail democratic institutions against potential wreckers. The Socialists' struggles against the Communist "Trojan horses," the fight against neo-Nazi writers and agitators, the banning of anticonstitutional parties, these were the acts of West Germans seeking to impose controls on their political system. In time psychological controls have come to be more important than legal and physical controls. West Germans were told by their own leaders and opinion-shapers that their rehabilitation in the eyes of the world required in effect voluntary abstinence from certain kinds of political behavior. The federal presidents, party leaders, and editorial writers have all acted to drive this message home, but Konrad Adenauer in particular has emerged in the role of a severe taskmaster ever ready to remind his pupils of their shortcomings. Perhaps in no other Western democratic country could an elected political leader express to foreign statesmen deepseated misgivings about the great political mistakes his own people might make when no longer able to benefit from his leadership, and yet be overwhelmingly re-elected and consistently named as the one individual whom his voter-pupils admire more than any other living person. By striving stubbornly to tie future generations together by a huge network of European and Atlantic military, political, and economic treaties and conventions, Adenauer has laid the basis for perpetuating a control grid beyond his own lifetime.

A much more effective functioning of external and domestic control mechanisms over the political system as a whole is only one of a complex of interrelated factors which have made Bonn different from Weimar. For the Federal Republic has possessed prerequisites for the establishment of a stable political system which its democratic predecessor did not have. Its founders were not discredited by charges of having accepted a dishonorable peace treaty, but rather were credited with cleverly speeding up the timetable toward the return of German sovereignty. The cold war also paved the way for the acceptance of Germany into the Western camp on a level of formal equality. By being based on the ego-restoring and profitable tie to the Western alliance, Bonn's foreign policy, again in sharp contrast to the experience of the Weimar regime, has had an over-all stabilizing effect on domestic politics (to whatever extent these two policy areas can be distinguished). An even more direct prerequisite for the maintenance of democratic institutions has been the fact that the political system could stabilize itself during a period of sustained economic growth, during which social tensions lessened and economic expectations could to a large extent be fulfilled. Finally, although democracy is still understood in varying ways among different West German political groups, there is no doubt that their leaders and chief instruments are sincere and single- minded in their commitment to the values of the Constitution. This, too, marks a vital difference with the Weimar "Republic Without Republicans."

Building on these prerequisites, the Federal Republic has developed effective instruments for keeping democratic institutions viable. The major German parties have established avenues of contact between the people and the government which, if far from ideal, are at least adequate. They have displayed greater powers of adaptability than their equivalents in almost any major European country, and this, together with the progressive de-ideologization of German politics, has caused a remarkable trend toward a two party system and a striking consolidation of political forces. Although the polarization of the party system has been based to a somewhat excessive extent on the role of personalities, it has served to present the voters with coherent alternative instruments for the exercise of political functions, and with individual candidates legitimized by their association with tested party labels.

Those governmental institutions which to the Germans exemplified the authority of the state have also proved very effective in stabilizing the system. The groups and individuals who have operated these institutions—Adenauer in the Chancellery, the civil servants in the bureaucracy, the judges on the Constitutional Court—are decidedly not new arrivals, but agents carrying over traditions from pre-Hitler Germany. The fact that these essentially conservative institutions should have become the mainstays of German democracy almost by default has perplexed many who expected the trade unions, progressive political groups, and variously voluntary organizations to shape new instruments to implement postwar democracy. However, even where such instruments were created, as in the case of the "codetermination" structure for heavy industry, they have not proved very influential. The cold war, the far-reaching German reaction against a planned economy, and the restoration of the traditional social structure have created a climate hostile to proposals calling for experiments in either the political or economic area. Even new or partially new institutions have become instruments for established forces or traditions. Thus the Bundesrat has become essentially an instrument allowing the bureaucracy greater scope for influence, while the Constitutional Court has served the purpose of adapting German legalism and the doctrine of the "rule of law" to democratic constitutionalism. Above all, however, it has been the office of the Chancellor and the personality of its first incumbent—both with strong Bismarckian traits—which have contributed the essential element of the stable pole around which the political game has revolved.

For many apolitical Germans these institutions have helped to transform the game of democratic politics from an unruly, dangerous amateur rodeo into a professional match supervised by a management which virtually guarantees spectators against injury, if not also against disappointment. With a professional captain drawn from an old family, with a coaching staff moulded by centuries of experience, with teams made up of licensed experts, and with rules enforced by legally trained referees, the German public has gradually come around to the view that this game can after all be observed with safety, and perhaps someday even participated in with all-around healthy enjoyment.

While professionalization in this sense has made democratic politics respectable, it also has deprived the game of attributes which add to its meaning and significance in countries with stronger amateur traditions. Although a relatively small number of *aficionados* remain close to it by enrolling as water-boys (party militants) or members of the cheering team (party members), the game by and large remains one for experts who are trained in either the regular legal-administrative route or the extension schools run by the parties. The general public, although it attends games as a matter of civic duty, does not really attempt to understand the rules. The rules have not been institutionalized—the public does not discuss them at home over the back fence; and the players frequently follow quite different versions until called to order by the referees, who laboriously decide on the correct one after consulting the law books.

Participants in the game know in a vague way that the rules are made up of an amalgam composed of conventions derived from the traditional German executive predominance, guidelines based on the formal acknowledgement of parliamentary prerogatives, and legalist taboos based on constitutional and statute law. But these various components have never been adequately synthesized by a body of solid and incontrovertible precedent such as exists in Britain, where elaborate parliamentary conventions set clear and definite limits to the way in which the government must permit Parliament and Her Majesty's Opposition to challenge its policies and the manner in which it executes them. In Germany the Parliament, and particularly the parliamentary opposition, frequently do not know from one instance to the next just which of the prerogatives they think are theirs will actually be respected by the executive when it comes down to a specific case.

Chancellor Democracy

This situation, when combined with the executive's strong constitutional position and the pattern established during the Adenauer period, has also left a very unclear picture of the way in which accountability is actually exercised under the German system. An intellectually inquiring minister must on occasion ask himself to just whom, other than the Chancellor personally, he is politically responsible. The people? But the voters have very little influence on his position as a minister, other than to elect him as an ordinary member of the Bundestag, which he owes much more to the assignment of a safe constituency by his party. Consulting the Basic Law, he would find that it says that ministers are "responsible" for the running of their departments, but it omits to specify to whom. He may conclude that it must be to Parliament. But on reflection he would have to decide that if indeed this were so, it must be a purely theoretical kind of relationship, for according to practice during the Adenauer era Parliament had no say in his appointment, no possible way of causing his individual dismissal, and not even a way of expressing a nonbinding vote of no-confidence. As a last resort, the minister might decide that he must be responsible to his party. But then a colleague might remind him of what happened in 1954 when the majority of the Expellees' party overruled its "ministerial wing," left the coalition and demanded that Adenauer dismiss the Expellees' party ministers. He would have to recall that Adenauer paid no heed to these demands, kept the former Expellees' party ministers in his cabinet, had them adopted into the CDU, and furthermore repeated exactly the same procedure in 1955 and 1960 when the same thing occurred with the Free Democratic and German parties. And so the minister would have to decide that he could not really be responsible to his party since he could be maintained in office against its expressed desire. Sadly he would have to draw the conclusion that, at least as long as Adenauer remained in office, he could be responsible only to the Chancellor, his conscience, and God, and he might well wonder in what order.

This then is part of the other side of the coin of the stability developed under Adenauer's "Chancellor democracy." Through the unforeseen development of a majority party, political factors which were to accentuate the executive's responsibility to Parliament have been weakened more than was probably intended by the drafters of the Basic Law. Accountability in the system is weak, and is in practice limited largely to infrequent election campaigns, in which the appeal of a dominant personality and the razzle-dazzle of public relations techniques have tended to dominate the picture. Between elections the Chancellor is largely insensitive to the wishes of his own party, and the party has learned from him that it can afford to be insensitive to short-term changes in public opinion. Thus the mechanisms which in Britain cause Parliament and its parties to be so responsive to the mood of the country are still largely inoperative in Germany. The political leaders do try to keep up with changes in public opinion, but their information rests more on public opinion polls than on the give-and-take with groups that articulate feeling at the grass-roots. The only groups well set up to channel specific demands are the centralized economic interest groups, whose leaders compete with the party politicians in seeking to influence decision-making at the place where most significant decisions are made, in Bonn.

These shortcomings of the substructure of West German democracy, it must be noted, are in good part bequests from earlier tradition. They could perhaps have been more nearly overcome if—without the cold war, the national dismemberment, and the overly hectic race for prosperity—Germans had had the incentive to really concentrate on fundamental domestic political reform. But given the situation that has developed, resistance against the Communist threat from the East has taken priority over disassembling authoritarian tendencies at home, and feuding with the regime in East Berlin has appeared more crucial than coming to terms with the inheritance of the Nazi period. Given that priorities have been dictated largely by outside influences, a good case can be made for the argument that West German democracy has developed about as well as might be expected, and certainly better than many had anticipated. Lacking a massive program of political education and citizenship training administered by Germans for Germans, it can be argued that it was wise not to repeat the error of the Weimar period by providing hyperdemocratic political institutions for an electorate not yet ready for them. Those limited institutional changes which were made have taken root. The tradition of the authoritarian national leader whom the people had been conditioned to yearn for during times of stress and strain—from Frederick the Great through Bismarck and Hitler—has not been eliminated, but it has been "parliamentarized" and fitted within a democratic constitutional system. The authoritarian state has been transformed into what under Adenauer has been a Chancellor democracy and what may gradually develop into a variant of democratic cabinet government. Given time and continued stability, the strong man at the top may prove increasingly dispensable and power may come to be shared more widely.

Indeed from the perspective of the average German many of these criticisms may not be at all apparent. For he naturally compares his system not with that of Britain or some other country deeply molded by democratic patterns, but with the predecessor regime, or with the political system in East Germany. In comparison with both, many of the blemishes of West German democracy seem insignificant. West Germany after all has effective civil rights guarantees, the executive power is contained by law and other political forces, there are functioning opposition parties and a free press; in short, all the basic formal requisites of democratic systems. By contrast the East German regime has imposed a system of totalitarian party rule which suppresses the freedom of individuals and minorities, thus continuing the old pattern of authoritarian rule under new ideological colors.

An analysis of the structure and relationship of the political institutions of the two states bears out the essential difference between them. Admittedly, some institutions in both West and East Germany display some affinity with regard to function. Thus, just as they have in earlier times, such institutions as the executive, the bureaucracy, and the judicial administration function as instruments of centralization and/or uniformity. In the West German system, however, other institutions check these centralizing elements in many ways. An element of checks and balances has been introduced through the Constitutional Court. Separation of powers plays less of a role since West German institutions have developed according to a pattern of interdependence. However, even if the political system is not formally segmented, such institutions and power groupings as the federal legislative organs, the interest groups, and the Laender tend to serve as decentralizing forces within the system.

The question of how the West German political equilibrium will be maintained depends—apart from vital economic and international prerequisites—largely on relationships between future Chancellors and the party system. Under Adenauer the Chancellorship has emerged as a powerful magnet, creating a "Chancellor following" which has shown some tendency to play the role of a "hidden" third party. As long as Adenauer funnelled this support to the CDU, the latter has remained numerically dominant, but it is not clear that his successors will succeed as well. In any event both major parties have declined in their ability to function as decision-making instruments by remaining too long in the Chancellor's shadow; the CDU by becoming too accustomed to playing a strictly supporting role, the SPD by trying too hard to present its programs and candidates tailored to the formula which Adenauer imposed. It remains to be seen whether they can recover lost initiative, and if not, what other institutions will take over the roles which they may leave vacant.

Political Systems, National and Supranational

Yet when all is said and done, when the politics of the two Germanies have been compared with each other and the political processes of other countries, a sense of contradiction remains. In the Western world today political systems exist on either the national or supranational level. It is difficult to place the German states within such a set of categories. They are rump states which have established pseudonational institutions at a time when, in Europe at least, the political significance of even the established nation-state is steadily declining. Much more so than its Soviet-sponsored competitor, West Germany has managed to create dynamic and stable economic and political systems. Yet even its leaders are in disagreement as to whether the Federal Republic remains essentially a provisional regime, sovereignty and political power notwithstanding.

The question of German unification will no doubt remain on

the international agenda, and some Germans will continue to seek
to deny legitimation to any government which does not represent
all Germans. But if the world powers find no way of breaking the
continuing deadlock over unification, and if the tendencies evident during the decade from 1950 to 1960 are projected into the
future, then all indications are that the two Germanies will move
further apart from each other and will become ever more closely
linked to their respective western and eastern neighbors. By
1965, for example, when East Germany is scheduled to complete
the basic revision of all prevailing law codes in line with
Communist ideology, the fundamental legal bond between them
will have been broken, and West German lawyers may find
even the technical aspects of pleading in an East German court
much more formidable than those in a French or Dutch court.

As regards East Germany, there is every reason to believe
that economic integration with the Communist bloc countries
will be increasingly accentuated, causing East Germany to
be dependent on the other Communist countries both for raw
materials and for the markets for her specialized products.
Further progress as regards political integration would seem,
however, to be dependent on the Communist bloc's being able
to solve some largely internal problems, such as the developing
ideological and leadership rivalry between the Soviet Union and
Communist China. A crucial condition for a further cementing
of East Germany into the Soviet bloc clearly lies in a settlement
of the "Berlin question" that is favorable to East Germany.

Further integration of West Germany into the Western
camp is also dependent on a number of variables, or rather
two sets of variables, since this process is taking place on two
levels—that of the larger Atlantic community and that of
"Little Europe." West Germany's place in the larger Western
alliance is likely to continue to be defined by her position in
NATO and by the question of whether American leadership
will help transform that body into a more closely knit political
organization. On the level of Little Europe, where considerable
economic integration has already taken place through the
ECSC and the Common Market, further progress depends to
a considerable extent on the leaders of France and Germany
and the kinds of policy they pursue. If De Gaulle and his successors pursue a policy of cooperation with the Germans in the
construction of a politically effective European community, then
both economic and political integration of Little Europe can
proceed quite rapidly, whether or not the British participate.

Thus the politics of the Federal Republic are likely to become increasingly a function of West European politics, while the relations between the world power blocs will surely continue to be vitally influenced by the confrontation of democratic and Communist forces on German soil.